CAPTAINS FILE: INDIA

FROM NAYUDU TO KOHLI: INDIA'S TEST CRICKET CAPTAINS

ROB HARVEY

Copyright © 2016 Rob Harvey
All rights reserved

First Published 2016 Kovac Publishing, 8-10 Pearson St, Naracoorte, SA

Second Edition updated content © Rob Harvey 2017

Third Edition updated content © Rob Harvey 2018

Fourth Edition updated content © Rob Harvey 2019

All rights reserved. No part of this publication may be reproduced, distributed, or transmitted in any form or by any means, including photocopying, recording, or other electronic or mechanical methods, without the prior written permission of the publisher, except in the case of brief quotations embodied in critical reviews and certain other noncommercial uses permitted by copyright law.

Kovac Publishing
www.kovac.com.au

ISBN: 1533052956
ISBN-13: 978-1533052957

ACKNOWLEDGEMENTS

No work of this nature could get by without standing on the shoulders of those who've gone before. Historians, commentators, writers of Indian cricket, one and all, have assisted me in this project either directly or indirectly. There are online archives, such as ESPN Cricinfo and the more traditional sources of cricket's bible, Wisden.

I pay particular homage to Mihir Bose and his comprehensive writings, likewise Boria Majumdar and his body of work and NS Ramaswami. Researching a project of this ilk is made far easier by these writers and others who have the history and culture of the game at heart.

I'd like to thank my selection panel, Tony Larder and Arunjit Singh, who assisted me with the final chapter. They studiously scrutinised all of the information I bowled at them and performed their roles with distinction.

I must acknowledge the man who fostered my love of cricket and cricket books, "criclit", as I call it, my father, GB Harvey. He was my first coach and my favourite captain.

On his deathbed in June of 2000, he left me his entire collection of cricket books. Many of those books are now missing jackets, pages yellowing, but they have been of enormous help as I delved back into days long gone.

Finally I acknowledge the 33 great men, about whom I have written. I know that through the years, each of them has been an inspiration to a nation, and more recently, an inspiration to me.

ROB HARVEY

CONTENTS

	Author's Notes	vii
	Introduction	ix
1	Cottari Kanakaiya (CK) Nayudu	1
2	Maharajkumar of Vizianagram	12
3	Iftikhar Ali Khan Pataudi	25
4	Nanik Amarnath Bhardwaj	30
5	Vijay Hazare	38
6	Mulvantrai Himmatlal Mankad	43
7	Ghulam Ahmed	49
8	Pahlan Ratanji Umrigar	53
9	Hemchandra Ramachandra Adhikari	59
10	Dattajirao Krishnarao Gaekwad	62
11	Pankaj Roy	65
12	Gulabrai Ramchand	68
13	Nariman Jamshedji Contractor	72
14	Mansoor Ali Khan Pataudi	80
15	Chandrakant Gulabrao Borde	97
16	Ajit Laxman Wadekar	99
17	Srinivas Venkataraghavan	108

18	Sunil Manohar Gavaskar	112
19	Bishan Singh Bedi	125
20	Gundappa Viswanath	141
21	Kapildev Ramlal Nikhanj	144
22	Dilip Balwant Vengsarkar	154
23	Ravishankar Jayadritha Shastri	158
24	Krishnamachari Srikkanth	161
25	Mohammad Azharuddin	164
26	Sachin Ramesh Tendulkar	174
27	Sourav Chandidas Ganguly	183
28	Rahul Sharad Dravid	191
29	Virender Sehwag	200
30	Anil Kumble	205
31	Mahendra Singh (MS) Dhoni	214
32	Virat Kohli	226
33	Ajinkya Rahane	249

SUNDRIES

34	The Best	257
35	The Centenary Tour 2032	261
	Bibliography	267

AUTHOR'S NOTES

The chapters 1 to 33, represent each of the Test cricket captains of India in order of their appointment, as the title suggests, from Nayudu to Kohli (to Rahane). This doesn't always run in a pure linear fashion. Captains get injured or replaced, only to return at a later date.

I wanted to preserve the order, but that means a little to-ing and fro-ing in some areas. I have endeavoured to maintain the flow despite the interruptions to careers.

There is a section at the back, Sundries, where I look at who were the best captains in my humble opinion and I couldn't resist the idea of putting them into a team, so I have constructed a team of captains with the assistance of my selection panel, Tony and Arun.

One of the joys of writing about these characters is that they weave in and out of each other across the generations. They intermingle with each other as players, as captains, they move into administration, management and selection. Some move into the commentary box and others into coaching. That provides a wonderful "glue", rather than 33 unrelated individuals.

I found, as I researched these men, through their own accounts, commentaries of others, the words of their opponents, that I was drawn in to the characters far more than was first imagined.

A word on place names. I have followed convention and used names as they were at the time, so Mumbai in 1932 is Bombay and Chennai is Madras. As we progress through history the names as they are represented today come into being.

This has been a thoroughly enjoyable exercise and I trust that you may also find yourself drawn to these characters every bit as much as I have been.

RJH
June 2016

PS: *Bonus Rahane chapter included July 2017*
   New content added August 2019

ROB HARVEY

INTRODUCTION

"Princes and pressmen, sportsmen and statesmen – all have played a big part in the muddle of Indian captaincy and, frankly speaking, I must say that they have not always played cricket." – CK Nayudu

For Indian cricket, the early twentieth century is about the tale of two princes: he Maharja of Patiala and an ambitious younger rival, Maharajkumar of Vizianagram. This rivalry was set against the backdrop of the simmering tension with the British Raj and the rise of the growing independence movement. By the end of the century the Raj was long gone, the princes had faded and India had become a dominant player in world cricket.

Cricket had taken a particular stronghold in Bombay from about the 1850's among the Parsis (descendants of Persians). They played their first match against the English residents in 1877, and lost, but were organised enough to send a team to tour England in 1886 and again in 1888. An English team visited India in 1890, but to play the local English, not the Indians, but one match was granted to the Parsis, who beat them by four wickets. It was the only loss by the English of the tour. Another tour by Lord Hawke in 1892/93 saw two games against the Parsis with one victory apiece.

An annual tournament between the Parsis and the Europeans, the Presidency Tournament began in 1892 in Bombay and was so popular, it attracted the attention of other communities. The Hindus joined in 1907 and the Presidency matches became known as the Bombay Triangular. The Muslims joined in 1912 and it became the Bombay Quadrangular, and was the premier first class competition in India. (In 1937, a fifth team was added, "The Rest" - Christians, Jews and other "strays" and the tournament became the Bombay Pentangular.)

The Maharaja of Patiala, firstly Rajinder Singh, like many of the princes during the British Raj, found sport as a way to cosy up to the British. He supported polo and cricket, but it was his son, Bhupinder Singh, when he became the Maharaja of Patiala, intensified the focus on cricket. He played the game himself and captained an unofficial tour to England in 1911.

During the first part of the twentieth century all teams touring India played a match at Patiala. It was one of the best wickets in India and the fixture was always a gala occasion.

Other princes also began to be involved with cricket, for they too saw the political advantage of patronage of the game. One of these was the Maharajkumar of Vizianagram. So keen to get a piece of the action, Vizianagram began to sponsor his own teams, just as Patiala, and naturally, like his rival, he was the captain. Other princes also began to get involved, the Maharaja of Porbandar, the Nawab of Bhopal, among others.

There was no cricket board at the time and the game was funded exclusively by the princes. In fact the generosity of the princes, despite the fact that there were other motives, is the main reason the game moved along so quickly. But these two particular princes, in their bids to outdo each other, in words, in deeds and in finance, had a major implication on the game and it caused the cricket community to be governed more by division than by unity. How well a cricketer fared quite often had less to do with talent and more to do with proximity to either of these two princes.

By the time the cricket board, the BCCI, was formed in 1928, both of these men had their eye on the biggest prize: captaining the first All India team against England in Test cricket. They positioned themselves politically and financially to ensure a positive outcome. Another prince, not as closely involved or as ambitious, the Nawab of Pataudi, was making his name in English cricket. His name was touted also.

Although this first Test was supposed to take place in India during 1930/31 season, political riots and uprisings against the British had the tour cancelled. Patiala arranged trial matches. Vizianagram put together a team of locals and overseas talent and toured Ceylon (now Sri Lanka) and India. As one prince made a move, so the other made a counter move. Surely one of these princes would be the captain of the first All India team. It had to be a prince, for the leader of commoners cannot be a commoner. And yet, it was a commoner after all.

CAPTAINS FILE: INDIA

1

COTTARI KANAKAIYA "CK" NAYUDU

During the final of the 1951/52 Ranji Trophy between Holkar and Bombay, when the 56 year old CK Nayudu was batting, fast bowler Dattu Phadkar bowled him a bouncer. It hit Nayudu in the jaw, dislodging a couple of teeth. The batsman spat the teeth out onto the pitch. Blood was streaming from his mouth, onto his shirt. Players rushed to his aid, as did a doctor who tended him for a short while. Nayudu brushed them all aside and continued to bat, but before he took strike, he brushed the teeth from the pitch with his bat, as if they were stray stones, and signaled to the bowler to send down another bouncer. He went on to make 66.

Who would want to rattle the cage of this older player? Perhaps the captain of the opposing team, Vinoo Mankad, upset at missing out on selection for India, for CK Nayudu was a national selector. Or was it a simple case of self-preservation on the bowler's part, for CK Nayudu's signature shot was the drive, and no-one hit the ball harder than this man. He also favoured the aerial route, a one man wrecking ball of destruction. One doubt's he received many half volleys.

Born in Nagpur in 1895, he was the son of CSPR Nayudu, a man who had a distinguished career in the legal profession and a love for the game of cricket. CK's grandfather was a landowner with considerable holdings in Nagpur. It was an easier upbringing than most for the young CK.

He began his cricket career at school at the age of seven in 1902, a year when Joe Darling's Australia successfully defeated England for the Ashes. No doubt the impressionable young Nayudu would have kept a keen eye on the performance of the Indian born English player, Kumar Shri (KS) Ranjitsinhji, for the only real pathway for an Indian player to play Test cricket at that stage was to play for England. The brilliant Ranjitsinhji was not the only Indian to play for the English Test team. India would not field a Test team for another thirty years.

CK's father and uncle were educated at Cambridge and were contemporaries of Ranjitsinhji, after whom the Ranji Trophy is named, and the father subsequently coached his young son, but with a level of unorthodoxy compared to the text books. His method? *The ball is there to be hit. Hit the ball hard.*

The young CK showed leadership ability from an early age and captained his high school team. He then went on to play for the Modi Cricket Club and was again appointed as captain.

Tall and lean, he was a powerful driver on both sides of the wicket and a nagging and miserly slow medium bowler who often opened the bowling. He had another nickname, Tiger, for his prowess in the field. He often patrolled the covers and had an excellent and deadly accurate throwing arm, but the truth is he could field anywhere, from slips to gully, on occasions even taking over as wicket keeper. CK Nayudu was the complete cricketer, perhaps the complete sportsman for he also excelled at hockey and football, but it was that punishing batting blade that had bowlers, fielders and spectators running for cover.

He made his first class debut in 1916 for the Hindus versus the Europeans in the Bombay Quadrangular Tournament. Batting at number nine, CK made 27 out of a team score of 155. He opened the bowling with SM Joshi and picked up a tidy 1-37 from 20 overs. Joshi destroyed the Europeans with 6-32 to have them behind on the first innings with only 112, however they rallied and the Hindus lost, despite Nayudu's three wickets in the second innings.

Nayudu continued to shine in the emerging first class scene, opening the bowling for the Hindus and progressively moving up the batting order. The hard hitting allrounder was making a name for himself and was chosen to play for a combined Indian team in an unofficial Test match against a visiting England team in 1918. Had normal rules applied the English would have been humiliated.

The All India team, under the captaincy of Maharaja of Patiala, were all out, 500/11 of which the youthful Nayudu scored 122, his first knock on the international stage. He bowled just eleven overs. England's reply, 158/11 and 140/10. One more wicket and England would have lost. This encounter with the English helped feed the growing Indian appetite for cricket. They had their own heroes now and Nayudu was at the centre. However it must be noted that India played an understrength England team. The English would not make that mistake a second time.

CK played first class level through the 1920's, bowling a little less but further cementing his place in the batting line-up for the Hindus under the captaincy of the Maharaja of Prahbakar. He was one of a rising number of very talented Indian cricketers: JG Navle, India's first Test wicket keeper and opening batsman, KM Mistry, regarded as one of the best cricketers of the early 1920's, Hormasji Vajifdar, a classy batsman as well as a clever medium fast bowler; the burley quick, Mohammad Nissar, allrounders Amar Singh and Lal Singh. Along with Nayudu, these players were helping to shape the landscape for India's entry into Test cricket.

In 1923 the Maharaja of Holkar invited CK to Indore to join his army making him a captain of that army but more importantly putting him in charge of the cricket teams.

In 1926, Arthur Gilligan's MCC team toured India, playing a number of unofficial Tests and other first class fixtures. It was in one of those first class fixtures that CK Nayudu made his presence felt.

On December 1st, 25,000 people packed into the Bombay Gymkhana Ground to watch the MCC take one of the local teams, the Hindus. The MCC batted first and made a respectable 353. In reply, at 84/3, CK Nayudu entered the ground. He got off the mark with a two. His next scoring shot landed on the pavilion. It began raining cricket balls as CK belted the MCC bowling attack to all parts. He smashed a (then) world record 11 sixes and 13 fours in a whirlwind of destructive batting, on his way to 153. He put one of Bob Wyatt's deliveries onto the roof of the Gymkhana. It delighted the crowd and it terrified the fielders. Oerhaps CK's father's words were ringing in his ears. *Hit the ball hard.*

The match was drawn, the MCC in shock and Cottari Kanakaiya Nayudu was the talk of the town, having announced himself as a cricketer to be reckoned with on the international stage once more. Unlike previous tours by the English, this time they were far stronger. Through the bat of CK Nayudu, India was a giant awakening in these first class fixtures.

The first official tour of India by the MCC and thus the first ever Test series, was due to take place in 1930/31 but local riots protesting against the British saw the tour cancelled. The two rival princes set to work.

In December 1930, Vizzy organised a tour in lieu of the cancelled tour by the MCC. The Maharajkumar of Vizianagram's XI toured India and Ceylon. It was a collection of local stars and international players pitted against local first class teams.

Naturally CK Nayudu was a key figure, but so too the Maharajkumar, for he is the subject of chapter two in this book and showed some very rare form in this series in 1930. Vizzy's team also included a couple of Englishmen in the side, superstars of any era, (Sir) Jack Hobbs and Bert Sutcliffe. If you are a prince, you get the best local talent, the best international talent and you build a team around yourself batting in the number three position.

Sutcliffe became ill scoring 144 in one match, missed the next and then came back with 165 in the following fixture, underlining his unmatched class in all conditions, all the while CK Nayudu making runs and often opening the bowling with his nagging medium pacers. He wasn't an international superstar of the likes of Hobbs and Sutcliffe, but the first man you would pick in your team. The Maharajakumar wasn't the best cricketer going around, but he was no fool and indeed he consulted CK on bowling changes and field placement for these were not areas in which that Vizzy shone. By all accounts the tour was a success and not only did it underline Vizzy's ability to both organise and underwrite a cricket tour, it placed him as a front-runner for the All India captaincy.

The first official tour of England by the All India team was to take place during the English summer of 1932 and it would include the first ever Test match played by India. In preparation for the tour there were two trial matches played in Lahore, organised by the Maharaja of Patiala. *Probables* versus *Possibles*: and *India* versus *Rest of India*. CK captained the Possibles which won by eight wickets and then went on to captain Rest of India. The captain of the India team was none other than the Nawab of Pataudi who by now had made a name for himself playing in England for Oxford University and it was hoped, expected even, that the Nawab would captain the team to England. An excellent batsman, Pataudi would have fitted the bill as captain of India, given his princely status, but ultimately he chose not to tour with India. Yes, Pataudi would make his debut in Test cricket in the same year, 1932, but not playing for India. His debut was for England under DR Jardine in the infamous Bodyline series.

Patalia's organisation of the trial matches was a rousing success. With Pataudi no longer in contention for the captaincy, it was given to the Maharaja of Patiala with KS Ganshyamsinhji of Limbdi as his deputy. Patalia had won the battle. Given the Maharajkumar of Vizianagram's status and invaluable contributions of finance, he was given the position of "deputy vice-captain".

The Maharajkumar was gutted. He didn't get first, or second prize. He withdrew immediately, citing his own poor form with the bat. He was broken-hearted. Had he not withdrawn his position might have improved, for Patiala withdrew two weeks later and captaincy for the touring team was bestowed upon Maharaja of Porbandar, a player of limited ability, but a prince, nonetheless, and he appeared to engender a good spirit amongst his men.

The team for India's first overseas tour was L N Amar Singh, S M H Colah, K S Ganshyamsinhji of Limbdi (vc), Ghulam Mohamad, S R Godambe, M Jahangir Khan, Capt S Joginder Singh, B E Kapadia, Lall Singh, Maharaja of Porbandar (c), Mohammad Nissar, N D Marshall, Naoomal Jeoomal, Lt. J G Navle, Capt. C K Nayudu, S Nazir Ali, P E Palia, Lt. S Wazir Ali.

The vice-captain for the tour was KS Ganshyamsinhji of Limbdi the brother-in-law of the captain and like the Maharaja was of limited ability when it came to cricket. In 19 first class matches he had a top score of 57 and an average of 17.41. Hardly beating down the door to represent one's country.

Despite the lack of ability governing the side, the Indians actually performed admirably. Notable stars with the bat through the tour were Nayudu, who topped the averages with 1618 runs at 40 in the first class fixtures, Wazir Ali, Nazir Ali and Naoomal Jaoomal. They were very well served in the bowling department by Mohammad Nissar, Amar Singh and Jahangir Khan. Keeping wickets was the reliable JG Navle.

In the very first match of the tour against T Gilbert Scott's XI, the captain of the opposing side was KS Duleepsinhji, nephew of Ranjitsinhji and another Indian who played Test cricket for England, a batsman of great skill. Had he and the Nawab of Pataudi been available for India, one wonders what the result of the tour would have been – in 26 first class matches they won nine, lost eight and nine were drawn.

It is worth noting that on the tenth match of the tour, against the MCC at Lords, Nayudu scored 118 and thus scored a century on debut at Lords.

By mid tour, it was evident that the team were carrying the captain and vice-captain and the Maharaja selflessly made way for Nayudu who celebrated by captaining India to victories over Norfolk, Northamptonshire and Worcestershire. Against Worcester, they played against Pataudi. Days later Pataudi would be playing university cricket and Nayudu would be leading the Indian team against England at Lords.

Nayudu wasn't a particularly popular choice among some of the players, who took their protest to Porbandar, but they were ordered to obey.

The First Test

On the 25th June, 1932, the Test careers of CK Nayudu and his ten team mates commenced, opening the door for every Indian Test cricketer to follow. It must surely be the most important day in the history of Indian cricket.

Destined to be a leader of men, to be a leader of India's Test cricket team, the "father" of Indian cricket, was a man whose time had come. A fine morning in what had already been a pleasant summer, saw Cottari Kanakaiya Nayudu, India's first Test cricket captain walk out to the middle of the pitch at Lords in front of 24,000 spectators for the very first coin toss. Not even in the running for the job – there were at least five other options before him – yet India could not have been better represented as they made their debut on the world stage.

Joining him for the toss is the England captain, Douglas Jardine. The name Jardine may send a shiver up the spine of every Australian cricket fan, but Jardine had a synergy with India, in fact he was born there and was at one stage, although only fleetingly, was considered an option for the captaincy of India. Jardine won the toss and elected to bat.

Despite the unavailability of the legendary Jack Hobbs, Jardine had a very strong English team to take on the Indians. Opening the batting to join Bert Sutcliffe was Percy Holmes, his Yorkshire opening partner. Despite the fact that Holmes had not represented England for eleven years, a week earlier Sutcliffe and Holmes had featured in a partnership of 555 for Yorkshire. English stalwart Frank Wooley followed at number three and then another giant of English cricket, Walter "Wally" Hammond at second drop, then Jardine, Eddie Paynter and the keeper, Les Ames. Bowes, Voce, Robins and Brown made up the bowling. This was a strong England team.

Opening the attack for India was the burley paceman Mohammad Nissar and the looping Amar Singh. Very quickly Nissar had dislodged both openers. Wooley was run out shortly afterwards and England were on the canvas at 19/3. Wally Hammond stuck around for a while but it was Jardine who held the innings together with a captain's knock of 79 and together with Les Ames, took the England score to 259, not exactly brilliant, but much better than it could have been. Significantly, Nayudu badly injured his hand while fielding, attempting a catch from Ames while in the gully. His hand was smashed. India, though, steady in reply through the openers Navle and Jaoomal, finished the close of play at 30/0. A very impressive first day for the newcomers.

India failed to capitalise on their good performance on day one and despite patient knocks from Jaoomal (33) and Wazir Ali (31 in 150 minutes), the Indian team struggled against the pace of Bowes and Voce. Nayudu, hobbled by his injured hand, batted bravely to top score with 40, but the team was bowled out for 189, a deficit of 70 runs.

Despite some early breakthroughs by Jahangir Khan and Amar Singh, England's captain again proved hard to dislodge, Jardine top scoring with 85 not out. He declared at 275/8, setting India the difficult task of chasing 346 to win.

It was an uphill battle from the outset. At 108/8, India looked humiliated, but some lusty blows from Amar Singh (51) in the lower order helped elevate the score to a slightly more respectable 187 all out.

England had won the Test by 158 runs, but India were not disgraced. Had a Pataudi and Duleepsinhji been available and CK not been hobbled by an injured hand – plus two of the bowlers were struggling with strains – the result may have been quite different. They had shown they were ready for the world stage and were led admirably by Nayudu.

India finished the tour with their heads held high, with the captain leading the batting and contributing over 100 wickets to boot. However, being a strict army man, Nayudu had put a few noses out of joint. He brought a discipline to the team that some players disliked. These inner ructions would play out loud and large over many seasons to come.

M. C. C. Tour of India, 1933-34

Earlier sides to tour India by England were a mixture of players on the rise and players past their use by date. That mix of experience and youth prevailed, but India was proving to be a stronger opponent by each year. As a result, the team led by Douglas Jardine was significantly stronger than any team to previously grace the shores. A team also buoyed by their recent demolition of Australia during the infamous Bodyline series. Would Jardine use the same tactics against India? Without Larwood on tour, it seemed unlikely, but Jardine had an affection for India in equal measure as his disdain for Australia.

Again the issue of the Indian captaincy arose. Patiala was slowly losing favour with the Viceroy, Lord Willingdon, but was busily promoting his son Yadav. The only other candidate was the ever scheming Maharajkumar of Vizianagram. Ultimately the BCCI voted for CK Nayudu.

The first Test, fittingly at Bombay, was the only Test match to ever be played at the Bombay Gymkhana. As it was a private English club, no Indians were allowed. The rule was set aside for the event and the crowd flocked in to witness the Test match. It was a quaint setting with the colonial style pavilion, no picket fence around the boundary, or barbed wire, just a few stray policemen to keep an eye on the crowd who had no fixed seating.

Nayudu won the toss and batted, but India struggled against the English bowlers, making just 219. Young allrounder Lala Amarnath top scored with 36. As he did in 1932, Jardine dined out on the Indian bowlers with a polished 60, but it was BH Valentine's century that was the backbone of the visitor's total of 438, exactly double India's first innings.

The second innings started poorly for India, openers Navle and Wazir Ali falling early, but a stirring partnership of 196 between the captain and the young Amarnath brought some pride back to the team. Nayudu scored 67, but the glory was for Amarnath, becoming the first Indian to score a Test century, in his debut Test no less. Unfortunately there wasn't much to follow. Vijay Merchant's 30 the next best, all out for 258. England polished off the required runs for the loss of only one wicket.

It was more of the same in the second Test, this time at Eden Gardens, Calcutta, with England dominant, but India managed to escape with a draw. At Madras England won by 202 runs. Jardine's team proved virtually indestructible, winning the series 2-0. Such was the inequality between Jardine's team and India that the English only lost one match of the tour, by 14 runs to the Maharajkumar of Vizianagram's XI.

In the four Test matches Nayudu had led India the result was three losses and one draw. He played one more tour to England in 1936. It is his good fortune that he was not the captain. Vizzy had finally gotten his way. We shall investigate that acrimonious tour in the next chapter, CK's last appearance in Test cricket and the last official Test cricket played by India before the Second World War.

Post Test Cricket

There was an unofficial tour by Lord Tennyson in 1937 with three fixtures against All India. Such were the rivalries, factions and politics that CK was left out of the first Test by the selectors, Pataudi, KM Mistry and Vijay Merchant, the captain. An uproar from both public and media, together with a poor showing by the team in the first match, led the selectors to pick CK for the second Test. However, his enemies rallied and as soon as CK arrived in Bombay he was inexplicably dropped again. Like many players over the years, CK found out in the media. The Maharajkumar of Vizianagram had been busy pulling the strings in the background and a number of players who held personal grudges were believed to have approached the selectors and refused to play with Nayudu in the team. Among them Lala Amarnath and Vinoo Mankad. It's also believed that some players also resented the adulation heaped on the aging star, by now 45 years old.

He continued to play first class cricket in India and over the decades he played he was a dominant figure within the game. He played in two first class fixtures just after WWII versus the Australian Services XI, captained by Lindsay Hassett. CK was 50 years old.

He captained Holkar to 8 finals in 9 years in the Ranji Trophy winning 4 of them. He played his last Ranji Trophy match at age 62, scoring 52 runs in his final innings. He returned to play a charity match in 1963/64 season at the age of 68.

Statistics don't tell the full story and while his Test record is modest, his six decades of service, from player to captain, from selector to coach, a genuine father figure for Indian cricket and it is little wonder he is known as the Father of Indian Cricket.

In 1955, at age sixty, CK Nayudu became the first cricketer to be awarded the Padma Bhushan, the third highest civilian award in the Republic of India.

CK Nayudu's innings finally ended in 1967, when he died in Indore at age 72, just a few short years after he'd finished playing his last cricket match.

Plaques, meeting halls and roads have been named after him. But perhaps the greatest honour is an honour bestowed on others. The most prestigious honour in Indian cricket, bestowed for lifetime achievement, is named the CK Nayudu Award.

Captaincy Record	Tests	W	L	D	%
England 1932 (in England)	1	0	1	0	0%
England 1933/34 (India)	3	0	2	1	0%
Total	**4**	**0**	**3**	**1**	**0%**

2

MAHARAJKUMAR OF VIZIANAGRAM – "VIZZY"

A masterful tactician. Crafty, shrewd and intelligent. Unfortunately, Vizzy displayed none of these attributes on the cricket field. His greatest skill came from his Machiavellian attempts to manipulate, bribe and marginalise. He conquered his rival, the Maharaja of Patiala, and he conquered the BCCI until he got his greatest reward: the captaincy of the All India Test cricket team. That he only played in one series is a blessing. He left a trail of destruction that had him sidelined for many years.

Lieutenant-Colonel Sir Vijay Ananda Gajapathi Raju, better known as the Maharajkumar of Vizianagram or Vizzy, was the second son born to Pusapati Vijaya Rama Gajapathi Raju, the ruler of Vizianagram. When his father died in 1922 his elder brother became the Maharaja, and Vizzy moved to the family estate in Benares.

He attended the Princes' College in Ajmer and Haileybury and Imperial Service College in England. He developed a great passion for cricket and hunting.

Using his considerable wealth, he attempted to follow in the path of the Maharaja of Patiala to influence the game of cricket in India and indeed donated huge sums to build stands and other facilities, funded tours and bought favours. The real game was not cricket, but his growing rivalry with Patiala.

He used his influence with dignitaries, in particular India's Viceroy

Lord Willingdon and cleverly exploited the differences between other key personalities. Such was his allegiance and loyalty to Willingdon that for a very short space of time, until Patiala managed to cleverly avert disaster, the Ranji Trophy was instead to be called the Willingdon Trophy at the insistence of Vizzy.

As a cricketer he was very ordinary and if ability counted for anything then the prince would never have been seen on a first class cricket field. That he used to bribe opposition captains to serve him a diet of full tosses and long hops is but one of the tales surrounding this bizarre prince.

The journey to Test cricket captain is one of bribes and manipulation, nothing more. He underwrote the 1932 tour to the UK and considered himself to be the frontrunner for the captaincy, ahead of his rival Patiala and the man most suited for the job, the Nawab of Pataudi.

He cosied up to Lord Willingdon which was clever, given the fact that the Viceroy was becoming increasingly frustrated by the well publicised womanising of Patiala. He used his money to bribe others to hurt his enemies and manipulated his way onto the Board.

The cancelled MCC tour of 1930/31, which was to feature the introduction of India to Test cricket, was used magnificently by Vizzy. He organised his own team, Maharajkumar of Vizianagram's XI, which included international stars Hobbs and Sutcliffe, (who had previously declined five previous offers to tour India) and local heroes, CK Nayudu, Vijay Merchant, Mushtaq Ali, among others, captained of course by Vizzy, who slotted himself into the number three batting position behind the two UK import openers. The tour was a success, played in major centres in India and also in Ceylon. Such was the organisation of same that Vizzy seemed a certainty to be the first captain of India.

However, shortly after that tour, Patiala gazumped him with the organisation of two trial matches for the tour to England in 1932. *"Possibles versus Probables"*, and *"All India versus Rest of India"*. Notably two of the captains were CK Nayudu and the Nawab of Pataudi. There was no involvement either as a player or an official by Vizzy, who had been sidelined by this manoeuvre. The move worked and Maharaja of Patiala was named captain of the All India team for the 1932 tour to

England, KM Limbdi vice-captain. Poor old Vizzy, despite all of his conniving best was given the lesser role of deputy vice-captain. It was a slap in the face and he issued a statement declining the role, in which he stated that while the position of Deputy Vice-Captain was an honour, his recent poor health was having a detrimental effect on his cricket form, and he could not possibly let the team down by playing when his form was not up to scratch. He was broken hearted and making an immense sacrifice for the future of cricket in India.

All that money, all the political game-playing and still no reward. Ironically Patiala pulled out, the Maharaja of Porbandar appointed and subsequently stood aside for CK Nayudu to lead the first Test.

CK Nayudu was a strict disciplinarian and upset some of the players on the 1932 tour by demanding adherence to rules such as returning to hotel rooms on time and to spend less time in the evenings partying. Amar Singh refused to play under Nayudu's captaincy after the tour remarking publicly, "*Nayudu wanted to win at all costs and had made the game into a killjoy pursuit.*" Curious. Others such as Wazir Ali were jealous of the Hindu captaining all India. If it has to be a commoner, why not me, why not a Muslim?

These divisions were gold to a master manipulator and Vizzy used them to great advantage. By manipulating players behind the scenes to attack Nayudu, an adored figure with the cricket loving public, while at the same time praising him publicly, he was really eating away at Patiala. Despite Patiala's own showering of gifts to the visiting English team, Nayudu was appointed captain of the home series in 1933/34. Patiala still coveted the role but in a sign of his weakening status with the likes of the Viceroy, tried to promote his son, Yadav, instead. Vizzy's support of Nayudu's appointment was simply a swipe at Patiala.

The two princes continued to wrestle for control and influence. By 1934, the need for a regional based first class competition as opposed to the communal teams of the Bombay Quadrangular became a hot topic for debate. Mahatma Gandhi announced that sporting teams ought not be divided by religion and his voice attracted support. Interestingly, despite the Board, the Viceroy and Gandhi wanting a new regional based competition, the players were united in keeping the existing one. And for good reason: the Bombay Quadrangular was very popular with both players and public. However politicians and administrators have more sway than player power alone.

Patiala was quick to act. He offered up £500 for a trophy for the new first class competition and wanted to honour the great Ranjitsinhji by naming the award, the Ranji Trophy. There was a delay in setting up the processes and this delay gave Vizzy some room to work his magic. He suggested a trophy to honour the Viceroy, Lord Willingdon, given that Ranji had played almost all of his cricket in England and had done very little for Indian cricket. For good measure, he would donate the trophy. The board, of which Patiala was a member, sat and voted in favour of the Willingdon Trophy, the premier prize for First Class cricket in India.

It was a major coup for Vizzy. He sold India's cricket soul for his own advance. Imagine at this time of political unrest with the British Raj, getting the nation's highest cricket award named after a Briton instead of the country's most celebrated and revered cricketers. It was a masterstroke, however it was short-lived. There were protests by the public and letters to newspaper editors. The players were likewise outraged.

Patiala, representing India at an ICC meeting in 1935 had done some manoeuvring of his own, one of which was to sponsor a tour to India by Australia. It was at this meeting that Patiala turned the tables on Vizzy and the Willingdon Trophy was relegated to a lesser competition and the Ranji Trophy was put in place.

Vizzy was gazumped once again, but his ability move in dark corridors allowed him to eventually claim the prize he most sought: the captaincy of the Indian cricket team for the 1936 tour of England. He was elected over Nayudu by the Board 10 votes to 4. The manager of the tour would be Major Brittain-Jones, the ADC to Lord Willingdon.

The All India Tour of England 1936

The summer of 1936 took the Olympics to Hitler's Germany during which India's men's hockey team won their third consecutive gold medal. In the same summer, England played host to Vizzy's All India cricket team. They did not enjoy the same success as the hockey team.

"Divide and conquer" has long been a tactic of generals of armies, leaders of industries and captains of sporting teams, however it is normally used on the opposition. Having finally reached the top of the mountain he was climbing, one could be forgiven for thinking that Vizzy might have mellowed, perhaps even matured, giving up his Machiavellian traits. One would be wrong.

From the very commencement of the England tour, Vizzy set about pitting his teammates against each other, creating factions, creating favourites and doing so with a renewed zeal using his old tactics. It beggars belief that he could have possibly thought this self-sabotage could work in the team's favour. It culminated in the most disastrous of cricket tours by an Indian team and created some permanent enemies. All touring groups naturally break off into different parties within a tour – team mates from previous fixtures, or from home states, it's natural that some players would gravitate towards old friends. But for the captain to play them against each other was a dagger through the heart of India's campaign. Vizzy and his sidekick, Major Brittain-Jones, would rule the tour with an iron fist inside a glove.

There were ructions under Nayudu's leadership, to be sure, but these amounted to maintaining discipline after hours and playing to win. Hardly too controversial. And Nayudu could play. Vizzy would struggle to be picked in a club team on merit alone. His comments from 1932 where he stated that his form was down and couldn't therefore let his team down were disingenuous. He never had any form of note outside of bribing opposition bowlers to bowl rubbish at him. After 47 first class matches he had an average of 18.60, with a top score of 77. During the tour he lavished gifts on opposition players and captains. He appeared more concerned with pleasing his hosts than winning cricket matches for India.

The All India team was a strong group on paper, captain aside. Nayudu, Wazir Ali, Vijay Merchant and Mushtaq Ali were all world class batsmen, and the bowling attack was strong also, led by Mohammad Nissar and joined when not on county duty by Jehangir Khan and Amar Singh. The wicket keeper was the accomplished Hindlekar and they were joined by a bunch of youthful players ready to make their mark, including the emerging allrounder, Lala Amarnath.

A good team on paper, but one that failed to win many games. Out of 28 played, they won four and were lucky to do that. There were some mitigating circumstances, not least of which was the weather, but some of the players also suffered injuries both before and during the tour. However, they would have performed far better without Vizzy's conniving ways.

Vizzy's Games

The relationship between Vizzy and Nayudu is important here. During the 1930/31 series of Vizzy's XI versus India and Ceylon – the replacement for the cancelled MCC tour – Vizzy as captain used Nayudu as his proxy. Nayudu was far more conversant with the nuances of field placements and bowling changes so it was a clever move. Nayudu became part of Vizzy's "favourites", showered with gifts. It was smart on Nayudu's part also – in those days cosying up with royalty was a good way to get ahead. Vizzy would also have enjoyed pulling CK away from Patiala. Also among the favourites was the young allrounder, Amarnath. The non favourites included Wazir Ali, his brother Nazir, and Amar Singh, who also had personal issues with Nayudu.

Vizzy then set about destroying his favourites group upon arrival in the UK. Those closely associated with Maharaja Patiala were set upon, and top of that list was CK Nayudu. The impressionable and precocious Amarnath was told not to associate with Nayudu or his party which also included Mushtaq Ali, MJ Gopolan and Cotar Ramaswami.

Amarnath did as he was told. Vizzy was pleased and continued to favour him, providing rides to the grounds in his car. Nayudu was furious and stopped talking with the young player immediately and that further alienated Nayudu from Vizzy.

Nayudu came in for some more treatment on the tour. Vizzy offered a Test cap to Baqa Jilana, a medium pace bowler of modest talent, if he would shower abuse at Nayudu over the breakfast table. The youngster obliged and won his Test cap. Vizzy was using younger players as pawns to humiliate the former captain.

This is most significant because it is noted in the Beaumont Committee Report following the tour that *Nayudu was aloof and failed to co-operate or support*. Given the games Vizzy was playing it would not be surprising if Nayudu kept to himself. It is also worth noting that Nayudu was neither the vice-captain nor asked to be in any senior role.

If Nayudu had any stray thoughts that Vizzy would copy his predecessor, Porbandar, and step aside in favour of him for the Test matches, surely they were distinguished early on.

Two of the Indian players to shine on the tour were openers Vijay Merchant and Mushtaq Ali. Merchant was "non-aligned" with any factions and Mushtaq in the Patiala camp. Vizzy promised Mushtaq a gold watch if he managed to get Vijay run-out. To his credit, Mushtaq declined, but it was just another example of the games that Vizzy played.

Taunting, teasing and manipulating his team while showering gifts upon the opposition. It got worse…

The Amarnath Episode

By mid-May, Amarnath was the leading run scorer and leading wicket taker on tour. The young allrounder was clearly the best performing player in the side. Useful runs in the middle order and a consistent wicket taker, opening the bowling with Mohammad Nissar. Against Northamptonshire, an unbeaten century, and then in the match against Leicester, cracks appeared in the relationship between Amarnath and his captain.

While bowling, Amarnath requested a fielding change from his skipper. Vizzy refused, telling him to stop wasting time. Amarnath bowled two more overs and was then banished into the deep.

The young man made the mistake of discussing the incident with some of his closer team mates but word got back to the captain. Vizzy pulled him aside and explained that as captain he could do whatever he liked. Amarnath protested that he did not expect rudeness from his captain especially when he was trying his best for the team, and reminded the captain that they were amateurs, not paid professionals.

Vizzy took the incident to the manager, Brittain-Jones who ordered Amarnath to apologize, which he did but the damage was done. In the following match Amarnath again fielded in the deep and was used sparingly as a bowler. Curiously, every time he got a wicket, he was taken off, however ended up getting 6-29. Perhaps a shrewd move on the part of the captain!

Amarnath scored twin centuries in the next fixture at Essex but had hurt his shin rather badly and had to leave the field to receive medical attention. Before the next match he sprained his back at practise but was ordered to play regardless and damaged his back further in the process.

He left the field in agony against Cambridge University but after an hour was ordered back to the field by Brittain-Jones. Bizarrely he was made to bowl and was in considerable discomfort. At lunch he made the mistake yet again, of complaining to his team mates. Brittain-Jones got wind of it and approached Amarnath, holding a letter in each hand, one to the Maharaja of Patiala and another to the Maharaja of Bhopal. The letters contained complaints against Amarnath. Brittain-Jones threatened to post them and at the same time send him back to India. This was understood to be a final warning.

The last nail in the coffin was in June during a tour game against Minor Counties. Amarnath, padded up and due to go in at number four, was repeatedly held back every time a wicket fell. Amarnath eventually went in at number seven and was furious at having had to wait so long. He was huffy on his return to the dressing room and muttered some words in Punjabi. It was beginning of the end for the young man who had so much to offer but struggled to keep his opinions to himself.

Brittain-Jones summoned him to a meeting and showed him a letter containing statements from fellow players complaining about Amarnath's behaviour and that the player would be sent back to India aboard the Kaiser-I-Hind the next day. Later that evening, a group of players including Nayudu pleaded Amarnath's case to the captain, but it was all to no avail. The most in form player in the squad would be sent home before the First Test.

Three days after this incident, in the King's Birthday Honours List, Vizzy received notification of a knighthood from the King to be bestowed at a ceremony between the first and second Tests.

The Amarnath sacking was widely reported in the British press who were just as confused as the cricket loving public. There were vague statements issued in the press but this did little to dampen speculation.

A statement issued by senior players, including Nayudu, Wazir Ali and L.P. Jai, supportive of their captain, made its way into the papers:

> *"In the cause of India cricket we, as senior members of the team in England, desire to state for publication that we have full confidence in our captain. Also we would like to take this opportunity of denying absolutely the rumours we have read that there is any dissention in the team."* – Daily Mail, Hull, June 25 1936.

Amarnath certainly had his detractors in the team, but his biggest mistake was getting offside with a character like Vizzy who would use whatever means possible to get his way. One wonders what strings he pulled to get Nayudu to agree to the press statement. That said, the extreme action of sending your best player home just before the First Test was unheard of.

On his arrival home, there were attempts by the Nawab of Bhopal, chairman of the BCCI, to have Amarnath re-instated, and had booked his return voyage, but Brittain-Jones and Vizzy held fast. Vizzy had used Lord Willingdon to threaten Bhopal if Amarnath returned. If Bhopal refused, Willingdon as Viceroy could make life very difficult for the Nawab. He no choice but to comply. The return ticket was cancelled so late that Amarnath's luggage went, but he did not. The cricket loving public in India were in shock. The whole affair was a public relations disaster and would be the subject of an examination when the team returned home, culminating in the Beaumont Committee Report.

Back to the Cricket

Days after Amarnath was sent home, Vizzy realised his dream: he would captain India in a Test match and it would be at the home of cricket, Lords. Things got off to a bad start when he lost the toss to new England captain, Gubby Allen, considered the fastest bowler in England at the time. He sent India into bat after rain had been lurking in the preceding hours.

Allen's appointment as skipper was considered controversial, for he was a fast bowler. In his debut match in charge, the England captain led the way taking 5-35 off 17 overs. India were all out for 147, with Vijay Merchant top scoring with 35 and a captain's knock from Vizzy of 19 not out, which would remain his highest in Test cricket.

All was not lost however as Nissar and Amar Singh were let loose among the English and bowled them out for 134, Singh capturing 6-35.

India's second innings was even worse, bundled out for 93. None of their star batsmen were any match for the pace of the England skipper. Set 106 runs for victory, the wicket having flattened out, England did it in a canter, winning by nine wickets.

Between the first and second Tests was a match against Lancashire at Liverpool, a match Vizzy missed on account of his knighthood in the King's Birthday Honours. While he was becoming Sir Vizzy, CK Nayudu filled in as captain and the Indian team minus Vizzy was winning. Upon hearing this Vizzy sent a cable instructing Nissar to bowl full tosses. When Nayudu figured out what was going on he replaced the bowler and India went on to win the game. Even in absentia Vizzy was pulling the strings.

The second Test went better for India, and Vizzy achieved the first drawn Test match on overseas soil, albeit on a flat wicket. The Indian skipper won the toss and chose to bat. This time it was the spin of Verity that caused the most difficulties and India were dismissed for 203. Then it was the Wally Hammond show as he amassed 167 before being bowled by Nayudu. Aided by Worthington and Hardstaff, and combined with some late order dominance by Robins (76) and Verity (66*) Allen declared the England innings 8 down for 571. The match petered to a draw, but not before Vijay Merchant (114) and Mushtaq Ali (112) had scored the highest partnership in Indian cricket to date, 203. At 390/5, it was a respectable finish to the drawn Test.

The final match in the series was played at the Oval. Allen won the toss, elected to bat and India was treated to another master class from Wally Hammond who scored 217. He had good support from Worthington (128) and England declared at 471/8. After a good start from Merchant and Ali, it went downhill quickly against the spin of Verity and Sims, India bowled out for 222.

Following on, India made a better fist of it in the second innings. Nayudu, for the first time in the Test series, showed some form with 81. In another display of his grit, he was hit in the heart by Allen and sought treatment on the pitch, but continued to bat on and in characteristic style seemed to hit the ball harder after the injury. He staved off the innings defeat, but India were all out for 312, Gubby Allen again the destroyer with 7 wickets, leaving England with a small total to chase. They won easily by nine wickets, taking the series 2-0.

A couple of minor fixtures to follow and thus ended the disastrous tour of 1936. It was the first and last series Vizzy would captain and the aftermath would leave eventually him in the wilderness for many years.

The Beaumont Committee Report

The "Amarnath Affair" was reported in the UK, it was reported in India and it even made the Canberra Times all the way to Australia:

"The Cricket Board of Control today issued the report of the Justice, Sir John Beaumont's Committee of Three, which was appointed in September to inquire into the circumstances into which Amarnath was sent home during the Indian team's tour of England. The report, discussing the tour generally, attributes lack of coordination and co-operation firstly to Naidu holding himself aloof from team and falling to support the captain; secondly to Captain Vizianagram forming his own party and not treating all members impartially; and thirdly, the feeling, whether or not justified, but shared by practically the whole team, that the captaincy on the field was faulty; and fourthly, too many idle players. The report adds that no blame for the team's failure attaches to the Manager, except that he should have formulated written directions regarding players in the match on or off the field, for example, the hours for returning to the hotel. The report points out that there were no breaches of discipline on the field, but Amarnath was guilty of ill manners and rude conduct in the presence of the captain in a private place. The captain and manager, in view of the warnings given Amarnath rightly took disciplinary action but the punishment was too severe. The report recommends the sentence on Amarnath, but as he committed neither a breach of discipline on the field or moral turpitude, he should be regarded as having expurgated the offence and ought not to be debarred from participation in Indian cricket, provided he apologizes to the board."

Vizzy came in for a lashing. "He did not understand field placings or bowling changes and never maintained any regular batting order." Yet surprisingly Nayudu was singled out. "Lack of coordination and co-operation firstly to Naidu (*sic*) holding himself aloof from team and falling to support the captain". This is the captain that ordered the young Amarnath not to speak with Nayudu. This is the same captain that promised a Test cap to a player if he abused Nayudu at the breakfast table.

Once again, reference to the hours kept after play, the time of the players returning to the hotel. This was one of the complaints about Nayudu's captaincy in that he was too strict, yet the management of this 1936 tour struggled with the same issue.

The evidence on offer seems to show that Brittain-Jones was merely a puppet of Vizzy; that Vizzy had no reasonable concept of man-management. Or cricket. That Amarnath was indeed talented, but also precocious. That if Vizzy had shown a little more respect to his players, particularly Nayudu, the tour would have been much more in keeping with India's first tour of England – a team on the rise. Under Vizzy, it was a team on the fall.

The evidence against Vizzy is emphatic. He was a talentless cricketer, but had money, power and influence. He donated much time and resources to the development of Indian cricket an undeniable fact for which he is to be congratulated, but his greed and ambition undid his good work, several times over.

Renowned writer and historian, Mihir Bose, when he asserts that Vizzy would have been a hero to Indian cricket if he'd kept his influence off the field. I have a different perspective. Vizzy was such a manipulator that he continued to harass Nayudu even after the Beaumont Report. This post report behaviour is the most damning. Vizzy used his position to deny Nayudu a return to the Indian team in 1937, when an unofficial tour was taking place and the entire country wanted the aging star to play. Between Amar Singh and some other players, with Vizzy's backing, Nayudu was publicly humiliated. The prince got his way. Or did he?

After the Beaumont Report, Vizzy faded from view. The report showed him for what he was and it was not a pretty sight. He did make an appearance a couple of decades later and seemingly made it up to Nayudu by appointing him as captain of the newly formed Uttar Pradash team in the Ranji Trophy in 1956. It would be Nayudu's last year of competitive cricket. Had the two rivals reconciled after all these years?

It is worth noting, that in every report I have found about Vizzy, they all end with his career in commentary. It's not good. He is described variously as pompous and verbose. When Vizzy had described how he had hunted and killed 300 tigers, former West Indian great, Rohan Kanhai responded, *"Really? I thought you left a transistor radio on when you were commentating and bored them to death."*

Vizzy loved shikar and his palace was decorated in some of the above mentioned tiger skins and heads. On a shikar in 1962, in the Nailani jungle, a tigress appeared out of nowhere and startled the hunting party. It was shot and wounded but appeared shortly afterwards as it lunged towards Vizzy's elephant. Vizzy fell to the ground, but his gun was out of reach. Luckily for him, the tigress just took off with his pith helmet and left Vizzy alone, however his injuries were considerable. He was rushed to hospital with a broken pelvic bone and his bladder punctured. He was successfully operated on, but he was never the same again. He died in 1965 aged 59.

Mihir Bose is right in one regard. Vizzy ought to have kept his influence restricted to promoting the game and not playing.

However, put yourself in Vizzy's shoes. You have money, power and influence and you are offered the position of Test cricket captain of your country. Would you refuse? No. Me either.

Captaincy Record	Tests	W	L	D	%
England 1936 (England)	3	0	2	1	0%
Total	**3**	**0**	**2**	**1**	**0%**

3

IFTIKHAR ALI KHAN
EIGHTH NAWAB OF PATAUDI

A prince who could not only captain the Indian cricket team, but one who could actually play… they wanted him in 1932, but instead he turned out for England, scoring a century on debut for Jardine's England team against Australia in Sydney. They wanted him in 1936. They selected him even, but ill health pulled him away. Then the war came. In 1946, the stars aligned and the prince who would be captain arrived, 14 years after India first entered Test cricket.

Iftikhar Ali Khan Pataudi – the eighth Nawab of Pataudi, known to his English mates as "Pat", was born in Pataudi House, Delhi, 16th March 1910. He succeeded his father in 1917.

The batting prodigy first learnt about cricket in India, with a private coach and then went to study at Oxford where he was coached by English Test stalwart, Frank Wooley. A slow beginning as he learnt to deal with English conditions, but gradually the young man followed in the footsteps of Ranjitsinhji and Duleepsinhji in setting English scoreboards ablaze. He starred for Oxford University, making a name for himself as a stylish batsman and he soon caught the eye of Worcestershire selectors. It is perhaps the promise of a contract with Worcestershire that killed off any idea that he would be a part of the All India team to England in 1932. So prolific was he for Worcestershire that he soon came into consideration for England.

In the year that India debuted on the world stage, Pataudi debuted for England at the SCG in the first Test of the famous Bodyline series, in December 1932. Australia, minus Bradman, helped themselves to 360 runs in the first innings of that Test, on the back of Stan McCabe's brave innings against the hostile pace of Larwood and Voce. England were even more at ease at the crease, Sutcliffe and Hammond dining out on centuries.

Pataudi came in at number four, at 300/2, and guided the team to 524, the last man out for 102 scoring a Test century on debut. Australia crumbled against Larwood, all out for 164. There were no heroics in the second innings from McCabe. Sutcliffe faced one ball and scored the one run for the victory for England.

Bradman returned to the Australian team for the second Test and scored a fighting century while O'Reilly and Ironmonger collected nine wickets to spin Australia to victory by 111 runs. The Test match was an unremarkable one for Pataudi, scoring just 15 and 5, losing his wicket to both the aforementioned bowlers. But it was remarkable in another sense. He refused to take his place in Jardine's Bodyline leg side field. "*I see His Highness is a conscientious objector,*" said Jardine. Pataudi was dropped and did not play in another Test match on the tour. His only other tour game was against NSW where he made 2 and 0. It has been reported that at end of the tour, Pataudi said of Jardine: "*I am told he has his good points. In three months I have yet to see them.*"

He played one last Test match for England, making 12 and 10 in a losing effort against Australia at Trent Bridge in 1934, under the captaincy of C.F. Walters, Jardine now a distant memory. He continued to play with Worcestershire until 1938, then returned to India and married the daughter of the Nawab of Bhopal in 1939.

The Second World War saw the cessation of international tours which meant the first class scene was the only available cricket, and as a result, flourished. The fledgling Ranji Trophy went from strength to strength. The benign pitches of the day made it a dreamtime for batsmen and a struggle for quick bowlers. Many records were broken during this era. Batting records, that is. CK Nayudu's Holkar team scored over 900 in one innings, the captain being one of six centurions.

Into that batting paradise came the first post war international engagement, the visiting Australian Services team in 1945/46, captained by Lindsay Hassett and featuring Keith Miller.

"Our batting looked reasonably strong until we came to compete with those superb and exciting Indian batsmen, Vijay Merchant, Lala Amarnath, Mushtaq Ali, Vinoo Mankad, Rusi Modi, Vijay Hazare, Imtiaz Ahmed and others in quick and frightening succession." – R.S. Whitington, The Lindsay Hassett Story

India, under the captaincy of batting machine Vijay Merchant, won the unofficial three match Test series 1-0. Pataudi did not play. In fact the war had taken a six year chunk out of his career. He had stopped playing for Worcestershire in 1938 and did not return to the crease until 1944 in India and even then, just for one match, teaming up with CK Nayudu, Vijay Hazare, HR Adhikari and Mushtaq Ali for Western India States versus Rest of India. Ill health continued to plague his career.

Nine months later he played his one and only Ranji Trophy match for Southern Punjab, opening the batting and making 7 out of a score of 472. He bowled one over, a maiden. He played in one more fixture, the Zonal Pentangular in Bombay, for North Zone, where he retired at the score of one.

Once again the captaincy of the upcoming tour to England was a hot issue. With commoners like Gandhi and Nehru as leaders in the political sphere, the idea of a prince needing to lead the Indian cricket team had begun to wane. Vijay Merchant had led the unofficial series against the Australians Services XI and won the three match series 1-0. His case was promoted by the Bombay Cricket Association, but despite the series win, his captaincy credentials were questioned.

Pataudi on the other hand had often changed his mind about the position and his health was questionable. It was a tough choice, but given the acrimony and division of the 1936 tour, Pataudi got the nod and Merchant was given the vice captaincy.

Pataudi's first match as captain of India was against Worcestershire, his old county team, in the first match of India's 1946 tour of England. The Indian team was a welcome distraction from the war years and Pataudi was a popular figure both on and off the field. There would be nothing like the turmoil of the previous tour under Vizzy.

The first Test at Lords was a massive occasion. After the destruction and devastation of the war, this first post war Test was a godsend for the people of London and 30,000 attended the first day.

Pataudi's team included Merchant, Vinoo Mankad, Lala Amarnath, Vijay Hazare, each of whom captained India in some capacity during their careers. Also in the team, another future captain, Abdul Hafeez, who later changed his name to Abdul Hafeez Kardar – in a few years he would lead Pakistan as their first Test captain.

For England, household names: Hammond, Len Hutton, Denis Compton and making his debut, Alec Bedser.

The Nawab won the toss against Hammond and chose to bat. Against the guile of Alec Bedser, who collected seven wickets, India were rolled for 200. England replied with 428 on the back of a Joe Hardstaff double century, Lala Amarnath toiling for 57 overs to pick up 5 wickets. Not faring much better in the second innings, India made 275 (Mankad 63) with Bedser picking up another 4 wickets. England with less than 50 to chase, Len Hutton and Cyril Washbook took little effort to clinch the win.

Pataudi won the toss at Old Trafford for the second Test and this time sent England in. Half centuries to Hutton, Washbrook and Hammond saw England to a modest 294, with five wickets each to Amarnath and Mankad. After a century stand between Merchant and Mushtaq Ali, India collapsed to Bedser and Pollard for 170 all out, a deficit of 124 runs. Trying to force the win, England declared 5 down for 153. India clung on to draw the match, 152/9 with that man Bedser the destroyer again taking seven wickets.

The third Test was a washed out draw, with Pataudi winning his third toss in succession. India batted and made 331, built on Merchant's 128. England were 95/3 when play stopped.

Poor health spoiled his tour and he did not have the strength to display his well-known talent against his old team. Often Vijay Merchant had to deputise and by comparison had a marvellous tour. It was a sad and unjust end to the career of the Nawab, although the good will generated by the tour is worth noting for it was a return to happier times with the resumption of Test cricket.

Pataudi was one of Wisden's Cricketers of the Year in 1932, his debut year, and was India's Cricketer of the Year in 1947.

Pataudi's son, the 9th Nawab of Pataudi, Mansoor Ali Khan, was celebrating his eleventh birthday when his father died of a heart attack playing polo on 5th January 1952 at the age of 41. So much talent, so much promise. Some of it realised, but much of it missed. Perhaps the newly anointed Nawab might be able to change that in the years to follow...

Captaincy Record	Tests	W	L	D	%
England 1946 (England)	3	0	1	2	0%
Total	3	0	1	2	0%

4

NANIK AMARNATH BHARDWAJ
LALA AMARNATH

A good allrounder is worth gold to any cricket team. It's as though you are fielding an extra player. A bowler, a batsman. What about one that can keep wickets as well? As an overall package, Lala Amarnath was one heck of a cricketer.

Born Nanik Amarnath Bhardwaj, in Kapurthala, Punjab on 11th September 1911, the precocious young talent was the first Indian to score a Test century, in his debut, against Jardine's touring team in 1933/34, at the Bombay Gymkhana Ground. He proceeded to gather a wide collection of firsts, especially as captain: the first Indian captain of Independent India, the first Indian captain to lead teams against Australia, West Indies and Pakistan. The first Indian captain to win a Test series.

His early Test career as seen in chapter two was plagued with turmoil after such a promising beginning. His other first, the first Indian player to be sent home from a tour, meant that after the third Test in Madras in February 1934, he would not play in another Test match for twelve years, with the Second World War, as for so many others, an interruption to his career. That 12 year gap is the longest between Test matches by any player.

That he was oozing with talent, there can be no doubt. Jardine is reported to have said that he was difficult to set a field to. But there is that nagging feeling that some of the difficulties on the 1936 tour of England were of his own doing. It's easy to understand in a team of divisions and rivalries: a young buck performing better than his older teammates is a recipe for a degree of cockiness and insolence.

After the team's return to India the Beaumont Committee reported in 1937 that while Amarnath was due for reprimand, he'd been overly punished for his crimes. One wonders if he'd had an old hand by his side, namely the one man he was ordered to avoid, CK Nayudu, whether the tour would have ended on a more productive note for all concerned.

But controversy continued to follow him throughout his career and also his post career activities as a selector. So did the runs and so did the wickets. He continued to plunder bowlers and baffle batsmen in the Ranji Trophy and the Bombay Pentangular, his highest score of 262, and best bowling of 7-27. He bowled off the wrong foot enabling him to generate prodigious in-swingers.

If one uses that old calculator that a batsman is at his peak at age 30, then, despite his wonderful career, the cricket world probably missed out on even higher levels of excellence that Amarnath could have reached. When that wretched war was over, a hastily organised tour to England saw Amarnath one of the first men picked for Pataudi's team. Not at his brilliant best with the bat, returning only one half century during the Test series, he was most effective with ball in hand, taking thirteen wickets at 25.38.

In 1947/48 Lala Amarnath was appointed captain of the first independent India team and the first to land on Australia's shores, although he was not the first choice. Vijay Merchant, who had deputised for Pataudi so often during the 1946 tour of England, was originally chosen only to withdraw at the last minute, so once again one of India's finest players was tantalizingly close to being captain but missed out. Merchant captained unofficial Test matches for India but not once in an official Test.

The tour to Australia would be no easy task at all for Amarnath and his men, facing a team led by Bradman which included Lindwall and Miller, Morris and Brown, to name a few. This was the nucleus of a team that would one year later be labelled the *Invincibles*. India would also be facing the unusual task of having to bowl eight ball overs, as was the rule in Australia at that time.

Amarnath was served up a bit of bad luck before the tour: not only was Vijay Merchant unavailable, but also RS Modi. They were the team's most accomplished batsmen and with them not joining the tour the team was short on experience. It was reported that the side was "unbalanced".

In somewhat of an unexpected own goal, Amarnath would not agree to Bradman's proposal of covered wickets. Amarnath's reasoning was that Australia had hammered the Indian bowling in the lead up games and if the Tests were played on flat wickets India would be flattened. His best chance was with the weather and catching Australia on a sticky wicket. This backfired dreadfully.

The poor run of luck continued into the first Test at Brisbane. Amarnath lost the toss and Bradman elected to bat, helping himself to 185 of Australia's 382. Then the rain came. And came. India, caught on a wet wicket had no chance, bundled out for 58 and 98 after following on. Ernie Toshack destroyed them with his left arm slow medium, taking 11 wickets for 31 runs and Australia won the match by an innings and 226 runs. Had India won the toss Vinoo Mankad could have exploited the conditions just as much as Toshack.

Amarnath won the toss in Sydney and got the best conditions in which to bat and India made 188 on another rain effected wicket. Australia displayed their vulnerability to be bundled out for 98, and India too followed with seven down for 61 before the weather was the victor, the match drawn.

Bradman won the toss in Melbourne and Australia batted first in what was a most unusual Test. Bradman and Hassett scored quickly and helped Australia to 394. India too replied brightly with Vinoo Mankad scoring the first century on Australian soil by an Indian, but a collapse left them at 291/9, 103 behind. Overnight it rained, and Amarnath cleverly declared, despite the deficit, hoping to crack through Australia's celebrated batting line-up as they had done in Sydney. It nearly worked, but Bradman swiftly made a counter-move, by reversing his batting order. At one stage a precarious 32/4 when Bradman was joined by opener Arthur Morris, batting at six, and both scored not out centuries before the declaration at 255/5. Facing an uphill battle to make the 358 required, India crumbled for 125, losing by 233 runs.

No rain in Adelaide for the fourth Test, but plenty of clouds for

Amarnath. He lost the toss again and Bradman chose to bat on a classic Adelaide Oval batting paradise. Bradman was out late in the day but only after he'd scored 201, bowled by Vijay Hazare. Lindsay Hassett and Sid Barnes also plundered the attack as Australia scored a massive 674. Centuries to Vijay Hazare and DG Phadkar helped India to 381 but they had to follow on, Hazare scoring another century in the second innings to underline his class, but India lost the match by an innings and 13 runs.

The final Test in Melbourne was the same result. Bradman won the toss and Australia won by an innings. As if they hadn't had enough of Bradman, a young man by the name of Robert Neil Harvey, playing in only his second Test, became the youngest Australian to score a Test century. India lost the series 4-0 but they would not be the only cricketing nation to struggle against Bradman's Australians.

But for a fair share of luck the result may have shown Amarnath's Indian team in a better light and the performances of Hazare and Mankad were enough to show that India had plenty of talent on offer. He'd led a well supported and popular team.

"Australia was too strong. To have been beaten by Australia is not a disgrace. We really came to learn - to worship at the temple of cricket. We've had a fine trip, and we've learned a lot about cricket. And that alone is worth coming for." Amarnath quoted in the Hobart Mercury, February 12th 1948

Although the tour was a happy one, Amarnath had his detractors. Prince Duleepsinhji, a board member but also covering the tour for Reuters, criticised the captain for his field placings for the bowlers. Amarnath took exception and it was reported in the Australian newspapers that he would confront the issue with the board upon his return home. However, Duleepsinhji was not the only board member Amarnath needed to worry about.

The issue of captaincy was still a contentious one and Amarnath was no certainty to continue. There was a continual push from some quarters for Merchant and a small but vocal support for Vijay Hazare who had performed so well with the bat on the Australian tour.

However, some nine months after that tour and there was another first: Amarnath was again appointed captain and would lead the first

Test series against the West Indies. Seeing the white captain of West Indies, John Goddard, must have made the cricketing public proud that the BCCI had not gone down the path of choosing a white captain themselves. West Indies would not see a black captain until Frank Worrell in 1960.

The West Indies, as has followed them through the different eras, were a popular and entertaining team. They possessed a strong batting line-up but a bit weaker with their bowling attack. This lack of pace on both teams made for piles of runs but very few results in what was a backbreaking series for bowlers.

Amarnath lost every single toss in the series and Goddard chose to bat on each occasion. Scores of 631 and 629 in the first innings of the first two Tests saw the Windies on top, but with no fire in their attack India also scored heavily. No result eventuated until the fourth Test which West Indies won by an innings and 193 runs.

A drawn fifth Test saw India lose the series 1-0. It was during the fifth Test that PK Sen, the wicket keeper, became injured and Amarnath, after having bowled four overs in the first innings, donned the gloves for the remainder of the match. He took five catches and no stumpings, with minimal byes let through. To be able to step up and keep wickets in nearly two innings of a Test just underlined how versatile this cricketer truly was. India was close to winning that Test and it might have gone that way if PK Sen was able to bat in either innings.

Aside from losing the series, there was more pain. The popular touring West Indies were treated to a better class of hotel and better facilities all round. When Amarnath complained he found himself at loggerheads with BCCI president, Anthony De Mello who angrily had the captain suspended for continuous misbehaviour and breach of discipline. De Mello had a shopping list of allegations and complaints against Amarnath and detailed them in a long document. It all amounted to matters of insubordination. The complaint about the hotels was the final straw for the president. Yet again Amarnath felt the wrath of the hierarchy, lost the captaincy to Vijay Hazare and went to cool his heels playing in the Lancashire League in England. He wasn't without his supporters however. In Bradman's, Farewell to Cricket he described Amarnath as a splendid ambassador, and while he spoke his mind, *"he always did so with the utmost courtesy and tact."*

By 1951, Anthony De Mello's power had drifted and Lala was back in the side under Vijay Hazare for the 1951/52 tour of India by England. That five Test series will be covered in the next chapter, as will the 1952 return tour by India minus Amarnath, again captained by Hazare.

In 1952/53, Lala was reappointed captain and the Indian team was to face its new neighbour, Pakistan, for the first time in Test match cricket. Curiously, a man by the name of Maharajkumar of Vizianagram - Vizzy - was instrumental in Amarnath regaining the captaincy. Was he trying to make amends for past deeds?

Following the political and humanitarian struggles between the two nations during the time of partition, the Test series itself was lifted to a new dimension. India/Pakistan Test series would always be hard fought and neither side would cope very well with defeat. This was more than just cricket.

The first Test was played at Delhi and Pakistan mostly had a team of debutants as this was that nation's entry into Test cricket. Captain AH Kardar and Amir Elahi had both previously represented India and there were a number of accomplished players, the likes of Imtiaz Ahmed, Fazal Mahmood and Hanif Mohammad, but as far as Test experience went, it was a team of greenhorns.

Amarnath won the toss – a pleasant change as he'd lost 4 of 5 to Bradman and 5 of 5 to Goddard - chose to bat, and despite a shaky start, at one stage 110/5, Adhikari (81*) together with the tail, particularly Ghulam Ahmed (50), got India to 372. Pakistan's reply was disastrous. Perhaps it was first match nerves, but apart from Hanif Mohammad, who made 51, the team crumbled against Vinoo Mankad's slow left arm medium bowling, the allrounder picking up 8-52. Following on, they fared little better with Mankad contributing another five wickets, supported by off spinner, Ghulam Ahmed with four. India won the Test by an innings and 70 runs, giving Amarnath another first: victory against Pakistan.

The second Test was played at Lucknow, the first and only Test ever played at the University Ground. The venue struggled to attract first class cricket, so it is puzzling to understand why it got a game in the first place, until you realise it came at the insistence of one Maharajkumar of Vizianagram.

Amarnath was dismayed at seeing the wicket. It was coir matting. Pakistan quick bowler Fazal Mahmood would be virtually unplayable and some of India's batsmen were not accustomed to a wicket of that type. Amarnath was successful at getting it changed to jute matting, which would play slower, but that was not enough to convince everybody. Hazare, Adhikari and Mankad all pulled out of the second Test, citing injuries. Amarnath felt their reasons lay elsewhere and was furious, but there was little he could do.

Missing the might of Hazare, Mankad and Adhikari saw another first: the first loss to Pakistan in a Test match. Amarnath won the toss and chose to bat, but the team collapsed against Fazal Mahmood and the other Pakistani medium pacers to be all out for 106. A century to Nazar Mohammad helped Pakistan to 331 and India in the second innings were again no match for Mahmood who picked up seven wickets. Pakistan won by an innings and 43 runs and the series was tied going into the third Test.

The return of the three missing players, particularly the batting of Hazare and the bowling of Mankad, saw India comfortably beat Pakistan by ten wickets at Bombay. Centuries to Hazare and Polly Umrigar and eight wickets for the match for Mankad got them home, now leading the series 2-1. Rain was the victor in the fourth Test and needing a win to square the series in the fifth Test, Pakistan was lucky to escape with a draw and thus India had won not only their first Test series, but importantly had won their first series against their new rivals.

It was a good time to hang up his bat, Amarnath finishing on top as a player and having gone further than any of his predecessors as a leader. He had proven to be good leader and a clever tactician and had engineered India's first series victory. Luck, or lack thereof, had a significant role to play, and had things turned a little differently – like coins, for example – Amarnath may have enjoyed more success as a captain, even against Bradman's Australians.

Like his predecessors, Amarnath continued to serve Indian cricket as a manager, a coach and a selector. Always committed, yet sometimes controversial, Amarnath remains as one of India's finest. He was India's Cricketer of the Year in 1947 and won the CK Nayudu Lifetime Achievement in 1994. A further legacy, two sons, Mohinder and Surinder, also played Test cricket for India. He died in 2000.

Captaincy Record	Tests	W	L	D	%
Australia 1947/48 (Australia)	5	0	4	1	0%
West Indies 1948/49 (India)	5	0	1	4	0%
Pakistan 1952/53 (India)	5	2	1	2	40%
Total	**15**	**2**	**6**	**7**	**13%**

5

VIJAY SAMUEL HAZARE

Vijay Hazare has the distinction of being India's first victorious captain, over England no less, in the 1951/52 series at home, guiding his team to victory to square the series in the fifth Test, after being one down. It was to be a lone victory as he recorded no other wins in his 14 Tests as captain.

A shy, retiring man, his batting suffered from having the responsibility as captain, preventing him from becoming India's greatest Test batsman. According to batting great Vijay Merchant it was one of the great tragedies of cricket. Despite that minor dip in form, Vijay Hazare is one of India's most cherished players, his name adorning the limited overs domestic competition with the Vijay Hazare Trophy.

Born in Sangli, Maharashtra, March 11th, 1915, Hazare was one of eight children to his school teacher father and was brought up as a Christian, educated at Presbyterian Mission Industrial School in Sangli and by all accounts was deeply committed to his faith.

He made his first class debut in September 1934, playing for Maharashtra versus Bombay, opening the bowling, oddly enough, and scoring 32 batting at number seven. In his next match he took eight wickets for the match and top scored for his team with 65, batting at number eight. His third first class match was for Central India, playing alongside CK Nayudu, Wazir Ali and Mushtaq Ali, against Jack Ryder's visiting Australian side. It wouldn't be the last time the Australians saw him bat.

In 1939/40 season he reached a peak of 316 not out, the first triple century by an Indian player on Indian soil. As he made his way into first class cricket with Central India in the Ranji Trophy, his batting became his main forte, his medium pace becoming less utilised. He also played for The Rest in the Bombay Pentangular and scored 309 out of a team total of 387 in a losing match against the Hindus in the final in 1943/44. In amassing that score, he became the first Indian to score two triple centuries.

Yet another career stalled by the Second World War, Hazare made his Test debut in Pataudi's 1946 team in England, making a modest debut with scores of 34 and 31. While the rest of the three Test series was unremarkable, he made some impressive scores against the counties, with 244 not out against Yorkshire in a stand of 342 with Vinoo Mankad.

He scored 1344 runs in first class matches at a tick under 50 per innings, with two centuries, definitely one of the better performers of the tour along with Merchant and Mankad.

In Amarnath's 1947/48 team to visit Australia, Hazare was second only to Bradman in Test runs scored, with 429 at 47.66, with two centuries and 1056 runs overall. In every respect as a batsman, the tour was a success for Hazare, if not for the team. He had the distinction of bowling Bradman in the Adelaide Test and scoring twin centuries in the same match, the first Indian to do so.

In the home series against the West Indies 1948/49, Hazare scored two centuries and topped the averages with 67.87. This was the tour where Amarnath and de Mello argued over hotels and payments and it resulted in Amarnath's dismissal as both player and captain, catapulting the reluctant Hazare into the role, becoming India's fifth Test cricket captain.

If he was a shy captain, it wasn't immediately noticeable. In his first two matches as captain, he scored centuries. Against Nigel Howard's visiting English team in 1951/52, the new captain lost the toss in the first Test in New Delhi, but his team bundled the English out for 203. He and Vijay Merchant then beat England's score on their own with a partnership of 211, both scoring centuries and India, with six down for 418, declared with a massive 215 run lead on the first innings. England rallied in the second innings on the back of 137 not out to AJ Watkins to achieve a draw that should have been a victory for India, who were guilty of dropping far too many catches. Hazare was criticized for his tactics, both the slow batting and the fielding.

So despite his batting heroics, Hazare was struggling in the new role. In the second Test at Bombay, Hazare won the toss and batted. India, on the back of centuries to Pankaj Roy and the captain, piled on 485. England replied with 456 and the match fell away to a draw, with England vastly improved on their first Test performance. The third Test in Calcutta, another draw, on a dull and lifeless wicket. Three Test matches into his new career as captain, Hazare was unbeaten, but that was about to change.

On a turning wicket in Kanpur, England made a couple of key changes, while India's selectors made even more, packing the side with spinners. Hazare won the toss and batted first, but it was a disaster, all out for 121. England didn't fare much better, rolled for 203, but in the second innings India continued to struggle against the turning ball, all out 157. In what was a miserable Test, Vijay Hazare had the unhappy distinction of scoring the first pair of ducks in Test cricket for India. England easily scored the remaining runs to win by eight wickets. What had started out so well for the new skipper had quickly unraveled.

The final Test in the series was held at Madras, and India came back in style to win the match, their first ever, and square the series – also their first ever. The selectors had made five changes and India, despite losing the toss, came out to play with intent. They had to win this Test match. On the first day the English made a steady start and finished with 224/5. During the afternoon it was announced that King George VI had passed away, so the second day of the Test was a rest day.

Mankad again weaved his magic and bowled England out for 257, taking 8-55. Pankaj Roy scored his second century of the series and with Polly Umigar's 130 not out helped India to a score of 457 and quickly enough to allow time to bowl England out, which they did, courtesy of Mankad and Ghulam Ahmed. India had won their first Test match and by the handsome victory of an innings and 8 runs. After a slow start, Captain Hazare had led his side to their first Test win and their first drawn series. It was a momentous occasion.

From the penthouse, to the cellar. India's tour to England in 1952 was a disaster, only rivalled by Vizzy's tour of 1936, but this time it was a strategic mess, as opposed to squabbling. For some reason the India brains trust chose to play in a very defensive manner, avoiding defeat where possible. This led to dull cricket, something that characterised the 1950's, and while it worked to a degree against the county sides, and had worked on the flat Indian pitches, the powerful bowling line-up of England's Test team were to prove far more effective, and the defensive tactics on lively wickets against the class of Trueman, Bedser and Laker were a tactical blunder.

India were minus key players. Merchant was injured and retired shortly afterwards, but Amarnath and Mushtaq Ali should have been selected on account of their experience in English conditions, notwithstanding the former still in the doghouse with the board. Most worryingly was that Mankad was playing in the Lancashire League and missed two of the Test matches because of a conflict of fixtures. And Hazare, despite there being no other contenders, was palpably weak as captain, despite his batting ability.

There were some bright spots. Polly Umrigar and Vijay Manjrekar enhanced their reputations, and Hazare did quite well with the bat. Off spinner Ghulam Ahmed had a good, if inconsistent tour, but the quicks failed to have the same penetration as their English counterparts. The English won the series handsomely and there was anger and disappointment at home at how poorly the team performed.

Hazare was dropped as captain and missed the second and fifth Tests in the inaugural series against Pakistan, where Amarnath led the side to triumph. Upon Amarnath's retirement following the Pakistan series, the reluctant skipper was called upon for one more tour. Hazare would lead the first Indian team to visit the West Indies.

Just as the West Indies were popular tourists in India, so too the Indian team was welcomed in the West Indies, and despite being on the wrong end of the Test series, which they lost 1-0, crowds flocked to see them play and at least one ground record was broken.

On a lifeless matting wicket at Port of Spain, a run feast by both sides saw a tame draw. The second Test was a victory for the West Indies, with India rolled for 129 by Sunny Ramadhin chasing an unlikely 276 for victory.

A delayed declaration by Hazare in the Third Test spoiled any hope of a result, and the fourth won by the weather. In the final Test at

Jamaica, India came across the full force of the three W's: Worrell, Walcott and Weekes, all scoring centuries, Worrell a double in another drawn batting fest. The West Indies could have pressed on for victory but surprisingly went on the defense.

Thus ended the Test career of Vijay Hazare, with a series dominated by batting. He himself had a career dominated by his own batting. The war and the captaincy both took their toll on his career, but even so, a test average of 47.65 is world class, and his first class average 58.38 with 18,740 runs is excellent.

His captaincy career consisted of a number of firsts, notably India's first Test victory, but one has to side with Vijay Merchant in his summation that Hazare would have finished with a far better Test record were it not for having the captaincy thrust upon him.

He served as a selector for the Indian Test team for a number of years and received a number of special honours; Padma Shri Award (the fourth highest civilian award in the Republic of India) in 1960, CK Nayudu Lifetime Achievement Award in 1996, and an inductee into the Wisden India Hall of Fame: 2015. His name lives on with the Vijay Hazare Trophy in domestic Indian cricket. He died in 2004, aged 89.

Captaincy Record	Tests	W	L	D	%
England 1951/52 (India)	5	1	1	3	20%
England 1952 (England)	4	0	3	1	0%
West Indies 1953 (WI)	5	0	1	4	0%
Total	**14**	**1**	**5**	**8**	**7%**

6

MULVANTRAI HIMMATLAL "VINOO" MANKAD

The Vinoo Mankad story is one of tragedy and controversy mixed with greatness. The tragedy is the death of his first wife, during childbirth, the controversy the runout of Bill Brown in a Test match for backing up, and the greatness is the fact that this supremely talented athlete rose above the undoubted traumas of life and became an outstanding international cricketer, one of India's finest.

One key thing that emerges immediately is Mankad's adaptability. He could bat in any position. Indeed, he did. He is one of only three players to have batted in every single position from 1 to 11 in Test cricket. (The other two being England's Wilfred Rhodes and Australia's Syd Gregory.) He could bowl on turf and on matting. It was this adaptability that made him such a dangerous player for opposition teams. His slow left arm medium wrought more destruction of batting line-ups than any other bowler of his kind in his era. On good wickets he'd pick up a few. On pitches that suited his bowling he was unplayable. He could bend, he could curve, he could twist, he could carve up teams. Then, as a batsman he could be exhilarating.

Such was Mankad's influence on Test cricket that India were quite the poorer for his absence. He was the glue. If Mankad was present, anything could happen. The impossible became the possible, such was his talent. When he wasn't in the team, he was sorely missed.

An example of this is the 1952 tour to England. He didn't play in the first Test match, probably just as well, for India lost their first four wickets in the second innings of that Test for none. Four wickets down with no runs on the board! It had never happened before and never since. England won easily by seven wickets. Mankad comes into the side for the second Test at Lords, makes 72 and 184 and with the ball bowled 73 overs in the first innings taking 5-196. He was the first player to take 5 wickets and score a century at Lords in more than thirty years and as such made it onto the honours board.

His 231 against New Zealand in 1956 was a record score for an Indian at that time and he also set a record with Pankaj Roy for the world record opening partnership of 413 runs, a record that would not be beaten for 52 years.

Outside of India and you hear less about his amazing all-round feats and more about the mode of dismissal that bears his name. It rightly irks Indian cricket lovers that the great man's name is synonymous with a way to dismiss a batsman and apparently against the spirit of the game.

In 1948 as Mankad was coming in to bowl he ran out Australian opener, Bill Brown, who was backing up too far. The action, within the laws of cricket, caused Brown to be out, run out. It had followed a warning by Mankad and one would think Brown might have learnt his lesson as it happened in a tour game earlier.

Some sections of the media howled in indignation. Under the heading, Run Out By Mankad Criticised: *"Mankad again ran Brown out backing up. Although by the laws of cricket it was justified it leaves a bad taste."* - KS Duleepsinhji – The Telegraph, Brisbane, Dec 15 1947

Yet respected cricket writer Ray Robinson's piece "Mankad Dismisses Eager Brown For Second Time. Crowd cheers alert bowler" – Brisbane Times, Dec 1947

From the Australian captain, Don Bradman:

"For the life of me, I can't understand why (the media) questioned his sportsmanship. The laws of cricket make it quite clear that the non-striker must keep within his ground until the ball has been delivered. If not, why is the provision there which enables the bowler to run him out? By backing up too far or too early, the non-striker is very obviously gaining an unfair advantage."

However, as in these modern times the media, all too powerful, managed to label this cricketer and the method of dismissal as "mankading" and Vinoo Mankad is more famous for this than his mighty deeds with both bat and ball.

The Australian public were vocal in their support of Mankad through letters to the editor:

"We wholly disagree with the notion that Mankad's "special method of dispensing with Brown's presence at the wicket" by running him out when he crept up the pitch in the Sydney Test was unsportsmanlike. Mankad more than satisfied the unwritten laws of sportsmanship by warning Brown in an earlier match. And if the batsman persists in a foolish habit he must take the consequences. It must be remembered that the batsman who backs up too early is often able to take a quick single, which is very irritating to a bowler. If the bowler is quick-witted enough to turn the tables, he deserves applause, not condemnation." - GG Noble CH Cocks, Brighton, Adelaide News

And more:

"The bowler is there to take wickets and the batsman is there to prevent him. Each knows the rules (or should). I sincerely hope that if any other batsman creeps down the pitch he will be dismissed as Mankad dismissed Brown. Or should we alter the rules for people like Brown, who is a vice-captain? If he is out of his crease so long as he has his fingers crossed he should be immune from being stumped. Failing this, the batsman would have to cry out "French forgets" or "slips" as boys do when playing marbles. As far as I am concerned, Mankad is no cad." - WF Doran

South Australian state vice-captain Phil Ridings said Mankad was quite justified.

"I consider it was a very sporting action of his in warning Bill Brown the first time. Anyway, all good coaches impress on batsmen that they must stand in the crease until the ball has left the bowler's hand."

This probably sums it all up best of all: "Brown clicked his fingers in disgust and swishing his bat in the air, obviously angry at his own foolishness, left the wicket." The Aussie captain, the player on the receiving end and the public had no qualms. If history were a little more forgiving, the term "Mankad" should be given more reverence and less disdain.

However, we are here to discuss captaincy and it was Vinoo Mankad, newly appointed captain who in 1954/55 led a team away for the first time to Pakistan. Like his predecessor, Vijay Hazare, he would manage to square his first series as captain. However, there is no real triumph here in the wider thought. Of the five Tests every one was drawn. Such was the importance of not losing, that winning never entered anyone's head. A dull and lifeless series, doing little justice to the abundant talent on both sides, was engineered to be five drawn Tests.

It would not be fair to apportion blame to Mankad for this dreary affair. Subsequent series against Pakistan that have not gone well have seen captains sacked. He would have gone in and achieved his master's objectives which would have been against his own more cavalier style of play. This series did no justice to Mankad on any level.

The first Test of this series, a four day fixture, was played at Dacca Stadium. Pakistan captain A.H. Kardar won the toss and elected to bat. Wicket keeper Imtiaz Ahmed top scored with 54 in a team total of 257, from 136.2 overs. It was painstakingly slow cricket. Subhash Gupte bowled 46 overs to take 1/79. Ghulam Ahmed bowled one less to take 5/109.

India batted ever more slightly slower, but were troubled by the pace of Mahmood Hussain (6/67) and Khan Mohammad (4/42). Gul Ramchand top scored with 37 in a total of 148 made from 82.5 overs.

Pakistan were 97/1 in the second innings at the end of day three. The following morning saw Gupte strike early, taking both overnight batters, Alimuddin (51) and Waqar Hasan (51). What followed was a complete collapse through Gupte (5/18 from six overs) and three calamitous runouts. 97/1 became 158 all out.

India's challenge was to score 267, the highest total in the match, from 82 overs. Given the lacklustre batting thus far, it was never going to be an option, with Pankaj Roy (67*) and Vijay Manjrekar (74*) negotiating the attack to see India to safety at 147/2. Oh for a fifth day! What could have been an exciting finish was denied by the negative tactics by both teams.

The second Test at Bahawal Stadium, Bahawalpur was played at the same glacial pace as the first and didn't even get to a fourth innings. Such a shame when you see the talent on offer. Mankad won the toss and batted first, promoting himself to number three in the process. Ramchand and Manjrekar each scored half centuries, as did wicket keeper Naren Tamhane who finished with 54*. The team scored 235 from 119.5 overs. The great Fazal Mahmood bowled 52.5 overs, collecting 4/86 while Khan Mohammad picked up 5/74 from a mere 33 overs.

Hanif Mohammad opened with Alimuddin and the pair put on 127 for the first wicket, the latter out for 64. Hanif was the ninth out having scored his first century in Test cricket in an innings of 142 over 510 minutes. Kardar declared the innings closed soon after, Pakistan 312/9 from 164 overs. Polly Umrigar took 6/74 from a marathon 58 overs.

Half centuries to Roy and Manjrekar saw India reach 209/5 when play finished on the fourth day.

The third Test at Lahore was a similar dull affair, two teams trying desperately not to lose. It does not seem possible, but the fourth Test at Peshawar was even more torpid. Pakistan's first innings of 188 came from 146.3 overs. The pace didn't pick up for the remainder of the Test and I shall spare you the fifth.

Manjrekar, Roy and Umrigar topped the batting averages for India, with Gupte the standout bowler. The captain had a fairly quiet tour by his standards with just 12 wickets across the five Tests along with just 51 runs from his bat.

India had a new captain in Ghulam Ahmed when New Zealand toured in 1955/56. Relieved of the captaincy, Mankad was back to his best, opening the batting in the second Test at Bombay with 223 and followed that with 231 in the fifth Test at Madras.

The Australians who toured India in 1956/57 kept the former captain quiet with the bat, struggling against the pace of Ray Lindwall and the spin of Richie Benaud. He was not alone – most of the Indian batsmen were kept quiet.

Vinoo Mankad played one more match as captain, the fourth Test against the West Indies in 1958/59, a match that India lost in a series where there were more battles at the selection table than there were on the pitch. Mankad's selection as captain was more about the various selectors, one of whom was Lala Amarnath, and their conflicting agendas. Mankad was merely one of the pawns being shuffled around on the chess board. We shall see more of that series in upcoming chapters.

A player who moved around, having played with no less than eight domestic teams, mainly out of economic need, Vinoo Mankad was a princely player and probably not designed to be a captain. In a workman like way, he followed the hierarchy and that ended in a mostly dull series against Pakistan. And his historic dismissal of Bill Brown is what he is most famous for. But if history has any justice, Vinoo Mankad will be remembered as a cavalier batsman, an excellent fielder and a deadly and destructive bowler. If you get out in cricket by Mankad, then you ought salute a clever and alert bowler.

In 1946/47 he was an Indian Cricketer of the Year. In 1947 he was a Wisden Cricketer of the Year.

In 1973 Mankad was awarded the Padma Bhushan. He died in 1978 in Bombay.

Captaincy Record	Tests	W	L	D	%
Pakistan 1954/55 (Pakistan)	5	0	0	5	0%
West Indies 1958/59 (India) *	1	0	1	0	0%
Total	6	0	1	5	0%

Not captain for full series

7

GHULAM AHMED

The 1950's had three key characteristics humming in the background of Indian cricket. One of those, although by no means on her own in this department, India began to play a more defensive style of "not to lose" cricket, highly visible in contests with Pakistan, but also against other nations. Secondly there was a revolving door of captains. Thirdly, happily, it was the genesis of a growing pack of high quality spin bowlers.

Ghulam Ahmed was part of all three. He bowled off-breaks with a high, fluent action and on the right wicket could be devastating and was a handy lower order batsman, but not your first choice as captain. If anything he was a seat warmer.

He debuted in the third Test match of the series against the West Indies in 1947/48, at Eden Gardens, under Lala Amarnath. He picked up 4-94 off 35.2 overs, including the prized scalps of Weekes and Walcott. He got Weekes again, caught and bowled in the second innings. With the bat he made a duck batting at number 10. He did enough to be in the fourth Test at Madras and was at the crease in the fifth Test when India could feel a little aggrieved when the umpire erred, pulling up stumps with a minute to go on the clock. India only needed another 6 runs for victory.

Although not used in the first three Tests of the 1951/52 tour of India by England, he showed his worth picking up 5 wickets in the fourth Test, helping Mankad bowl England out for 203 and in the fifth Test again partnered Mankad in bowling England out and celebrating

India's first Test win.

He went on the disastrous 1952 tour to England, but was able to hold his head high to a degree, returning figures of 15 wickets at 24.73.

Returning to India for the 1952/53 series against Pakistan, Ahmed scored 50 in the first Test, batting at number ten in a rescue mission with Hemu Adhikari. Together they put on 109 runs for the tenth wicket, a record that stood for 61 years. Ahmed was overshadowed by Mankad's brilliant bowling, but chipped in with 4 wickets in the second innings. His contributions with bat and ball were significant in the first Test victory.

He had a quiet time of it in the second and third Tests, missed the fourth and chipped in with some handy runs and wickets in the fifth. He missed the 1952/53 tour to the West Indies, but returned to the fray for the 1954/55 tour of Pakistan, but had a quiet tour (as did most bowlers) and missed the final Test. The captain, Mankad, was relieved of duty at the end of the series.

The first touring team from New Zealand came to India in 1955/56, under the captaincy of quick bowler, Harry Cave. Not only was Ahmed back in the team but he was selected as captain. Mankad was no longer captain but was opening the batting with Pankaj Roy, with Polly Umrigar at three, Vijay Manjrekar at four, Kripal Singh and Gulabrai Ramchand making out a very strong top six.

Umrigar dined out on the Kiwi bowlers in the first Test, with 223, Manjrekar likewise with 118 and Singh picked up a round 100 in his debut. Ghulam Ahmed declared 4 down for 498.

With the bowling, Ahmed picked up one wicket as did Mankad and Ramchand. Leg spinning sensation Sabash Gupte the remaining seven as New Zealand were forced to follow on. The Kiwis settled down in the second innings and played out time with Sutcliffe, their best batsman, not out 137 at the end, Ahmed and India unable to force for victory.

Ahmed unfortunately suffered an injury and missed the remainder of the series. Polly Umrigar would take over for the remainder of the series and we shall investigate that further in the next chapter.

Ahmed returned to the team for Ian Johnston's Australian tour of 1956/57. Umrigar had retained the leadership, but India were manhandled by Benaud and Lindwall and were handed a spanking in the First Test. Dropped for the second Test in Bombay which was drawn, Ahmed returned for the third. He picked up his best bowling figures, 7-49 in the first innings and 10 for the match. Benaud went one better with 11 wickets as Australia clinched an exciting win, winning the series 2-0. In many ways it was a watershed tour for the Australian leg spinner.

Speaking of watersheds, the 1958/59 tour of India and Pakistan by the West Indies was one such moment for that team, featuring a new dynamic squad, following on from the era of the three W's, under the captaincy of Gerry Alexander. Conrad Hunt, Cammie Smith, Rohan Kanhai and Garry Sobers were the new breed of batsman. Sunny Ramadhin, a bit past his prime but still a potent spinner and two dangerously fast men in Wes Hall and Roy Gilchrist. It was a strong, well balanced team.

India on the other hand were going through a bit of turmoil at the selection table. Chairman of selectors and no stranger to controversy, Lala Amarnath was pushing for the team to be selected more on merit than on regional factors. Most would argue in Amarnath's favour, but regional rivalries were still running rife. Amarnath used his casting vote to elect Ghulam Ahmed, a friend, as captain for the first Test. Ahmed withdrew seven days before the Test due to a knee injury.

Controversially, mainly due to the ructions within the selection committee, Polly Umrigar was named as captain of the first Test, which was drawn.

Ahmed returned for the second Test and was named captain. He might have been better nursing his sore knee. While both sides made 222 in each of their first innings, a rampant Sobers scoring 198 out of 443, and a hostile Wes Hall, eleven wickets for the match, trampled the Indians.

It got worse. In the third Test Rohan Kanhai smashed 256 while Butcher and Sobers assisted, both with centuries, getting the Windies to 5 declared for 614. Hall and Gilchrist murdered the Indian batting and the Windies won by a whopping innings and 312 runs. It was a comprehensive and humiliating thrashing.

Ahmed fell on his sword, suggesting it was time for a younger player to take over. He was, after all, 36 and it was time to move on. In keeping with the man he quietly drifted away and left the Indian Test team returning into the hands of Vinoo Mankad, who would captain one last time.

Ghulam served as team manager for the Indian tour to Australia and New Zealand in 1967/68, became an administrator, secretary of the Indian Board from 1975 to 1980, and served twice as a selector. When India won the 1983 World Cup he was chairman of selectors.

He died age 76 in 1998. As a side note, former Pakistani batsman Asif Iqbal is his nephew.

Captaincy Record	Tests	W	L	D	%
New Zealand 1955/56 (India)*	1	0	0	1	0%
West Indies 1958/59 (India)*	2	0	2	0	0%
Total	**3**	**0**	**2**	**1**	**0%**

Not captain for full series

8

PAHLANJI RATANJI "POLLY" UMRIGAR

Polly Umrigar was one of India's finest cricketers and a vision of brightness through the dull cricket played during the 1950's. Unlike the run machines of the older generation, like Merchant and Hazare, careful and steady accumulators, Polly had more dash and style to his batting, one of those types who draws crowds. He put his broad shoulders to good effect, was a powerful driver, and yet was a delicate cutter of the ball. He was also a very effective off spinner, an occasional swing bowler opening the bowling and a versatile fieldsman, making him an excellent allrounder.

A product of the cricket powerhouse of Bombay, and a Parsi, meant Polly had a very rich vein of cricketing DNA. He made his first class debut for the Parsis in the Bombay Pentangular in 1944 in the semi-final against Hindus. He made nine runs and failed to take a wicket. It was his only game that season but over the next few years, while his batting developed slowly it was with the ball that he enjoyed most success which led him to his Test debut in the second Test in the series against the rampant West Indies in 1948/49. His bowling was hammered, like all of the bowlers, by the Windies batsmen as they marched to 629 for 6 down. Polly batted only once, at number eight, a patient knock of 30 in 122 minutes. It was a quiet debut and he took no further part in the series.

He didn't appear on the Test scene again until the tour by the English in 1951/52 and played every Test match in the series, under the captaincy of Vijay Hazare. This time he was selected for his batting and was at number three in the First Test at Delhi, when a run feast by

Merchant (154) and Hazare (164) stole the show. On a tough pitch for bowlers, Polly was one of two run-outs and failed to join in the glut of runs.

He failed in Bombay, scene of the second Test, when another batting festival was on offer and again in the third Test in Calcutta. He made a duck and 38 in the lost fourth Test, but finally showed his class in the winning fifth Test at Madras, with 130 not out.

The return series in England in 1952 was a disaster for the team and particularly so for Polly. He scored 43 runs with a top score of 14. The team was up against "Fiery" Fred Trueman and it was on this tour that it was suggested that Polly "ran away" from the fast bowler and was thus not equipped to play fast bowling. It was a monkey on his back, but he would prove in the ensuing years, against the express pace of the West Indies that he held no fear of the quicks – in fact rose to the challenge and thrived on it.

In the victorious home series against Pakistan in 1952/53, he picked up a century in the third Test at Bombay, but had modest returns outside of that and was little required in the bowling department.

On the 1952/53 tour of the West Indies, Polly topped the batting, both the aggregate (560) and averages (62.22). Finally the potential and the talent was beginning to be realised. Those runs were also scored against pace and away from home.

For the drawn five Test series against Pakistan away in 1954/55, Polly again topped the averages for India (54.20) and scored the only century on the tour. He also picked up his best bowling figures, 6-74 in the second Test at Bahawalpur.

He had now become a senior member of the team. In the 1955/56 home series versus New Zealand, he was named as captain from the second Test onwards, taking over from Ghulam Ahmed. In the first Test of that series he ran the Kiwis ragged with a new Test record high score for India with 223, making him the first Indian player to score a Test double century.

The new skipper celebrated his elevation to the captaincy in the second Test, at Bombay, by winning the toss against New Zealand captain Harry Cave. Vinoo Mankad celebrated by equalling Polly's new record of 223, exactly the same score as the skipper in the first Test. On the back of Mankad's double ton, India passed 400 and Polly declared 421/8. New Zealand started well, but were all out for 258. Following on, they crashed and burned to be all out for 136, against the leg spin of Subash Gupte (5-45) and that man who won't be kept quiet, Vinoo Mankad (3-57). Polly Umrigar won his first Test match as captain of India.

On a flat track at Feroz Shah Kotla, Delhi, for the third Test, New Zealand's opener, Sutcliffe, dished up some punishment of his own, scoring 230 not out and Cave declared at 450/2. India then upped the ante, Polly declaring at 531/7, just about everyone bar the skipper was amongst the runs, but the highlight Vijay Manjrekar's 177. Suffice it to say, the match ended in a draw.

Despite a horrid start in the fourth Test at Eden Gardens, winning the toss and being bundled out for 132, Polly nearly engineered a victory after being 204 behind on the first innings. In fact, so great was the turnaround, New Zealand were lucky to escape with a draw.

Polly chose to bat first but the Kiwi bowlers masterfully exploited the early morning dew and India were soon out for 132, well short of expectations. Held together by Reid, who scored 120, New Zealand made 336. Gupte toiled away and took six wickets. In better conditions, centuries to Pankaj Roy and Gulabrai "Ram" Ramchand, a 90 to Manjrekar and a handy half century from new opener, Nari Contractor, India replied with 438. With just under half a session remaining, Polly declared 234 ahead and set Gupte and Mankad loose. When stumps were drawn, the visitors were 6 down for 75 with not much batting to come. The captain had nearly conjured up a victory after what had seemed like certain defeat after the first two days.

In the fifth Test at Madras, Polly won the toss and batted and was 79 not out when he declared at 3 down for 537. Records tumbled.

Mankad and Roy had put on a record 413 run opening partnership, the former helping himself to his second double century, 231, and the latter with 173. The partnership was a Test record, surpassing the 359 made by Len Hutton and Cyril Washbrook for England against South Africa in 1948-49. The innings total was also India's highest ever total in Test cricket to that point.

Gupte and Patel spun New Zealand out for 209 and following on, they crumbled against the spin of Gupte and Mankad.

Success for India, winning the five Test series 2-0, and Polly having overseen the last four Tests had a captaincy record of two wins and two draws. It was very nearly three wins and one draw. Not a bad start to one's captaincy career.

New Zealand's antipodean cousins toured India in 1956/57 under

Ian Johnson. It was a strong unit, featuring a mix of experienced players from the 1948 Invincibles and some new young kids on the block, namely one leg spinner called Richie Benaud.

Polly won the toss and batted in the first Test at Madras. Australia, having been on the road for quite some time, had stopped off at Pakistan after a lengthy tour of England were down in their pace bowling attack, minus Keith Miller and Alan Davidson both ill, but they weren't needed. The young Benaud routed the home side, getting 7-72, India all out for 161. Australia were also looking poor on the same batting surface until some spirited lower order counter attack from Johnson (73) and Crawford (34) saw Australia reach 319. Benaud was kept fairly quiet in India's second innings, but it was Lindwall who took over, taking 7-43. Australia won by an innings and five runs, and Polly had suffered his first defeat as captain.

The second of the three Test series was in Bombay. Polly again won the toss, this time against Lindwall, filling in for Johnson, and India batted first. It was another struggle for the home team, inching their way to 251, buttressed by Ram Ramchand's 109.

Then it was the Neil Harvey show. Australia's second wicket partnership of 204 was ominous enough, with RN Harvey scoring 140 of those. At the other end Burke helped himself to 161 and Lindwall, not out on 48 after 21 minutes, declared at 5 down for 523.

India went into lockdown. After 137 overs, they were 5 down for 250 when stumps were drawn on the fifth day. Polly had batted for nearly nine hours to save the match, in partnerships with Roy, Manjrekar and finally Adhikari. It wasn't popular with the spectators, who jeered the slow batting, but Polly had saved the match for India.

Three from three winning the toss in the third Test, at Calcutta, and Polly sent the Australians in on a track that was spinning from the outset. Ghulam Ahmed picked up a career best of 7-49 and Australia were bundled out for 177, vindicating Polly's decision to send the opposition in. At 15/0 at the close of day, all was good.

Overnight rain delayed the start of the second day and things were going along ok until Benaud got his hands on the ball. India were skittled for 136, 41 runs behind. Australia fared marginally better in the second innings scoring 189 with the help of Harvey's 69, aided by the lower middle order.

Set the modest target of 231 to win, India had a chance to square the series. The top order all got starts, but no-one went on with it and

India were bowled out for exactly the same as their first innings score, 136, spun out by Benaud and Burke. Australia won the Test, and the series 2-0. It was a far cry from the success against the New Zealanders 12 months earlier.

Returning to the troubled series of 1958/59, the home series against the West Indies, where there were heated battles at the selection table. As Chairman, Lala Amarnath used his casting vote to change the captain. He chose his friend, 39 year old Ghulam Ahmed who had not really shown much form as a skipper previously. It was an odd choice. As it turned out, Ahmed injured his knee before the first Test and had to withdraw, leaving the captaincy in Umrigar's hands.

The West Indies team was not considered particularly strong before their arrival with the retirement of the run machines Walcott and Weekes, replaced with untried youngsters, Rohan Kanhai, Garfield Sobers and WesleyHall, to name a few. India were a far more settled outfit, selection table tiffs notwithstanding.

At the first Test at Bombay, Polly lost the toss and Windic's skipper Gerry Alexander chose to bat. Good spells by Ramchand, and the leg spin of Gupte saw the visitors all out for a modest 227. Alexander then unleashed Hall and Gilchrist upon the Indian batting line-up and they were reduced to 156. It would have been worse but for Polly's stoic half century.

Courtesy of a blazing 142 not out by Sobers, the West Indies declared at 323/4, leaving India 399 to chase, a seemingly impossible task, and as such, Polly's team shut up shop and anchored themselves to the crease. Pankaj Roy batted for over seven hours to make 90. When stumps were pulled on the final day, India were 289/5 from 132 overs. Perhaps with a little more enterprise the result may have been a victory rather than a draw.

And that ends the captaincy career of Polly Umrigar, one of four captains used during that season. Ghulam Ahmed returned to captain the next two Tests, then suddenly retired. Polly was restored as captain for the fourth Test, but arguments over selection saw him resign on the eve of the Test match. Vinoo Mankad, who hadn't played a Test match in the series was quickly drafted into the side and made captain. The team got belted.

While the end of his captaincy, it wasn't the end of Polly, who went on to become one of India's finest players, finally pulling up stumps in 1962. At the time of his retirement, he held the Indian record for the most Test matches played (59), the most runs scored (3631) and the most Test centuries (12). Those records stood for 16 years and took none other than Sunil Gavaskar to break them.

Following retirement he stayed with the game and moved into administration and selection.

He was Indian Cricket Cricketer of the Year in 1948/49 and was awarded the Padma Shri in 1962 on his retirement and the C.K. Nayudu Trophy in 1998-99 for contributions to cricket. He died in 2006.

Captaincy Record	Tests	W	L	D	%
New Zealand 1955/56 (India)*	4	2	0	2	50%
Australia 1956/57 (India)	3	0	2	1	0%
West Indies 1958/59 (India) *	1	0	0	1	0%
Total	8	2	2	4	25%

Not captain for full series

9

HEMCHANDRA RAMACHANDRA "HEMU" ADHIKARI

If the 1958/59 West Indies tour of India, and the selection dramas that ensued couldn't become more bizarre, then the fifth Test in the series reached new heights of the ridiculous.

Let's recap. Ghulam Ahmed is appointed on the back of the casting vote by chairman of selectors, Lala Amarnath. Prior to this Polly Umrigar had been the Test captain. Ahmed pulls out injured and Polly skippers the first Test. Ahmed returns to captain the next two Tests, India gets hammered and he falls on his sword. Umrigar is due to captain the fourth Test but resigns after a selection squabble. Vinoo Mankad, who hasn't been playing in the series due to a pay dispute with the BCCI is returned to the side and the captaincy. Three different captains in four Tests.

By the time the fifth Test rolls around, it's chaos. The team is getting whipped by the Windies and it is more than reasonable that while the Windies turned out to be a very strong team, India would have performed much better with some stability particularly in the captaincy ranks.

Ghulam Ahmed, with the best of respect, was only a fill in captain when he skippered his one and only previous Test match, before this series. He was pushed aside in 1955 for Umrigar, a younger player who rose to the occasion and was someone that others looked up to. Ahmed, at 36, was not going to be a long term option either as player or captain. It beggars belief that Amarnath was such a strong advocate.

It is little wonder that there were arguments at the selection table if this was Amarnath's stance. Stranger still when he was the one arguing for merit over bias when that he was pumping for his friend.

Umrigar was back at the helm for the fourth Test after Ahmed was "standing down for a younger man." At least *Ahmed* was showing some common sense. Umrigar would have remained as captain, but for another selection bungle. Star batsman Vijay Manjrekar was unavailable and a BCCI board member informed Polly that the batsman would be replaced by off spinner Jasu Patel. An angry Umrigar stated, quite rightly, that a batsman should be replaced by a batsman, not a spin bowler. The argument ran on and on and ultimately Polly resigned as captain the night before the Test. With time of an essence, they recalled Mankad and the team was thrashed.

With an upcoming England tour, Amarnath quashed any thoughts of retaining Mankad as captain, suggesting he was too negative in his approach, and they needed an eye to the future. This "eye to the future" appointed the 39 year old Hemu Adhikari.

Hemchandra Ramachandra "Hemu" Adhikari, born in Pune, Maharashtra, July 31st 1919, was a right handed batsman and spin bowler who was yet another cricketer whose career was effected by the Second World War. In fact he served in the Indian armed forces.

He continued to juggle cricket and army duties when in 1947 he was called up for service in the Indian Test team, heading to Australia. He had modest returns, it must be said, with both bat and ball but was retained for the tour of India by the West Indies and in the first Test scored 114 not out batting at number seven which was to prove the high point of his batting career.

Hemu was in and out of the side during his 21 Test career and his batting average of 31.14 indicates that he struggled to retain his place consistently. He was obviously respected enough to be made captain in that final Test match in 1958/59, but at 39, it was an odd choice. He had not even played in the first four Tests of the series, yet was parachuted into the captaincy.

He won the toss at Feroz Shah Kotla, Delhi, on what was a flat track for batting and a batting fest ensued. Despite losing Pankay Roy for 1, it was plain sailing for the Indian batting lineup. The express pace of Wes Hall and Roy Gilchrist was nullified by Nari Contractor

(92), Polly Umrigar (76) Chandu Borde (109) and Adhikari (63) to see India all out for 415.

Runs also flowed for the West Indies with centuries to Kohn Holt, Cammie Smith and Joe Solomon for a total of 644 for eight declared. It was a run fest alright!

With his half century in the first innings and 40 in the second, Adhikari held his head high and also managed to salvage a draw for India which, all things considered, was a pretty good result. It would be his last Test for India.

It is his leadership after his playing career that is worth a mention.

He moved into coaching and assisted with the development of players such as Sunil Gavaskar, Kapil Dev and Ravi Shastri. Being a military man, he was straight forward and he brought this quality to his coaching and administrative roles and it's those positions that earned him the admiration and respect more so than his playing career, although he most definitely played a couple of key innings, notably the 81 not out against Pakistan in the first Test between the two countries, which went a long way towards achieving victory for India; and of course his aforementioned century not out against the Windies.

Hemu died in in October 2003, aged 84.

Captaincy Record	Tests	W	L	D	%
West Indies 1958/59 (India) *	1	0	0	1	0%
Total	**1**	**0**	**0**	**1**	**0%**

Not captain for full series

10

DATTAJIRAO KRISHNARAO "DATTA" GAEKWAD

If the 1958/59 West Indies series taught the selectors anything, it was that instability at the top of the tree impacts team performance. After the poor showing against the West Indies, the selectors wiped the slate clean and selected not Mankad, not Umrigar, not Adhikari, not Ahmed. They went for an entirely new captain, one without any baggage.

Born in Baroda in 1928, Dattajirao Krishnarao "Datta" Gaekwad was a right hand batsman with a sound technique and a solid drive and was a versatile fieldsman. Datta made his Test debut at Leeds against England in 1952 in the first Test of that series. Opening the batting with Pankaj Roy, he was cleaned up by Alec Bedser for 9 and 0 and played no further part in the Test series.

He opened the batting against Pakistan in the second Test in 1952/53 scoring 6 and 32 and was dropped for the next two Test matches. He returned for the fifth Test where he made 21 and 20 not out.

He was selected to tour with the team for the West Indies tour in 1953 and was picked to play in the first Test where he batted at number seven and made 43 and 24. He bowled one over which cost four runs. In the next Test he made a duck and didn't bat in the second innings – absent injured. He took no further part in the Test series.

In the return series, the debacle at home with the captaincy swapped around 4 times, Gaekwad did not play until the 5th Test. He made 6 in the first innings and in the second made his highest Test score and his only Test half century, scoring 52.

Looking at the above resume, just seven Tests across four series and seven years, it is hard to see how the selectors had room for Datta in the team at all for the upcoming England tour in 1959, let alone reward him with the captaincy, but that is exactly what they did. Was Datta a serious choice or was he designed to keep the seat warm? Or was he a compromise, given the heat at the selection table?

Unfortunately for Datta, he came across a very strong England line-up led by Peter May which included high quality batting in Colin Cowdrey and Ken Barrington, a legendary keeper/batsman in Godfrey Evans and one of the most lethal fast bowling combinations of all time in Fred Trueman and Brian Statham.

Gaekwad lost the toss in the first Test, at Trent Bridge, and the tour went downhill from there. May chose to bat and England piled on 422, courtesy of a captain's knock of 106, with half centuries to Barrington, Horton and Evans. Subhash Gupte chipped in with four wickets.

Despite Pankaj Roy's half century and the captain's 33, India folded for 206 against the pace of Trueman and Statham, and followed on. To make matters worse, allrounder Chandu Borde broke a finger while batting and would not bat in the second innings. England won by an innings and 59 runs.

Datta was absent for the second Test, captained by Pankaj Roy and again India was on the wrong side of the result. The most positive thing to come from that game was the gutsy innings of 81 by opener Nari Contractor, who batted most of the innings with a cracked rib.

Fortunately there was no Statham in the third Test, at Headingley, and Datta won the toss and batted, however India collapsed against Trueman, Alan Moss and Harold Rhodes to return only 161 which was quite good considering they were 75/6 at one stage. Cowdrey then helped himself to 160 runs as England applied the pressure by scoring 473/8. Gupte again with 4 wickets was the best bowler. India were rolled for 149 in the second innings to lose by an innings and plenty.

The fourth and fifth Tests were just as depressing as India fell in a heap to lose the series 5-0. It was their worst result in their 27 year history.

It does seem from various reports that Datta Gaekwad was a passive captain, happy to let things drift. This is unfortunate as the English clearly ran rampant with their strong line-up; but India were not without their own stars who underperformed. Umrigar, Roy and Contractor could have been more useful with the bat and it seemed as though the only bowler to perform was the leg spinner, Subhash Gupte. It was a sad and sorry tour and it did not help that Datta was ill for much of the time. That he was able to play in four of the Tests is testament to his courage.

Datta Gaekwad played one more Test, against Pakistan in 1961, scoring 9 runs. He won Indian Cricketer of the Year in 1957/58 and is the father of the former Indian Test opening batsman Anshuman Gaekwad.

Captaincy Record	Tests	W	L	D	%
England 1959 (England) *	4	0	4	0	0%
Total	4	0	4	0	0%

Not captain for full series

11

PANKAJ ROY

Calcutta born and raised, Pankaj Roy was a workman-like opening batsman with a solid defense and a patient mindset, but with the ability to go on the attack when the need arose.

The bespectacled and pugnacious opening batsman scored a century in his first class debut and when he was given the opportunity at Test level against England in 1951/52, he grabbed it with both hands. He finished with two centuries and a number of other useful scores to top the aggregate runs for India with 387 at an average of 55.28. One of those centuries was in the fifth Test, India's first Test victory.

It seemed as though India had found a reliable replacement for the retiring great, Vijay Merchant, but Roy suffered at the hands of Fred Trueman, as did most of the team, on the return series in England in 1952 with only 54 runs over seven innings at 7.71. Hard for any opening batsmen against a fresh Fred Trueman. The fast bowler got him four times for a duck and for good measure, Bedser got him for a duck also to give him five ducks out of seven innings. His up and down form saw him get a total of 14 ducks across his Test career.

He struggled for form in the 1952/53 home series against Pakistan and that scratchy form had him dropped for two Tests. He was included in the team to tour West Indies in 1953/54 but wasn't picked for the first Test and struggled for form until the fifth Test where he scored 85 and 150.

Against Pakistan away in 1954/55 he scored 273 runs at an average of 34.14 with two half centuries. He scored a century against New Zealand in the fourth Test in the 1955/56 series and for good measure backed up with a century in the fifth Test, only this time it was a big one, 173 in the record partnership of 413 with Vinoo Mankad (231).

He had modest returns against the visiting Australians in 1956/57 but some reasonable knocks against the Hall and Gilchrist pace attack of the West Indies in 1957/58.

The tour to England in 1959 saw Roy with scores of 54 and 49 in the first Test against Statham and Trueman. The unwell captain Gaekwad was unable to play in the second Test and Pankaj Roy became the eleventh Test captain for India.

Captain Roy won the toss against Peter May and elected to bat on a lively pitch at Lords. Roy and Contractor batted patiently for the first hour, taking the shine off the ball. Contractor was struck by a rising ball from Statham and cracked a rib. He fell to the ground but after some attention got up and continued to bat.

Soon Statham struck and Roy was out for 15. Two more wickets fell before lunch and then the leg spin of Greenhough set about the rot. Contractor batted bravely to top score with 81, but India were all out for 168.

Down, but not out, India's quick bowlers, Ramakant Desai and Surendranath also took a liking to the pitch, and supported by Gupte bowled England out for 226.

The second innings began badly however, the skipper getting a duck and Trueman and Statham causing all sorts of trouble. Some resistance from Vijay Manjrekar and Kripal Singh, but India, crippled already by the injured Contractor batting at number eight, were all out for 165 leaving England 107 for victory which they did for the loss of two wickets, Cowdrey 63 not out.

So our eleventh skipper, in his only Test as captain showed spirit but unfortunately his record stands as one Test, one loss. Gaekwad returned as skipper for the remainder of an unforgettable series for India.

He scored two half centuries against the visiting Australians in 1959/60 and got his only test wicket in the third Test: Ian Meckiff bowled Roy, 0. His last Test was against Pakistan in December 1960.

Despite his modest Test record Pankaj Roy was an opening batsman in an era that included Trueman and Statham, Lindwall and Miller, Hall and Gilchrist, all household names in the history of fast bowling.

Pankaj Roy became a Test selector, representing the East Zone. He died in 2001 in Kolkata.

Captaincy Record	Tests	W	L	D	%
England 1959 (England)*	1	0	1	0	0%
Total	1	0	1	0	0%

Not captain for full series

12

GULABRAI "RAM" RAMCHAND

Born in Karachi and powerfully built, this right hand batsman and medium fast bowler had only one series as India's Test captain, but he will always be remembered as the first captain to lead the team to victory over Australia in a Test match.

Though a quick glance at Ram's overall Test statistics shows modest returns, it was the manner in which he scored his runs, rather than the number of them, that counted. He was very good at counter attack. He was also a brilliant fieldsman, particularly close to the bat.

He made his debut in the disastrous 1952 tour of England. In the first Test he made a pair batting at number nine, but picked up two wickets. He made 42 batting at nine again in the second Test, but like all of the team his returns for the series were quite limited and the tale was the same for the 1952/53 series at home against Pakistan.

Promoted to first drop in the first Test against the West Indies at Port of Spain 1952/53, Ram finally realised his enormous potential and hit 61 runs on the matting wicket and 62 in the third Test at the same ground. He opened the bowling throughout the series but there were slim pickings for any bowler flinging leather against the batting might of the Three W's.

A quiet series with both bat and ball against Pakistan in 1954/55 until the fifth Test when he picked up his best bowling figures of 6-49 at Karachi. His century in the fourth Test against New Zealand in 1956 was a counter attacking and match saving innings.

He got his first look at the Australian team in 1956/57 in Polly Umrigar's team and scored a century in the second Test but lacked penetration with the ball.

The notorious selector's bun fight in the 1958/59 home series against the West Indies saw Ramchand selected as captain for the fifth Test but that was withdrawn because of another argument between the selectors and ultimately he didn't play. He went from captain to being dropped from the team altogether! He was also not selected for the 1959 tour of England, but that was a blessing in disguise as India were on the receiving end of a hiding.

When the Australians toured in 1959/60, not only had Ram returned to the team, he was now appointed as captain. It was a strong Australian team skippered by Richie Benaud who had been so effective on the previous tour. The team included Neil Harvey, Norm O'Neil, Ken McKay, Alan Davidson and was a good balanced outfit.

Ram won the toss against Benaud in the first Test at Delhi, but that was about as good as it got. He chose to bat but India were no match for the bowling of Davidson, Ian Meckiff, Gordon Rorke, Lindsay Kline and Benaud and were bundled out for 136 with Contractor top scoring with 41. All but one of the Australians reached double figures as they scored 438 runs. India, after a fighting opening stand between Roy and Contractor, eventually collapsed all out for 206, leaving victory to the Australians by an innings and 127 runs. Not the best of starts for the new captain.

In the second Test at Kanpur Ram won the toss again, elected to bat, and once more the Indian batsman were dominated by the Australian bowlers, all out for 152. Australia were cruising at 127/1 and looking at a huge total when they collapsed badly against the spin of Jasu Patel who took an incredible 9-69, all out for 219. This was just the sort of luck India needed and they rode the momentum into their batting, scoring 291, with Contractor again amongst the runs with 74 and Ramnath Kenny with 51, but there were also useful contributions from Chandu Borde, Abbas Baig and Bapu Nadkarni, leaving Australia with 225 needed for victory.

The Australians started steadily enough but as soon as Patel came on they were mesmerised, just as they were in the first innings. Patel picked up five, Polly Umrigar four and the Aussies were dismissed for

105, giving the hosts victory by 119 runs. India had beaten Australia for the first time in Test cricket. There were jubilant scenes and no-one was more satisfied than the skipper.

With the series still alive, at Bombay for the third Test, Ram continued his happy knack of winning the toss and elected to bat. On the back of yet more runs from the gutsy opener, Contractor, 108, India put together a competitive total of 289. Australia replied with 387, courtesy of centuries to O'Neill and Harvey. The tradition of spectators running garlands of flowers, along with lemons to centurions bemused Harvey.

"I can understand the garland of flowers but for the life of me I don't know why one gets the lemons as well. In front of 30,000 people a batsman can feel a little ridiculous with flowers round his neck and a handful of lemons."
– Neil Harvey *"My World of Cricket"*

With time running out Ram declared at 226/5, having seen the team to safety, leaving Australia an impossible target in too little time. Benaud reversed the batting order and Grout opened with Ian Meckiff. Ram responded in the same spirit and allowed some lesser bowlers to have some fun. Pankaj Roy picked up the only wicket to fall, bowling Meckiff for a duck.

At the fourth Test in Madras, Benaud won the toss and elected to bat. Hard hitting South Australian opener Les Favell scored his maiden Test century as Australia made 342. Benaud and Davidson then destroyed the Indian batting line-up – twice - to give Australia an innings victory. It was a big letdown after the highs of the previous two Tests.

There was still hope however, if India could rally there was still a chance to square the series in the fifth Test at Bombay. Normal service resumed, with Ram winning the toss and electing to bat. But normal service also resumed for the Australian bowlers, who bundled India out for 194. Plenty of starts, but no-one went on with it. A century to O'Neill helped Australia to 331. However India rallied in the second innings and fared much better with the bat, scoring 339, leaving Australia the victory target of 203, but time was the enemy and the Test drawn.

The series showed that India could indeed compete against

Australia, even against the might of Benaud, Davison and Harvey. Ram was rightly lauded for his captaincy, but the series would be his last. And what a way to go out, having matched it with the Aussies.

Ram had a career with Air India and was also manager of the Indian team during the first World Cup in England in 1975. He died in September 2003.

Captaincy Record	Tests	W	L	D	%
Australia 1959/60 (India)	5	1	2	2	20%
Total	5	1	2	2	20%

13

NARIMAN JAMSHEDJI "NARI" CONTRACTOR

It's been described as a tragedy. I prefer to look at it from a different perspective: it was a bloody miracle. In a tour match in which he was not supposed to take part, but did so due to another player's illness, Nari Contractor found himself at the crease in Barbados, facing the unpredictability of Charlie Griffith and his frightening pace. He was dropped by Conrad Hunte at forward short leg. He then became distracted by something behind the bowler's arm and didn't pick up the next delivery until too late. It struck him in the head and he dropped to the ground, bleeding from the nose and ears. His international cricket career ended right there. He nearly died. That he lived, is the miracle.

A compact, neat, left handed opening batsman, Nari Contractor was born March 7th 1934 in Godhra, Gujarat. At the age of 21 did what Australia's Arthur Morris had done before him: scored a century in each innings of his first class debut. Batting in the middle order for Gujarat against Baroda in the Ranji Trophy, he scored 152 and 102 not out, but it would be, like Morris, as an opening batsman where he would make his mark in Test cricket.

The opening batting positions were a struggle for India in the 1950's. Retirements of some big names, plus a plethora of outstanding fast bowlers from other nations meant that getting a steady and consistent opening pair seemed elusive. Contractor debuted against New Zealand in the second Test of the 1955/56 series, playing in the middle order, out for 16 in his only innings. By the time the next Test rolled around, he was opening the batting and made 62.

He missed the first two Tests of the 1956/57 series against Australia, and contributed a couple of twenties in the third Test.

By the time the 1958/59 series against the West Indies at home, India had settled on the opening batting pair of Contractor and Pankaj Roy. In a series beset by off field dramas, the openers did pretty well and Contractor secured his spot, finishing the series with a personal high of 92 in the fifth Test at Delhi.

His sterling and courageous innings of 81 in the second Test in England in 1959, after he'd cracked two ribs while batting, was one of the few highlights for India on that tour.

Against the touring Australians in 1959/60 he had his best series to date and hit his highest Test score of 108 in the third Test at Bombay. *"...was easily India's most accomplished batsman in the series."* – Neil Harvey

By now he'd become someone very dependable at the top of the order and with the retirement of Gulabrai Ramchand, Nari Contractor was rewarded with the captaincy for the home series against Pakistan in 1960/61. At the age of twenty-five, the 13th Test captain of India was the youngest skipper ever to be appointed.

With the 1950's a period with the record as one of the dullest cricket decades on offer, despite a couple of bright spots, nothing came duller than a Test series between India and Pakistan. The anticipation of such series was great and the expectations high, but the sheer nature of the battles between these neighbours away from the cricket field meant that ceding on any level was not negotiable. India and Pakistan could have a Test series of marbles, or tiddly winks, and these too would end as draws.

For an outsider looking in, it is frustrating. Two countries with such an abundance of talent ought to be producing exciting cricket every time they play. But equally, an outsider just does not know what is at stake. Losing is simply not an option.

The 1960/61 series between the two sides ended in five drawn Tests and created from the template created in 1954/55 under Vinoo Mankad. The formula was very simple: win the toss, bat and then shut up shop. The team batting second would do the same and thus there would be no time for two completed innings. No possibility of forcing a win, but then, no way to lose.

In the 1960/61 series, Pakistan's Fazal Mahmood won the toss in the first Test at Bombay and chose to bat. 137.4 overs later they were dismissed for 350, courtesy of centuries to Pakistani great, Hanif Mohammed (160) and Saeed Ahmed (121) at 2.54 runs per over. Once the centurions were out, the team folded. They went from 301/1 to all out 350.

Contractor declared the Indian first innings closed when they were 9 down for 449 from 176.4 overs, also scored at 2.54 runs per over. The ninth wicket partnership between Ramakant Desai and Nana Joshi realised 149 runs. India's innings was closed on the morning of day five. Pakistan were 4 wickets down for 166 runs in the second innings, scored at 2.07 runs per over, when the Test ended. Hardly what you would call an advertisement for Test cricket.

In the second Test at Kanpur, Mahmood again won the toss for Pakistan and again they batted first, only this time with far less flamboyance than the first Test, scoring 335 in 188.4 overs at 1.77 runs per over. India were far more brisk as they amassed 404 runs at a more hurried 2.08 runs per over. Opener Motganhalli Jaisimha was unlucky to be runout for 99 after having batted for over eight hours. India were all out in their first innings just before lunch on day five!

Fazal Mahmood won the toss in the third Test at Calcutta and Pakistan were actually on top of India at one stage but India fought back. Had rain not intervened, with over one day's play lost, both sides were in with a chance of winning the Test.

Some records tumbled in the fourth Test at Madras – batting records, that is. Once again Nari Contractor lost the toss and once again Pakistan batted first, making 9 declared for 448 in just over two days. India then batted until day five, scoring 9 declared for 539, a new high for them in Test cricket. Chandu Borde's 177 over nine hours was the highest individual score to date between the two countries. Pakistan successfully negotiated eighteen overs in the second innings and the Test ended in another draw.

But for a little hurry up from India in the first innings, the fifth Test could have been an Indian victory. Contractor finally won a toss and India batted first and continued batting into the third day for 463 runs. The captain himself made 92 of those in just under six hours – at the end of the first day he was 54 not out. In reply, Pakistan were all out for 286 and were made to follow on. In the second dig they made just 250, leaving India just 73 runs for victory, but only two overs were available to score them. Another draw. Five from five.

With that series thankfully over, England toured in the 1961/62 season with series against both India and Pakistan. A rushed itinerary organised at the last minute, a tour to the West Indies by India, meant that England would play both Test nations in a split itinerary. They would play one Test in Lahore, Pakistan, then five Tests in India, one more against Pakistan in Dhaka, East Pakistan (now Bangladesh) before completing the tour in Karachi. Probably not ideal.

The India v England series would be a far cry from the five Test bat-athon between India and Pakistan. Ted Dexter won the toss in the first Test at Bombay and chose to bat, with England making 500 on the back of a Ken Barrington century. India scored slowly but steadily and made 390, still 114 behind. England, looking for quick runs in the second innings declared at five down for 184. India played out time, 180/5. Approximately 200,000 spectators turned up over the five days.

On a flat wicket in Kanpur, Nari Contractor won the toss and batted first in the second Test making eight declared for 467, Polly Umrigar amongst the runs with 147 not out, however the scoring was quite slow, the whole innings at 2.35 runs per over. Making his debut in this Test, young wicket keeper Farokh Engineer, was ironically stumped by his opposite number after making a useful 33.

Again, this slow scoring hurt India. England collapsed against the leg spin of Gupte and for the first time in their history, were forced to follow on against India. However the nature of the wicket allowed England to escape. Centuries to Pullar, Barrington and Dexter saw them five down for 497 when play stopped on day five.

The third Test at Delhi was washed out after three days. Had the rain not appeared it is unlikely that the match would have had a result, such was the snail's pace at which both teams were scoring. A young fellow by the name of Mansoor Ali Khan, aged twenty, made his debut in this Test match. The ninth Nawab of Pataudi, son of the third Test captain of India, would make his own impact on the game and Indian cricket over the coming seasons.

The fourth Test, at Eden Gardens Calcutta, broke a streak of nine drawn games for India. Contractor won the toss and batted first on a pitch that was taking spin on the very first day. Spinners Tony Lock and David Allen sent down seventy overs between them as India scored 380 runs with honours shared amongst the batsmen. Chandu Borde topped with 68 runs, along with the Nawab who scored 64.

Borde and Salim Durani spun England out for 212, leaving a deficit of 168 runs. In their second dig, India also succumbed to spin, with Lock and Allen picking up nine of the wickets to fall as the home team were all out for 252, Borde again top scoring with 61. Left 421 for victory, England showed patches of resistance, but the climb too great and pitch too volatile, India winning their second ever Test match against England, victors by 187 runs.

In the fifth and final Test, now in a position of authority, captain Contractor was in a position to advance further forward. He won the toss and batted, leading the way with 86 in good time, followed up by the Nawab of Pataudi's debut century and India finished with 428 at good clip. Nadkarni and Engineer contributed valuable runs in the lower order with 63 and 65 respectively.

England struggled against the left arm spin of Durani and were bowled out for 281 leaving them 147 runs behind on the first innings, Mike Smith's 73 the top score.

Before he was runout, Vijay Manjrekar was the sheet anchor for India's second dig of 190, as Tony Lock had them in a spin, leaving England with 338 to win. It would prove too much. The spin of Borde and Durani meant it was too big an ask on that wicket and India won the Test match by 128 runs.

Not only had they won the Test, but they also won their first ever series against England. Nari Contractor had inflicted on the English something that none of his predecessors had ever come close to. His place in history was assured.

West Indies Tour 1961/62

With a series victory over England, India would have been full of confidence heading to the West Indies for a five Test tour in February 1961. New players such as Pataudi and Engineer gave the team new verve. In fact, those two players had not even tasted defeat in Test cricket.

At Port of Spain, scene for the first Test of the five match series, Nari won the toss against Frank Worrell and chose to bat but conditions conducive to fast bowling suited Wes Hall and Chester Watson, and that impossibly good allrounder, Garfield Sobers, to have India bundled out for 203. Without the same pace firepower, India toiled hard through the spin of Durani, Umrigar and Borde, knocking the hosts over for 289.

The second innings was a disaster, Hall bowling eight overs with figures of 3-11 and that man Sobers with 4-22 off fifteen. India were blown away for 98 runs. Conrad Hunte and Cammie Smith knocked over the requisite 13 runs without bother.

Contractor won the toss in the second Test, at Sabina Park, Jamaica, and elected to bat. After a wobbly start, Polly Umrigar and Chandu Borde bolstered the innings with 50 and 93 respectively, Borde proving to be an outstanding allounder, especially when the chips were down. Valuable contributions from Nadkarni (78*) and the young 'keeper, Engineer (53) and India ended their first innings with a well-made, if a little fractured, 395. It was all too little. An avalanche of runs to the West Indies with centuries to Easton McMorris, Rohan Kanhai and Sobers had Frank Worrell declaring at eight down for 631, a lead of 236 runs.

India put up little resistance against Wes Hall, who took 6-49, and were bundled out for 218, losing the Test by an innings and 18 runs. The top score was wicket keeper, Engineer, with 40 runs. It was Nari Contractor's last Test match.

After the second Test, a tour game against Barbados, a match which was supposed to be a rest for Contractor, disaster struck, but he was forewarned by Frank Worrell. Charlie Griffith was fast and unpredictable at times and that was amplified on the Barbados pitch. Worrell suggested he sit out the match and not risk playing against Griffith, but injuries to the touring squad meant that Nari had to play. It very nearly cost him his life.

Opening the batting as usual, Nari Contractor faced up to Griffith. There was no sight screen and the skipper was having some issues with some movement in the crowd behind the bowler's arm but resolved to deal with it at the end of the over. He negotiated the first two balls well and was dropped by Conrad Hunte off the third. Contractor struggled to see the fourth ball. He got behind it to play it, but his lack of vision caused him to swerve too late and it smacked him on the head. Having been hit behind the right ear by a Charlie Griffith missile, Nari dropped to the ground. He was bleeding through the ear and through the nose.

Contractor was immediately taken to the pavilion by team manager and former captain, Ghulam Ahmed. He was mopped up, but the bleeding would not stop.

Twenty minutes later, Vijay Manjrekar was also felled by a short delivery, the ball hitting him on the bridge of his nose. *"I've been blinded! I cannot see a thing,"* he cried in the dressing room. Fortunately his eyesight returned after a short while, but with Contractor bloodied and Manjrekar blinded, it was not much fun waiting to go and bat.

"The atmosphere was tense, waiting to bat was almost like waiting for the executioner's axe." – Nawab of Pataudi *"Tiger's Tale"*

Contractor was taken to hospital where he became unconscious. There was no surgeon at the hospital – he would not be available until tomorrow, but by then it might be too late. The pressure on Nari's brain was enormous. Something had to be done.

A local doctor did enough to stabilise the batsman so that he would still be alive when the neurosurgeon arrived in the morning. He just had to hold on overnight. He was losing blood fast and needed a transfusion. Fellow players Polly Umrigar, Chandu Borde and Bapu Nadkarni gave blood. So too did the West Indies captain, Frank Worrell, in a gesture that comes as no surprise from the great man.

The neurosurgeon arrived in the morning and completed the procedure but Nari remained unconscious for six days. Griffith came to visit him every day. Nari's wife came from India to keep a bedside vigil.

Nari Contractor survived and lived to tell the tale, but he would never grace the Test arena again. He tried, he desperately tried, for you cannot keep a man of his courage and commitment in a cage. He returned to first class cricket, and despite a mountain of runs the Test selectors would have nothing to do with his return. It was too risky. Ghulam Ahmed, the man who helped him from the field and one of the selectors, would have none of it. It's not hard to understand Ahmed's point of view. Think in more recent times of Australian batsman Phillip Hughes – there's just no way you would be prepared to let someone go back into the fray. It's a human life. Cricket is but a game.

Despite his efforts to return to the Test arena it was never going to happen. And so, one of cricket's bravest batsmen was never to play Test cricket again. He was awarded Indian Cricket Cricketer of the Year in 1955/56, the Padma Shri Award in 1962 and the CK Nayudu Lifetime Achievement Award in 2007.

Captaincy Record	Tests	W	L	D	%
Pakistan 1960/61 (India)	5	0	0	5	0%
England 1961/2 (India)	5	2	0	3	40%
West Indies 1961/62 (WI) *	2	0	2	0	0%
Total	**12**	**2**	**2**	**8**	**17%**

Not captain for full series

14

MANSOOR ALI KHAN
NINTH NAWAB OF PATAUDI

Mansoor Ali Khan's father, the eight Nawab of Pataudi, died when Mansoor was eleven. The captain of his cricket team Nari Contractor, nearly died ten years later, thrusting the young prince into the role of India's Test cricket captain at the tender age of 21, after having represented India in only three Test matches, the youngest Indian Test captain ever. On the surface, it could have been the most ridiculous appointment in the history of Test cricket. As it turns out, it was one of the best, Pataudi described as arguably India's greatest captain.

Nicknamed "Tiger" by his parents, the moniker stuck and this much loved cricketer was called Tiger by just about everybody. The name referred to his movements as an infant, but it became more associated with the man and his character as he grew.

As we learnt in an earlier chapter, Mansoor Ali Khan's father was Iftikhar Ali Khan, the former Indian captain in charge during the 1946 England tour. Mansoor had limited opportunities to learn cricket from his father, but he reports that he played in one or two matches with him.

Pataudi's captaincy can be defined by two key components. Firstly, he was about unity. The team represented India, not the parts there-of and as such should work together as a unit. Secondly he set about to change the mindset of the team to chase victory as opposed to avoiding defeat. It was a refreshing change and Pataudi heralded a new era, however it was also a time characterized by his creativity in making the best use of the resources at hand, for in an age of great fast bowling attacks, India's stocks were limited.

Like his father, he was schooled in England, and he was coached by former England player, Frank Woolley. The young prodigy played his debut first class match at the age of 16 for Sussex in 1957. In a handful of games that year he scored 67 runs at 17.25. He continued playing for Sussex, but in 1960 played for Oxford University and became the first Indian captain of that team.

In the summer of 1961, disaster struck. Tiger was involved in a car crash in which he was a passenger. While no major injuries were evident initially, a tiny shard of broken glass from the windscreen had become dislodged in his right eye. Despite surgery he effectively lost vision in that eye. Permanently. It was thought that the twenty year old would never play cricket again, but that idea never occurred to Tiger.

Though he had double vision and a lack of visual perspective, Tiger was back playing in the nets within weeks. He made some minor adjustments to his stance but probably the most important thing was covering his damaged eye, which mitigated the blurred vision. He tilted his cap to cover the right eye. Some thought the prince was being stylish when in fact the angled cap was Tiger being practical.

Remarkably, not only was he back playing first class cricket, but six months out from the injury he made his Test debut for India against England in the third Test at Delhi, at the age of twenty. He made just 13, but in the next Test a bright 64 and followed up with a century in the fifth Test at Madras. The next time he stepped into the Test arena, he would be leading his country.

Selected as vice-captain for the 1961/62 West Indies tour under Nari Contractor, Tiger Pataudi didn't play in the first two Tests, nursing an injury. He was to be the understudy for a few years before taking over, but was thrust into the captaincy upon the injury to his skipper. The bouncer that felled Contractor reverberated around the ground and into the dressing room. It was the end of Nari's Test career and Mansoor Ali Khan, the ninth Nawab of Pataudi, became the 14th Test captain of India.

To receive the captaincy in that context for one so young and inexperienced must have been quite a shock to the system. He was the youngest Test captain India had ever chosen. *"I was fortunate to have a few senior players around me."* In fact every single player on the tour was senior in terms of age and experience, but Polly Umrigar, a former captain himself, was one of the first to offer support.

"You have got to do the job, but I will be at your elbow at all times giving all the help I can," Polly told the young captain and was good with both word and deed for he had a pivotal role to play in a number of important times in the remaining three Test matches.

His first Test in charge, the third match of the series, was played at Kensington Oval, Bridgetown Barbados, the very ground where Nari Contractor was felled. Pataudi lost the toss and was sent in to bat by West Indies skipper, Frank Worrell.

Pataudi and Durani both top scored with 48 runs each, but the batsmen generally struggled against the pace of Wes Hall and India were all out for 258. While there were no centuries in the Windies reply, they still managed 475 runs and left a lofty deficit to chase down. India crumbled against the spin of Lance Gibbs who picked up 8-38, and were all out for 187, a loss by an innings and 30 runs. It was a tough initiation for the young skipper.

In the fourth Test at Port of Spain, Pataudi again lost the toss, with the Windies piling on 444 after Worrell chose to bat. The innings was built around Kanhai who blasted 139 and good backup from Worrell batting at number nine, making 73 not out. Polly Umrigar toiled tirelessly for his young skipper, bowling 56 overs and taking five wickets.

Wesley Hall had accounted for the top five Indian batsmen when the score was only 30. A 94 run fightback between master and apprentice, Umrigar and Pataudi, helped settle the innings but they were all out for 197. Following on, the batsmen showed more spunk in the second innings, and on the back of a century to Durani, and 172 not out from Umrigar, India had restored pride and even gave themselves a whiff of victory with 422, leaving a modest chase of 175. It was not to be however, with West Indies victors by seven wickets.

Sobers had a fine match in the Fifth Test, with the double of a century and a five wicket haul helping the West Indies to a 123 run win. It had been a tough tour for the visiting Indians and they'd have been very glad to get on the boat to sail home. It had been a cruel tour for the original captain and a tough initiation for the new one.

A New Era

Back at home, the new captain began to assert himself and shape the team in his own way. It was a new team, a new breed. He wanted to stamp his authority, not in a belligerent fashion, but the young man had ideas. One of those was that the Indian cricket team need to be "more India" and less regional based. That meant selection was to be more about merit than the regional biases: the exact same thing Lala Amarnath as a selector had been arguing about previously. Only this time, it was a prince in charge and Tiger Pataudi was not without influence.

Tiger's first full series was on home soil, against the English. It has to be said that it was an unfortunate spectacle, although crowd numbers were excellent, to finish with no result after five Test matches. Both teams were guilty of passivity, it must be said, but the conditions were also not conducive to bright cricket.

India were at times overly defensive and this negative policy must rest with the young captain, still finding his feet. England were suffering from players being down due to illness, so they too, by necessity, tended towards defensive cricket. Had Tiger been a more seasoned campaigner (note, to this point he had played only six Test matches in total before this series) he would have likely been quicker to seize the opportunity when England were on their knees with missing players. In the fifth Test, England had to borrow a fielder from India as they only had 10 fit men. It was a throwback to the boring cricket of the 1950's and out of character for the young Pataudi. This would not happen again.

Bobby Simpson's Australian team toured in 1964/65 and this was a much brighter spectacle than the tour by the MCC. Simpson and Bill Lawry shone for the Aussies with the bat and pace bowler Graham McKenzie was the standout bowler. The leading light for India, their young skipper, Pataudi.

The three Test series began in Madras where Simpson won the toss and Australia batted first. They were looking very comfortable at 160/3 but Bapu Nadkarni's spin spoiled the party and the visitors collapsed to be all out for 211. To be sure, India were slow in reply, but coming in at 76/5, Tiger Pataudi's 128 not out meant that India, with 276 runs, took a handy first innings lead.

Australia performed much better in the second innings and made 397. McKenzie then ripped through the Indian openers and it went further downhill from there, bundled out for 193. It was a disappointing loss after the promising start to the Test. The Aussies just ran them down.

Simpson won the toss at Bombay for the second Test and opened the batting with Lawry, both openers contributing very little but the Australians scored a good 320. In that innings they met for the first time a spin bowler by the name of Bhagwat Chandrasekhar. He picked up the wickets of Simpson, Brian Booth, Tom Veivers, and Johnny Martin. India replied with 341, Pataudi top scoring with 86.

Half centuries to Lawry, Bob Cowper and Booth saw Australia finish with 274, Chandrasekhar picking up another four wickets to give him eight for the match.

Set 254 to win, India were staring at defeat at 122/6, but Pataudi held things together with a fighting half century, and with assistance from Vijay Manjrekar, turned the tables and India won a gripping contest by two wickets. It was a courageous victory and the young prince's first as captain. Australia could only blame their poor catching. Pataudi was dropped by Burge when only 9, and by Simpson twice in the slips, when the batsman was 24 and 28. It was a most satisfying win for the young skipper.

The third Test was won by the weather. The ground at Calcutta had turned into a quagmire by the fourth day, so the series was squared. It was new territory. This was the first time India had squared a Test series with Australia. Tiger Pataudi's century in the first Test was the only century by either side during the series. The young man, and his transitioning team, were beginning to find their feet.

New Zealand, under the management of Walter Hadlee, toured in 1964/65 for a four Test series. They would follow that series with one against Pakistan and then on to England. They played thirteen Test matches in six months and faded through that period. However, they were at their freshest when they started in India.

Unfortunately it was another Test series of overwhelmingly negative and defensive cricket. The first three Test matches produced no result. The first two Tests, rather dull, but the third match, at Bombay, was an exciting see-sawing match that was thrilling up to the last minute with either team well within grasping victory.

John Reid won the toss for New Zealand and Graham Dowling's 129 helped them to a score of 297. India collapsed badly in reply, all out for 80, thanks to 5-26 from the fast medium pace of Bruce Taylor and were asked to follow on. Admittedly the wicket was conducive to faster bowling and many balls simply spat off the pitch.

In the second innings, had Taylor been more alert in the slips off of Bevan Congdon's bowling, Indian opener, Sardesai, would have been out for 20. Add another zero and he makes 200. Borde chips in with 109 and India are right back in the match, scoring 463, the target for New Zealand, 254. At eight wickets down for 80 runs when stumps were drawn on day five, what had seemed like a possible win for New Zealand was in fact a lucky escape in the end. It had been a great comeback by India.

In the final Test at Delhi, Reid again won the toss – 3 from 4 – and chose to bat. A young spinner, yet another one, Srinivasaraghavan Venkataraghavan, "Venkat", took eight wickets as New Zealand fell for 262. Another century to Sardesai and one for the Nawab saw India in front on the first innings, declaring at 8 down for 465. Venkat picked up another four wickets to give him twelve for the match as New Zealand were bowled out for 272. India made the 73 for victory with only three wickets down and won the series 1-0. The skipper had led from the front during the series with the blade of his bat and his crooked cap, with 316 runs at 52.66 with two centuries.

The Indian skipper had now gone from the disaster in the West Indies, to a drawn series against England at home, a drawn series against Australia and now a victory against the Kiwis. The trend line was upwards, however it was to dip back sharply in the next three series, home to West Indies, and away to England and Australia and with each loss, the skipper was never given a guarantee of the captaincy beyond the first Test or two. He was fighting to retain the role, his plight made all the more difficult because of the lack of fast bowling stocks.

The home series against the West Indies, or to put it more pertinently, against Garry Sobers, was a disappointment, with the home side going down 2-0 in the three Test series. The search for quality pace bowlers meant that India was now becoming ever more reliant on spin. The first Test in Bombay a case in point. The quicks bowled three overs. Chandrasekhar bowled 61.5 and Venkat 52. In the second innings the quicks got 1.1 overs and Chandra and Venkat 50 between them. The Indian quicks simply had no penetration, certainly not on Indian pitches, yet Hall and Griffiths got wickets for the West Indies. Pataudi had no quick bowlers remotely in that class.

In the second Test, another spinner was added to the team, a young Sikh named Bishan Singh Bedi, a slow left armer, but because India's batting was so out of sorts, he only bowled in one innings, West Indies winning by an innings and 45 runs. The third Test was a run fest, the most notable feature, Erapalli Prasanna in for Venkat.

The Indian team was now regularly playing three spin bowlers. Tiger Pataudi was struggling with a dearth of quality pace bowlers, yet there was a seemingly endless line of high class spin bowlers becoming available. Who said you had to have quick bowlers at all? Was Tiger proving to be a master tactician, as he crafted his team over the ensuing years around his quartet of tweakers or was he simply bereft of alternatives? Whatever that answer may be, let there be no mistake: he was now in charge of one of the most potent bowling attacks of all time – it was just that they were spinners and not the ferocious fast bowling combinations cricket was used to.

The 1967 tour to England was an unhappy one, mainly due to the English weather. So bad was it that the Indians had barely fired a shot in anger to adjust to the conditions before the first Test was upon them. They were also beset by injuries and the continual lack of pace bowling options a perennial plague.

England's Brian Close won the toss and batted in the first Test at Headingley and the crowd were treated to a Geoff Boycott marathon, the English opener unbeaten on 246 when Brian Close declared four down for 550. India were rattled by the English bowlers, out for 164 with Pataudi top scoring with 64. Following on, they fared much better with a magnificent fightback making 510 and again the captain led from the front with 148, with good support from Ajit Wadekar and Farokh Engineer. It wasn't enough to hold England back, reaching the victory target of 125 with only four wickets down. Pataudi again made his spinners toil, probing for wickets, with Chandrasekhar 19 overs opening the bowling and Prasanna 21.3 overs – out of 47.3 overs.

Of Boycott's 246 not out, it was the highest individual score for any Test between England and India to that time. However, despite not making a false stroke, his slow and patient batting was criticised and the selectors dropped him for the next Test. That's tough! Make a double century and get dumped for the next Test. Australia's Jason Gillsepie and Geoff Boycott share more than just their Yorkshire connection.

Pataudi won the toss for the second Test at Lords and batted first in murky conditions. The pace of John Snow and David Brown proved too much and India were routed for 152, Ajit Wadekar providing the only real resistance with a patient 57 from two hours and thirty minutes. England in reply treated the spin trio with extreme caution and the scoring rate was only 2.5 runs per over. (Compare that to the first Test where England scored at 3 runs per over during Boycott's marathon.) They painfully crawled to 386, but the pain was India's, for in the second innings they were bamboozled by the spin of Ray Illingworth and rain stoppages, all out 110. Victory to England by an innings and 24 runs.

Beset by injuries, bad weather and a strong opposition, Pataudi must have been happy to be at the end of the tour. By the time the third Test came around he'd lost three quick bowlers, and the stocks were so thin that for the first time he bowled his awesome foursome, the spin quartet of Chandrasekhar, Bedi, Prasanna and Venkat, and he opened from one end with the team's reserve wicket keeper, Budhi Kunderan.

Brian Close won the toss and batted and on a pitch taking spin on the first day. Pataudi opened with the pace of Kunderan and Subramanyam but the spinners did the job, restricting England to 298.

Unfortunately the batsmen didn't do their job. Overnight rain suited the English pace attack and the Indians collapsed to be all out for 92. Brian Close was criticised in some quarters for not enforcing the follow-on, but it wasn't widely known that one of his key fast bowlers, Brown, was suffering from a back strain and could do with a rest before resuming duties. The Indian spinners, led by Prasanna, bowled England out for 203, although it must be said that England were much more carefree with their batting, given the considerable lead. India were never going to make the 410 required but some stoic batting by Wadekar and the skipper gave them a respectable 277, however losing the Test by 132 runs and the series 3-0. They would be glad to leave the rain, John Snow and Geoffrey Boycott.

The tour to Australia in 1967/68 went about as well as the tour to England. Again India were under-resourced in the fast bowling stocks. Rusi Surti and Umesh Kulkarni were honest toilers and Abid Ali just above medium pace, but this trio were not going to be able to fire out the strong Australian batting line-up in Australian conditions. Simpson, Lawry, Paul Sheehan, Ian Redpath, Bob Cowper, Ian Chappell. It was a very strong top order. India's best chance was with their spin quartet, but they would not be much good without a strong effort from their batsmen to back them up and despite a few glimpses of joy, mostly it was a forgettable tour. So much so that they lost all four Test matches and every first class game they played.

The tour got off badly when Pataudi injured his hamstring and the team missed his guiding presence in the early matches where he was absent. He also missed the first Test in Adelaide, Chandu Borde deputising for him. Australia won by 146 runs. Leading bowler Chandrasekhar was also injured.

The second Test, despite being a loss for India and a number of excellent performances from the Australians, notably Simpson and Lawry with centuries, 151 to Chappell (his first Test century) and ten wickets for Graham McKenzie, this will always be remembered as Pataudi's Test, such was the courage and audacity he displayed in both innings. Not only was he hampered by the permanent injury to his right eye, he was still hobbling with the temporary issue with his hamstring.

Tiger won the toss, and despite the green tinge to the pitch, elected to bat. Batting at number seven, Pataudi hobbled to the crease when the score was only 25 for the loss of five wickets, McKenzie running rampant. Unable to run properly, Tiger had two options, defend or hit boundaries. Against incredible odds, he top scored with 75 out of the team total of 173. He batted for nearly four hours, facing 194 balls. He hit 8 fours and had the understandably low strike rate of 38.65. It was a courageous knock.

Prasanna took six of the Australian wickets to fall, but not until they'd amassed 529, adorned with the aforementioned centuries to Simpson, Lawry and Chappell. There was a bit more fight in the Indians in the second dig, and knocks of 42 (Engineer) and 99

(Wadekar) but a mini collapse brought Tiger to the crease and from number seven, he bettered his first innings performance, scoring 85 of the innings total of 352. Australia deservedly won the Test by an innings and four runs for they had well and truly outplayed India, but the Test will always be remember for the bravery and the audacity of those two innings from Tiger Pataudi.

Two changes to the Australian team for the third Test in Brisbane. Doug Walters came in for the resting Bobby Simpson, with Bill Lawry taking over the captaincy and South Australia's fast-medium pacer, Eric Freeman, came in for the resting McKenzie.

Pataudi won the toss and sent Lawry and his team into bat. Untroubled by India's pace bowlers, the Australians made 379, Walters top scoring with 93. The burley Freeman, batting at nine, made sure his first scoring shot in Test cricket counted: a six from the wily Prasanna. When the Indian innings got underway, Freeman then sent two of them packing early as the visitors slumped to three wickets down for only nine runs.

A middle order fightback rescued the day and again Pataudi was in the thick of things, scoring 74, ably supported by Surti (52) and Jaisimha (74) as India recovered to 279 all out. Still 100 behind but it could have been so much worse, given some of the poor batting in the previous Tests.

Australia were cruising at 4 down for 240 when Prasanna picked up Chappell and then proceeded to run through the rest of the order, taking six wickets. Australia all out for 294, leaving India a run chase of 395 to win. At 61/3, it looked like a forlorn hope, but a brilliant display by the middle order, led by Jaisimha (101) following up on his first innings success, with support from Borde, Surti and Pataudi assured the match would be a tight finish. India fell short by 39 runs but had truly lifted their performance to give Lawry's Australians a real scare.

The fourth and final Test was in Sydney and was to be the farewell of Bobby Simpson, who starred in the match, not with bat, but with ball. Pataudi sent the Aussies in to bat and a similar circumstance to their second innings in Brisbane. Cruising at 5 down for 242, Chappell was run out for a duck and another collapse left Australia short of where they were heading, ending up with 317.

India likewise were going along nicely and also collapsed. Pataudi was the ninth man out, for 51, as he was running out of partners. Simpson with his leg spin, and Freeman with his pace, bundled India out for 268. Australia's second innings was bankrolled by Bob Cowper's 165 but they collapsed once again. Good fielding and poor running resulted in three runouts as the Aussies tumbled towards 292. The pattern had been set in the previous three innings. India, heading steadily towards the victory target of 341 at 145/2, fell into a spin themselves against Australia's trio of spinners: Gleeson, Cowper and Simpson. Simpson picked up 5-59. Australia won the series 4-0, but Pataudi had fought hard and topped the batting averages for India with 56.50.

The First Away Series Win

A quick trip across the Tasman Sea from Australia to New Zealand for a four Test series against the Kiwis and what would turn out to be a far more pleasing result than the previous two series against England and Australia, so much so that this series was the first time an Indian team had won a Test series away from home soil. It was also the first visit to New Zealand shores by an Indian team. New Zealand's captain Barry Sinclair, was dumped after one Test for Graham Dowling who skippered the remaining three matches.

Sinclair won the toss for New Zealand in the first Test at Dunedin on the South Island and had no hesitation in batting. A steady, albeit slow gathering of runs saw opener Graham Dowling score 143 and New Zealand finished with a more than respectable 350. India batted a little more briskly on the foundation laid by Engineer and Wadekar and the team total ended nine runs more than the Kiwis in the first innings.

Prasanna picked up six wickets as New Zealand laboured to 208 all out off 104 overs. (Pause to reflect on the axing of Geoff Boycott for slow scoring, again...) India were untroubled in the chase and on the back of another half century to Wadekar, won the first Test by five wickets.

Pataudi sent New Zealand in to bat in Christchurch, also on the South Island for the second Test after the pitch looked a bit green. Looks deceived and new captain GT Dowling again piled on the runs for the Kiwis, this time a double century to get the team to 502, Bedi picking up six wickets. Between Bedi and Nadkarni, they bowled 113.3 overs. India's reply was patchy and Kiwi quick Dick Motz picked up six wickets as the team was bowled out for 288. Forced to follow on they fared slightly better in the second dig, ending with 301. Chasing only 88, New Zealand got the wobbles, but a sterling 61 from Bevan Congdon got them home by four wickets. Series level, heading to Wellington on the North Island.

Dowling won the toss in the third Test and batted but Surti and Prasanna saw to it that the innings was an abbreviated one and bundled the Kiwis out for 186. Wadekar again showing his class at number three scored 143, providing India's backbone as they scored 327, a substantial lead of 141. Spitting cobras, those Indian spinners, Bedi, Prasanna and Nadkarni, rolling New Zealand for 199. India won with only two wickets down. 2-1 in the series with one to play.

Dowling won the toss in Auckland and sent India in to bat. They struggled against the pace of Motz and Bartlett all out for 252, top score being the skipper who'd had up to this point a fairly lean series after his good form in Australia. To be fair, there were rain stoppages and conditions not conducive for batting. Indeed, Dowling and his team found that out to their detriment as they were routed for a dismal 140.

Tiger Pataudi declared the India second innings at five down for 261, leaving New Zealand the task of chasing down 374 in just under five hours on a pitch now taking sharp spin. Dowling provided some resistance but it was too much for the Kiwis and India won by 272 runs and the series 3-1. A most important day in the history of Indian cricket: their first series win away from home. Tiger Pataudi had done something no Indian captain had done before. He was rewarded later that year as a Wisden Cricketer of the Year and deservedly so. His courageous batting in Australia and his aggressive captaincy in New Zealand were high points for the cricketer and the nation.

He celebrated that success on his return home by marrying Bollywood star, Sharmila Tagore. It was a glamorous affair and it captured the country's imagination: India's princely Test cricket captain marrying a movie star. It was a match made in heaven and continued for the rest of his life.

Downward Slide

The return series by New Zealand in India in 1969 was a bit of a letdown after the highs of the overseas victory. It was a stronger bowling and fielding outfit from a side that had played a lot of cricket. These Kiwis were match hardened and had played some tough cricket over the previous 18 months against England and the West Indies.

Pataudi won the toss for the first Test at Brabourne Stadium, Bombay and batted. (The Test was originally scheduled for Ahmedabad but rioting forced a last minute change) Hadlee (Dayle) was almost unplayable and received good support from Bob Cunis and Bevan Congdon, India all out for a paltry 156. Congdon's 28 helped New Zealand get to 229, but they failed to really capitalise and the wicket was beginning to take turn. It was tough going in the second innings as India ground out a laborious 260, with the skipper top scoring with 67 in four and a half hours, leaving New Zealand to score 188 on a turning pitch. It was a bridge too far. Bedi was brilliant and backed up by Prasanna, New Zealand never in the hunt, losing by 60 runs.

New Zealand reversed the result in the second Test at Nagpur, the first Test match to be played at Vidarbha Cricket Association Ground. Dowling won the toss and New Zealand batted cautiously, laboriously, but battling the spin of Bedi, Prasanna and Venkat on a pitch that took spin on day one, they did a good job, scoring 319. India were rolled for 257. It could have been worse but for Anjaj Roy (nephew of former captain, Pankaj Roy) and Farokh Engineer batting in the lower order. Glenn Turner top scored with 57 in New Zealand's second innings of 214. The match was now set up, India to chase 277. They didn't even come close, Pataudi top scoring with 28 as India collapsed against Hedley Howarth and Vic Pollard to be all out for 103, victory to the Kiwis by 167 runs.

The third Test at Hyderabad, ending in a draw, is best forgotten. It was marred by rain, bad umpiring and riots. It was a match that should have been won by the Kiwis and it did not display Indian cricket in the best light. The series was squared 1-1.

Crowds flocked to see the visiting Australian tourists, led by WM Lawry in 1969/70. It was a strong team despite the retirement of

Bobby Simpson and they were well known to Pataudi and his players.

Disappointing crowd scenes marred an otherwise absorbing contest in the first Test at Bombay. Pataudi won the toss and batted, and top scored with 95 as India made 271. Fast bowler Graham McKenzie toiled hard and was rewarded with five wickets and well supported by Alan Connolly and John Gleeson. Australia batted steadily, if a little slowly in reply, but the spin trio of Prasanna, Bedi and Venkat made life difficult. The Aussies ended up with 345, with a century to new opener Keith Stackpole and good contributions from Doug Walters and Ian Redpath, a lead of 74 runs. Australia's own spin twins, John Gleeson and Ashley Mallett destroyed India's batting in the second innings, all out for 137.

A catch by wicket keeper Brian Taber off Connolly to dismiss Venkat caused some excitement in the crowd late in the day. Bottles hurled, chairs set fire, a low point for Test cricket, but play continued. Australia won the Test by eight wickets.

Gundappa Viswanath, one of a number of changes the Indian selectors made after the first Test, was making his Test debut in the second Test, at Kanpur. Pataudi won the toss, batted, and India made their way to 320 all out. The debutant Viswanath was out for a duck. Paul Sheehan held the Australian innings together with 114, his maiden Test century and the visitors were slightly ahead on the first innings with 348.

India replied with 312 in the second innings, and Viswanath was the star of the show. After his duck in the first innings, he cut and drove powerfully to score a century on debut. His 137 was the backbone of the innings and left Australia 284 to score in two hours. Pataudi could not afford to be more generous with the declaration and it was a wise move: in that two hours Lawry and Stackpole put on 95 for no wicket and no trouble, and the match ended in a draw.

In New Delhi for the third Test, on a pitch that favoured spin, Lawry won the toss and batted. Prasanna and Bedi had their way with most of the Australian batsmen – except for Ian Chappell who batted for over four hours and made a fighting century, his second against India, with Stackpole in support at the top of the order. The spinners ripped through the bottom half, save for 46 by Taber and the Aussies were all out for 296. Mallett and Gleeson then had their way with the

Indian batsmen who also struggled on the turning pitch. Ashok Mankad (son of former captain, Vinoo Mankad), who had already proven to be a fighter in this series, top scored with 97, but India were well short of Australia's total, bowled out for 223.

India's quick bowlers sent down a total of 3 overs between them before Tiger unleashed his two most potent weapons. Australia were all at sea against Bedi and Prasanna and there were no heroics from Chappell this time, scoring a duck. There was stubborn resistance from captain Lawry, who not only top scored but also carried his bat, remaining not out in the carnage as Australia were bowled out for 107. With just over two days to score the 181 runs, India lost Engineer to be 13/1 at stumps on day three. Bishan Bedi came in as night watchman and made an invaluable twenty runs in partnerships first with Mankad and then with Wadekar, whose 91 not out guided India to victory with support from the young Viswanath. India won the Test by seven wickets and proved that if conditions were conducive to spin, Pataudi had supreme firepower at his disposal. The series was level at 1-1 with two Tests to play.

The fourth Test at Eden Gardens, Calcutta, was a letdown after the heroics of New Delhi. Lawry won the toss, and in heavy conditions and poor light, sent India in to bat and they were made to struggle against McKenzie who took six wickets as the home team folded for 212. Again the young Viswanath top scored, with 54. A good start by openers Lawry and Stackpole before another fine innings from Chappell, desperately unlucky to edge Bedi to slip when he was on 99 and Australia made 335. Freeman and Connolly bowled India out for 161 and the Aussie openers had no trouble knocking off the 39 required for victory. Australia ahead 2-1.

Despite six days being scheduled for the final Test in Madras, it was over after lunch on the fourth day. Once again a low scoring affair and Australia won by 77 runs, giving them the series 3-1 and that would be the last we would see of Tiger Pataudi for a few years.

A Triumphant Return

There had been some unrest among the selectors about his captaincy, and the series against Australia was not his best for batting. However, having laid the groundwork for India's new outlook, he was dropped completely for the 1970/71 tour to the West Indies and the 1971 tour of England as the selectors wanted to press on with younger players and a fresh outlook. 1971 continued to be a bad year when he was stripped of the family title, when an amendment to the Constitution of India abolished the titles enjoyed by Indian royalty.

Pataudi was left out of the team until 1974/75 when the West Indies toured. Not only was he back in the team, but he was restored to the captaincy. (We shall cover the period while he was out of the team in chapter sixteen.) However, he was now getting on, despite being only 34 years old, but had been out of the Test team for nearly four years. The team had changed and so had Pataudi. And so had the West Indies, now on the cusp of their glorious twenty year reign. Clive Lloyd's team would not hit the summit for a few years, but apart from the skipper himself, with names such as Fredericks, Greenidge, Richards, Kallicharran, Roberts – this was a team on the rise.

But for a bit of luck India would have won the series 3-2. They lost the first two Tests, won the next two, but the losing of the toss in the final encounter was pivotal. Lloyd won the toss and chose to bat in the fifth Test and the first Test match to be played at the newly built Wankhede Stadium. And bat he did. He contributed 242 not out and declared his team six down for 604. India were never in the match and lost by 201 runs. Pataudi's final innings in Test cricket a subdued nine runs. He was no longer listed as Nawab of Pataudi in the scorebook, but simply M.A.K Pataudi.

It could have ended so much better. Had he been left to lead the team for another season at least, he could have not only gone out on a high, but also left the game on his terms. The final period of his time as a player did not do the man justice.

Tiger stayed in touch with the game he loved and continued working off the field for many years as an administrator and was generous with his time and comments about the game of cricket. Was he India's most successful Test captain? Statistically, no. Did he put India on the right road? Undoubtedly.

Tiger Pataudi's legacy to Indian cricket was enormous. As a player he was Indian Cricketer of the Year in 1962, and a Wisden Cricketer of the Year in 1968 and all of that with one eye, but his greatest contribution was as a leader, giving the Indian Test team the belief that they could win, and fighting the opposition as a united force.

In 1967 he received the Padma Shri Award and in 2001, the CK Nayudu Lifetime Achievement Award, and what a lifetime it was. Tiger passed away in September 2011.

Captaincy Record	Tests	W	L	D	%
West Indies 1961/61 (WI *)	3	0	3	0	0%
England 1963/64 (India)	5	0	0	5	0%
Australia 1964/65 (India)	3	1	1	1	33%
New Zealand 1964/65 (India)	4	1	0	3	25%
West Indies 1966/67 (India)	3	0	2	1	0%
England 1967 (England)	3	0	3	0	0%
Australia 1967/68 (Australia)*	3	0	3	0	0%
New Zealand 1967/68 (NZ)	4	3	1	0	75%
New Zealand 1969/70 (India)	3	1	1	1	33%
Australia 1969/70 (India)	5	1	3	1	20%
West Indies 1974/75 (India)*	4	2	2	0	50%
Total	**40**	**9**	**19**	**12**	**23%**

Not captain for full series

15

CHANDRAKANT GULABRAO "CHANDU" BORDE

Chandu Borde was an accomplished allrounder who scored important runs for India and picked up wickets with his leg break bowling when they were most needed. His career was almost entirely under the captaincy of Mansoor Ali Khan and with over 3000 Test runs and 52 wickets, he was an instrumental player in that team.

Born in Poona, Maharashtra, July 21st 1934, he debuted at age twenty for Baroda in the 1954/55 domestic season. It was a modest start, but he broke through in his second season, scoring his maiden century against Bombay, and a half century and five wickets in the Ranji Trophy final of 1957/58. By now the selectors were taking notice and Borde played his debut Test match in 1958 against the West Indies. Dropped after two Tests, but returning to the team for the fourth, he made a half century and then backed that up with a century in the fifth Test of the series. It was a roller coaster start to his international career.

It was in Australia in the season of 1967/68 that Chandu Borde was called upon to represent his country as captain of the Test team, in the absence of Tiger Pataudi. It would be his one and only Test match as captain.

Bobby Simpson won the toss and batted on a perfect Adelaide Oval wicket. He and Bill Lawry got Australia off to a good start with a stand of 99 runs. Both were out within ten runs, Simpson for 55 and Lawry for 42, but the Australian batsmen prospered on the easy pitch and against a friendly pace attack. Paul Sheehan helped himself to 81 and

Bob Cowper 92, but the Indian bowlers pegged things back, Abid Ali taking six wickets and Prasanna three as Australia collapsed to be all out for 335.

Farokh Engineer got things off to an electric start after the early loss of Sardesai to Dave Renneberg before eventually falling for 89. He received good support from Wadekar (28), Borde (69) and Surti (70) as India muscled up with 307 in reply.

Centuries to Simpson and Cowper underwrote the strong Australian second innings of 369, leaving India the uphill climb of 397 to win. It began badly and it never gained any reasonable momentum as India were all out for 251, Renneberg picking up five wickets and Subramanya top scoring with 75. Thus ended the captaincy career of Chandu Borde, the Australians victorious by 146 runs.

It wasn't the end of Chandu Borde however and he continued to be a strong performer for India in Test cricket. His last Test was against Australia, a team he'd played against in four series, in the first Test at Bombay in 1969.

After his celebrated career, Borde went on to be a team manager and was in charge of the team which toured Pakistan in 1989 that included teenage sensation, Sachin Tendulkar. He went on to be a selector and continued his involvement with Indian cricket no matter what level. The consummate allrounder on the cricket field was the consummate allrounder even after he'd hung up his playing boots.

Chandu Borde won Indian Cricket Cricketer of the Year 1958/59, the Arjuna Award in 1966, the Padma Shri Award in 1969 and followed that with the Padma Bhushan in 2002. Finally, in 2003, the most important award for an Indian cricketer, the CK Nayudu Lifetime Achievement Award.

Captaincy Record	Tests	W	L	D	%
Australia 1967/68 (Australia)*	1	0	1	0	0%
Total	**1**	**0**	**1**	**0**	**0%**

Not captain for full series

16

AJIT LAXMAN WADEKAR

Ajit Wadekar had big shoes to fill: he was the replacement for the much loved and heralded Mansoor Ali Khan. The elegant and aggressive left handed batsman did more than fill the shoes. He took the team crafted by Tiger Pataudi and turned them into a winning unit. He became India's most successful captain by the time he retired. Ironically, the man who took over after him was Mansoor Ali Khan.

So successful was Wadekar that he won his first three Test series as captain. No man before him had done that for India. What makes it even more impressive is that the first two of those Test series were precious victories away from home.

Wadekar came from the cricketing powerhouse of Bombay and despite a very good track record in domestic cricket, he had to wait eight years before he was called up for his country in 1967. He debuted under Pataudi, against a bowling line-up consisting of Hall, Griffith and Sobers. His debut was unspectacular. Trying to occupy the important number three position, it wasn't until the third Test in that series that he passed fifty, scoring 67, indeed top scoring at Madras.

He toured England in 1967 and scored a duck in the first innings of the first Test, but backed up with 91 in the second innings. Half centuries in the second and third Tests proved that he was capable at this level.

Another overseas tour, this time to Australia in 1967/68, he struggled to find his feet in the first Test and again fell short of a century in the second, scoring 99 in Melbourne. In Pataudi's successful series against New Zealand, he was a consistent performer, half centuries in each innings of the first Test and a breakthrough century in the third. He had made the number three spot his own.

In the home series against the visiting Australians in 1969/70, he got half centuries in each of the first two Tests and his unbeaten 91 underwrote India's victory in the third. By the end of the series he was India's most reliable batsman and given the selector's ongoing concerns with Pataudi, they promoted Wadekar, now 29 years old, to the captaincy for the upcoming tour to the West Indies making him the 16th Test captain of India.

The team was bristling with youth and experience. Still to find a new opening pair, but fortified by the older pair of Sardesai and Durani in the middle, new wicket keeper, Krishnamurthy, and the experienced, wily pack of spin sensations, Bedi, Prasanna and Venkat. Wadekar's strategy was simple: bowl tightly to the batsmen with the spinners and the West Indies would eventually lose patience, getting out to rash strokes.

Before the first Test, Wadekar hatched a plan to nullify the strength of the West Indies pacemen. The strategy was to go for a draw, and wait for more spin friendly tracks further into the series.

The first day of the first Test at Sabina Park, Kensington, was lost due to water getting in through the covers. When play was allowed to begin, Sobers won the toss and put India into bat. At 75/5 it looked as though the West Indies captain made the right decision, but a courageous fightback led by a nearly eight hour stay at the crease by Sardesai who scored 212, and assisted by the tail India ended the first innings with an excellent 387. The West Indies were the total opposite. They started solidly, cruising at 200/4 and collapsed suddenly against the Indian spin trio to be all out for 217. For the first time in a Test match against this opposition, India enforced the follow-on, however the West Indies fared much better and Kanhai's 158 not out ensured they reached the safety of a drawn Test.

Sobers again won the toss for the second Test in Trinidad but this time chose to bat. It was a regrettable decision. Opener Roy Fredericks was clean bowled off the first ball of the match and the Windies never recovered, bundled out for 217. A Test debutant by the name of Sunil Gavaskar got his first entry into a Test scorebook. He bowled first change, one solitary over that cost nine runs. His second entry a little more to type, opening the batting he shared a good partnership with Mankad (44), and then with Sardesai (112) before the young opener fell to the spin of Noreiga, but not before making 65 runs. He was dropped by Sobers at slip when he had only 12 runs to his name. The skipper Wadekar got a first ball duck but it was immaterial. India finished with 352 runs, a lead of 135.

The Windies had a better go at it in the second innings, but some poor running between the wickets and the spin of Venkat left them with just 261 and a lead of just 124 runs. Gavaskar was there at the beginning and was still there at the end, 67 not out, guiding India to a first ever victory against the West Indies, winning by seven wickets. It was the first win in 25 Test matches against this opposition.

The third Test was notable for slow scoring scores of 350+ by both teams in the first innings which spoiled any real opportunity by either side to push for victory. It was also notable for the continued batting success of Gavaskar, a century in the first innings and 64 not out in the second.

Wadekar won his first coin toss in the fourth Test at Bridgetown, Barbados, and sent the West Indies in to bat. His reasoning behind the decision that in an earlier tour game against Barbados, the batsmen struggled on a green wicket. Better to let the West Indies bat first. And bat they did. Finally flexing some muscle with the bat, particularly the captain Sobers who scored 178 not out, the Windies declared at 501/5. The Indian top order collapsed, at one stage 6 down for 70 runs. Sardesai once again came to the rescue and together with Solkar helped get the score to 256, far more respectable. He then had partnerships with the lower order and in particular a tenth wicket partnership with Bishan Bedi, not only avoiding the follow on but netting 62 runs. Well short of the Windies first innings, but you'd take 347 after being 70/6.

Quick runs from Fredericks and Clive Lloyd allowed Sobers to declare 6 down for 180 leaving India to score 334 to win in just over five hours. Sobers used ten bowlers in a bid to press for victory, but the one wicket they really needed was Gavaskar, who guided the team to safety with a not out century.

Needing just a draw to win the series in the fifth Test at Port of Spain, Wadekar won the toss and elected to bat. Gavaskar's century helped the visitors to 360, about good enough to guarantee that they would not lose, despite the match being extended to six days. Sobers had other thoughts however and his 132, along with 105 from Charlie Davis gave the West Indies an excellent advantage with 536, a lead of 166. India lost Abid Ali early but that man Gavaskar again nailed himself to the crease and scored a brilliant double century. Sobers and his team must have been utterly sick of the sight of the little opener by then! The skipper finally made some runs, 54, and India were all out for 427. It left the delicious scenario of West Indies needing to score 262 in two and a half hours.

Wickets tumbled too frequently for the West Indies and by the time they shut up shop, they were 165/8. It has been suggested that Wadekar left it too late to introduce his spinners, but that is a moot point. India had won their first Test series against the mighty West Indies and only their second overseas victory.

A matter of months later, in June 1971, Wadekar and his team were on another overseas tour, this time to England to face Ray Illingworth's outfit. There were many familiar faces – Geoff Boycott, John Edrich, Basil D'Oliveira, John Snow. It was a solid England team, bolstered by their thumping demolition of Australia six months earlier. Illingworth had proven to be a master tactician and cleverly used his number one pace weapon, John Snow, to good effect against the Aussies. England had not tasted defeat in their last 24 Test matches.

Illingworth won the toss in the first Test at Lords and but for rain, a thrilling victory was on offer to either side on day five, but the match ended in a draw. Happily there were runs for Wadekar, who had struggled with the bat in the West Indies, scoring 85. Honours were about even for both teams and it set up an enticing contest for the rest of the series.

Illingworth, on the back of his own century, nearly crafted a victory for England in the second Test at Old Trafford. Had rain not wiped out the entire fifth day, it is doubtful whether India could have held on, 65/3 chasing 420. They been given a lucky break after having been outplayed on the first four days.

Illingworth won his third toss in succession for the third Test at the Oval and batted. Despite a mini collapse in the middle order, England were rescued by pugnacious wicket keeper, Alan Knott (90) and

Richard Hutton (81) to post a respectable total of 355. Gavaskar and Mankad fell early, but good contributions throughout most of the batting helped India to 284, 71 runs short of England's total. Wadekar then went on full attack with his spinners. It was the Chandrasekhar show, taking 6-38 and spinning the English batsmen into turmoil, all out for 101, their lowest ever total against India, and indeed, their third lowest since the war.

It left India with a chance of victory, chasing 174, if they could negotiate their way through the pace of Snow and Price, and the probing darts of Derek Underwood. Not to mention the wily Illingworth.

Snow picked up young gun Gavaskar, for a duck. Underwood took out Mankad for eleven and the small fightback from the skipper Wadekar, who made 45 was needlessly snuffed out by runout. Illingworth kept ringing the changes, himself leading from the front, while Underwood was constantly probing, nagging. India were 76/3 with 100 to go, but fourth innings runs are the hardest to score.

Sardesai and Viswanath put on a valuable 48 run partnership before the former was snared by Knott from the bowling of Underwood. 124/4. The runs came painstakingly slow, but they were gathering one by one. Solkar came and went, another victim for Underwood. 134/5.

Vishy and Farokh Engineer, continued slowly, steadily, before Illingworth threw the ball, and the dice as it were, to Brian Luckhurst. After nearly three hours at the crease, Vishy's vigil ended. His 33 run innings ended, caught Knott bowled Luckhurst. However, his wicket fell at 170 and a mere four runs from victory. The man who would one day captain this team had played a dogged captain's knock.

Abid Ali came in and wasted no time. He hit a boundary and with Engineer, steered India home to victory by four wickets.

India had won its most famous prize: victory over the English in England. It snapped a 26 Test streak of non-defeat by England. It clinched the series. India had won a Test series away from home against the most powerful team on the planet. Wadekar had done the seemingly impossible: he'd registered two series victories on the trot away from home.

England in India 1972/73

Under new captain Tony Lewis, and bolstered by new talent such as South African born allrounder, Tony Greig, the MCC toured India and Pakistan in 1972/73. Pakistan aside, England were hell bent on revenge for the last series.

The English were lacking training in local conditions, a bit underdone, before the first Test at Delhi but came out firing on all cylinders. Wadekar won the toss and batted, but were fired out by the swing and pace of Geoff Arnold who took 6-45. India in tatters, all out for 173, but they fired back themselves, Chandrasekhar mesmerising the visitors with his spinners, bettering Arnold by taking 8-79, England all out for 200.

England fought back, again with Arnold, backed up by Pocock and Underwood, skittling India for 233. It left England with a 207 run target and a tantalising finish to the Test match, given their wobbles against Chandrasekhar in the first innings. They struggled early, losing Amiss and Fletcher to Bishan Bedi, but were eventually home by six wickets, thanks to knocks from Tony Greig and the England captain, Lewis. England had wiped away their pain from the previous series and arrived in India ready for revenge and had landed a lusty first blow.

It was another, tense and low scoring Test match in Calcutta for the second of the series. Wadekar won the toss and batted. Wickets fell regularly – the English had kept that pesky opener Gavaskar quiet, unlike their West Indies counterparts – but a rear-guard innings once again from Engineer, helped India to a modest 210.

This was battle, neither team taking a backward step. Wadekar let loose with the pace attack for seven overs and then tossed the ball to his spinners, Bedi, Chandrasekhar and Prasanna. Whether attacking or defending, England lost wickets at a quick rate. Resistance by Greig, Knott and Chris Old, but not enough, the team rolled for 174, India with a crucial first innings lead of 36.

A fiercely fought contest such as this one means that England came back even harder at India. Chris Old, who was making his debut in place of the injured Geoff Arnold, after his batting heroics came out and bowled like a champion, taking four wickets; and his batting partner in crime, Tony Greig, bowling off cutters, knocked over five more, taking his best figures to date of 5-24. India all out for 155, seemingly on the canvas, but this drama had one more act to play and once again Tony Greig was front and centre. England needed 191 runs to take a 2-0 lead in this riveting series.

Wadekar wasted little time with his pace bowlers and the first four English wickets fell for 17 runs. But Tony Greig was nothing, if not a fighter, and between him and Mike Denness put England back on track for victory. Chandrasekhar knocked him out when the score was 114 and struck again when he took out wicket keeper Alan Knott. Shortly after the last line of resistance, Denness, fell too. Pocock, Underwood and Cottam were out soon after and India had pulled off a remarkable victory in this absorbing Test match, victors by 28 runs. Not only that, but they were now back in the series.

Forced changes to both sides for the third Test at Madras and Lewis, winning the toss for the first time, elected to bat. Coming into the Indian side, an old hand, Mansoor Ali Khan. He'd belted a century against the MCC in a tour game and he was rewarded with selection. The Tiger had returned to the fold.

Wadekar opened the bowling with Solkar (2 overs) and Sunil Gavaskar (1 over) before tossing the ball to his trio of tweakers. One wonders why the charade to even bother with the quicks. Chandrasekhar with 6-90 was too hot to handle for the English batsmen, and apart from a fine 97 not out from Keith Fletcher, England struggled to be all out for 242. Lots of starts for India but only one score over fifty. Tiger Pataudi, receiving a hero's welcome to the crease from the adoring crowd, was back and at his brilliant best, top scoring with 73 as India ground out 316.

Wadekar dismissed any notion of fast bowling by opening with Solkar at one end and Bishan Bedi at the other. Solkar bowled two maidens and was replaced by Chandrasekhar and was not required any further. His four overs for the match were plenty for an Indian pace bowler!

England tried desperately, slowly, somehow trying to find a way against these dastardly spinners, but only Denness could provide any resistance. They batted for 106 overs but could only muster up 159 runs. It left India an easy target for victory of 86 runs, but with both openers in the sheds early, and Wadekar for a duck, there was a fair bit of panic. Fortunately they scraped through, a belligerent 38 by Durani, and the calm guidance of an old hand, 14 not out to the Nawab, India victors by 4 wickets to take a 2-1 series lead.

Rather uninteresting draws in the final two Test matches of the series gave India its third series win on the trot and its second successive series win against England. It was as though nothing could stop them and the victorious skipper, Wadekar, despite his own form not being as well as it was prior to taking the captaincy, was a on a roll. Next stop England to continue the dominance, but it wasn't to be.

The 1974 tour to England began badly. The weather was appalling, just as it had been on the 1967 tour. England had a new captain, Mike Denness, and was bolstered by the return of Geoff Boycott, John Edrich and Bob Willis. Tellingly their batsmen had learned to use their feet when facing spin bowling. It was a dramatic and emphatic turn around. Gavaskar had a welcome return to form, but the rest of the team went in the opposite direction.

The first Test was lost by 113 runs, the second and third by an innings. India was thrashed comprehensively, 3-0. England had learned how to play spin and had tamed India. (They would take their new found confidence in spin bowling to Australia where they would meet a challenge of a different kind: Lillee and Thomson.)

His own form shy of his best and leading a badly beaten team Ajit Wadekar retired from Test cricket at the end of the series. It was not a glorious departure, following the series against England, but his leadership was the most successful so far, with three series wins from four, and particularly overseas and against the old enemy. His cherished place in the history of Indian cricket is indeed well deserved.

Like many of his predecessors he continued to serve Indian cricket. He was a manger of the team during the 1990's and was a chairman of selectors.

On the awards front, he was Indian Cricketer of the Year in 1963, awarded the Padma Shri in 1972 and the CK Nayudu Lifetime Achievement Award in 2011.

Wadekar passed away in August of 2018.

Captaincy Record	Tests	W	L	D	%
West Indies 1970/71 (West Indies)	5	1	0	4	20%
England 1971 (England)	3	1	0	2	33%
England 1972/73 (India)	5	2	1	2	40%
England 1974 (England)	3	0	3	0	0%
Total	**16**	**4**	**4**	**8**	**25%**

17

SRINIVAS "VENKAT" VENKATARAGHAVAN

It is hard to find something Srinivas "Venkat" Venkataraghavan has not done in cricket. First and foremost the gifted off spin bowler was a member of Test cricket's most potent quartet of spin bowlers, along with Bhagwat Chandrasekhar, Bishan Singh Bedi and Erapalli Prasanna. He captained his country. After twenty years of first class cricket he retired in 1985, and moved into cricket administration. He was a team manager. He made his second debut in Test cricket when he started a new career as an umpire. He also became an ICC referee. This is a man who has served the cricket world with distinction.

Born in Madras in 1945, he made his first class debut for Madras in 1963. Just over one year later, Venkat made his Test debut against the visiting New Zealand team in season 1964/65 at his home ground and went on to play the entire series. He had fairly modest returns bowling in tandem with Chandrasekhar, until the fourth Test of the series when he destroyed New Zealand singlehandedly with 8-72 and 4-80, helping India to win the Test.

He was in and out of the team over the next couple of seasons, as fitting four quality spin bowlers into a cricket team meant that someone had to miss out. He toured Australia in 1969/70 and played every Test, bowling alongside Prasanna and Bedi. Opportunities to bowl were few and far between, the bulk of the bowling handled by his two spinning mates, but he chipped in with key wickets and his batting improved, making handy runs and also being used as a night watchman.

There was a pattern emerging – Venkat was having much greater success as a bowler in home conditions than away, which might have resulted in getting less opportunities with the ball. A case in point is the tour to England in 1974 where he failed to take a wicket at all in the two Test matches in which he played.

Following that disastrous tour he was picked to play in the first Test against the West Indies at Bangalore in 1974/75, in the returning Pataudi's team, bowling alongside Chandrasekhar and Prasanna. Although the team was thrashed by an innings and plenty, Venkat himself performed well and when Pataudi was absent for the second Test, the off spinner was promoted to the captaincy becoming India's 17th Test cricket captain.

It couldn't have happened at a worse time. Gavaskar was missing, along with Pataudi, and the rain lurking about was more likely to be friendly to Andy Roberts and company than India's spin attack.

Venkat won the toss at Feroz Shah Kotla, Delhi and batted, but India collapsed to be all out for 220. I.V.A. Richards then launched a ferocious attack, hitting 6 sixes on his way to 192 not out, the West Indies all out before he could get his double century, for 493. Rain again played havoc with the Indian innings and they did perform marginally better, but all out for 257 gave the West Indies victory by more than an innings.

Pataudi returned for the third Test to lead the team, while Venkat was dropped and took no further part for the rest of the series.

Again Venkat found himself in and out of favour with the selectors over the next few seasons. He played the first Test against New Zealand in 1975/76 and was dropped for the rest of the series. Against West Indies also in 1975/76, he missed the first Test and played the next three but struggled for wickets. He played all the tests against the visiting Kiwis in 1976/77, picking up thirteen wickets for the series. He played the first Test against the visiting English team in 1976/77 and missed the remaining four. He toured Australia in 1977/78 and played only the second Test on the pace friendly WACA ground in Perth.

Seemingly back in favour he played all six Test matches against the visiting West Indies team in 1978/79 and gave a good account of himself with twenty wickets at 24.75. Indeed, Venkat's four wickets in each innings of the fourth Test was a major reason why India won the only Test match in the six Test series to end in a result. It was a tussle between two sides trying to find their way; India blooding some new players after retirements, the most noteworthy the emergence of young fast bowler Kapil Dev, and the West Indies weakened by the absence of their star players who had defected to World Series Cricket.

Venkat was rewarded with the captaincy of the 1979 tour to England, but far from being the honour it should have been, it was a poisoned chalice. Sunil Gavaskar had captained the side against the West Indies but had given it up for this tour. Wise move. They were up against the shrewd Mike Brearley, a middling performer as a batsman but a master tactician as he would prove time and again over the ensuing years and indeed wrote an entire book about the subject, the Art of Captaincy.

India struggled in the ODI World Cup fixtures preceding the Test series and this had a spillover effect on the main game. Chandrasekhar was carrying an injury, Venkat himself struggled to be effective. The attack lacked cohesion and potency and the one bright spot, Kapil Dev, suffered from lack of support at the other end.

Brearley won the toss in the first Test and declared when David Gower reached his double century, 633/5. Kapil Dev was the only bowler to take a wicket, ending with 5-146 from 48 overs. India were never in the match and lost by an innings.

The second Test was equally horrific and India were lucky to escape with a draw. Ian Botham took five wickets as India were bowled out for 96 after Venkat won the toss. England replied with 419 but centuries each to Viswanath and Vengsarkar helped India regain respectability and fall over the line to draw the Test.

Rain won the third Test, and a classy double century by Gavaskar in the fourth ensured another draw. Overall India only lost the series 1-0 but the truth is they were lucky to walk away with that result, despite the excitement of the final Test at the Oval, where India nearly chased down a record 438 to win the match.

And thus ended the captaincy career of Venkat. In truth he was handed a hot potato, but his cricket career is littered with so many other highlights that his captaincy period is left in the shade. He continued to play into the 1980's, his last Test against Pakistan in

September 1983. He'd have probably played more Tests and gained more wickets were it not for the fact that he was one of four colossal spin bowlers all born in the same era.

One of that awesome foursome, a captain of his country, a globally respected umpire and match referee, Srinivas Venkataraghavan has been an ornament to the game, not just for Indian cricket fans but followers of the game overall, for many decades.

Captaincy Record	Tests	W	L	D	%
West Indies 1974/75 (West Indies)*	1	0	1	0	0%
England 1979 (England)	4	0	1	3	0%
Total	**5**	**0**	**2**	**3**	**0%**

* *Not captain for full series*

18

SUNIL MANOHAR "SUNNY" GAVASKAR

A casual glance at the statistics will show a mountain of runs the likes of which had never been previously seen – the first man in history to pass 10,000 Test runs. Thirty four centuries and forty five half centuries across 125 Test matches at an average of 51.12.

What the statistics don't tell you is the other side of the story: every shot in the book, a classic technique and near impossible to remove from the crease. The stats also don't tell you that he was the world's leading batsman when it came to confronting the fearsome West Indies pace battery of the 1980's and the Australian's of the 1970's. He had courage beyond words, and all this before helmets. His head "protection" was an old, floppy off-white sun hat.

Three times he scored centuries in both innings of a Test match. By the time his career was drawing to a close, it seemed he was breaking a record every single time he went out to bat.

Born in the cricketing stronghold that was Bombay, he was awarded India's Best Schoolboy Cricketer of the year in 1966, debuted in first class cricket in 1966/67. He played his first Ranji Trophy match for Bombay in 1968/69 and scored a duck, but in his second match he scored 114.

In 1970/71 at the age of twenty one, he was chosen for the tour to the West Indies, under the captaincy of Ajit Wadekar. He missed playing the first Test but made his debut at Port of Spain in the second Test scoring half centuries in each innings. He went on to score 774 runs for the series at an average of 158.80, breaking a string of records along the way: the first Indian to score 700 or more in a Test series, the highest runs in a debut series, only the second man to score a century and a double century in the same Test match. Only Don Bradman ever had a higher series average. All those runs and he missed the first Test! India had unleashed a batting superstar upon the cricketing world.

A little more subdued in the English conditions of the 1971 tour, but the team continued on its winning ways, this being the second of two consecutive series wins overseas for India. Still struggling to find the form from his first series, he had a quiet series at home against England in 1972/73 but much better on the tour to England in 1974 with 217 runs at 36.16. He'd now played against the same opposition in three consecutive series. Injured in the tight series at home against the West Indies in the first Test in 1974/75, he returned for the deciding fifth Test and found immediate form with 86 runs.

Rumblings within the administration and the selectors over the captaincy following the retirement of Wadekar after the England tour – both Bishan Bedi and Farokh Engineer were considered the likely options, but neither was chosen. Engineer was not considered on account of him living overseas in the UK. Bedi missed out due to a supposed disciplinary reason and did not play the first Test. Hence the return of Mansoor Ali Khan, Tiger Pataudi, despite his absence from Test cricket for the previous two years, to guide the team in the home series against the West Indies in 1974/75. It was Pataudi's last series in Test cricket.

An Early Victory

The team to leave India's shores for the tour of New Zealand of 1975/76 was of a mix of the past, present and future. Team manager was former captain Polly Umrigar. Two of the sons of former captain Lala Amarnath, Surinder and Mohinder were in the squad. New captain Bishan Bedi was ready to take the reins in his first Test in that capacity, but an injury kept him out of the match and so he was denied a second time, but returned for the rest of the series and is the subject of the next chapter. Once he was unavailable, India had a stand-in skipper, and Sunil Gavaskar became the eighteenth man to take on the role of India's Test cricket captain.

Persistent rain in Auckland prior to the first Test meant that the pitch at Eden Gardens had been under cover for nine days. The grass underneath was dead, a major bonus for India's spinners. Glenn Turner won the toss for New Zealand and chose to bat first.

Madan Lal and Mohinder Amarnath were able to bowl nine overs between them before Gavaskar followed the template of captains past and tossed the ball to the three spinners, Chandrasekhar, Venkat and Prasanna. The ball was already turning sharply on the first day which saw the spinners take all ten wickets, Chandrasekhar six of them, and New Zealand were all out for 266.

As if he didn't have enough records already, Gavaskar helped himself to a century in his first match as captain, successfully negotiating the pace attack of Richard Collinge and Dayle Hadlee. He was joined by Surinder Amarnath who top scored with 124. They were assisted by some dreadful catching by the fielding team, dropping nine in all. Not to be outdone, Mohinder Amarnath scored a stubborn 64 batting at number seven. Lala would be proud. India finished all out 414, a lead of 148. Former Kiwi captain Bevan Congdon picked up 5 wickets for 64 runs.

Madan Lal and Mohinder Amarnath bowled six overs between them before Gavaskar tossed the ball to Chandrasekhar and Venkat. He might have tossed it first to Prasanna, the fifth bowler used, for he took the first five wickets to fall and the last three to register the brilliant figures of 8-76.

India lost two wickets chasing down the 67 runs for victory and the skipper was there at the end, 35 not out. A brilliant match for the spinners and a marvellous captaincy debut for Gavaskar: a century and a victory in his first Test as captain. We shall visit the rest of that series in the next chapter, for it is the captaincy debut of the returning Bishan Bedi. Gavaskar finished the tour averaging 66.50.

He showed good form in the following tour to the West Indies who were smarting from their 5-1 drubbing at the hands of Australia and their fast men. Captain Clive Lloyd was in the building process of his own pace battery and they practised on the visiting Indians who resembled an emergency ward as they boarded the plane to head back home. In the face of that attack Gavaskar stood tall with two Test centuries and an average of 55.71 during an exciting series which will get more coverage in the next chapter.

He showed good form at home in 1976/77 against New Zealand with another century, but struggled against Tony Greig's visiting England team, not really hitting his straps until the fourth Test where he scored 108.

He toured Australia under Bedi in 1977/78 against Bob Simpson's team, essentially a second XI as the Australian team had been decimated by the defections to World Series Cricket. He scored centuries in Brisbane, Perth and Melbourne and finished the series with an average of 50. To Pakistan in 1978/79, he was again amongst the runs with 447 at 89.40 in a losing series.

Full Time Captain

After three series losses in a row, the board felt it was time for a change at the top and Gavaskar was handed the captaincy for the West Indies tour of 1978/79. Former skipper Bishan Bedi would continue to play, but no longer as captain.

The West Indies team, like Australia the previous season, were weakened considerably by the absence of their players who were playing in the breakaway World Series Cricket. Only five of their players had received Test caps before.

Alvin Kallicharran was only appointed as Test captain following extraordinary exchanges between the WSC players and the West Indies Board. The Windies had just hosted the weakened Australia team, captained by Bobby Simpson, and the full strength Windies team flattened them in the first two of a five Test series.

There was a dispute at the selection table, which also involved West Indies skipper, Clive Lloyd. It went unresolved and Lloyd resigned. The rest of the WSC players withdrew leaving a vastly weakened West Indies team captained by Kallicharran. The immediate beneficiaries were Simpson and his Australian team, two Test matches into a five Test series, but it would also give India a leg up, for the unknown and untested players in the West Indies squad were galaxies away from the full strength West Indies team. It was this team, which included veteran Vanburn Holder and a heap of youngsters that Kallicharran began a six Test tour away from home, in India.

At Bombay for the first Test, India's new Test captain Gavaskar lost the toss and Kallicharran sent India in to bat. Gavaskar celebrated his second stint at captaincy by responding with a double century. His aggressive stroke play laid a platform for the team's total of 424. So positive was he that when he was out for 205, the team score was 334.

Pace bowler KD Ghavri picked up both Windies openers for ducks, but the Windies recovered through their skipper who made 187 not out and the team piled on 493. Bad weather and lack of spice in the bowling of both teams led to a draw.

The second Test, in Bangalore, marked the debut of West Indies paceman, Malcolm Marshall, in a bid by his captain to bolster the fast bowling stocks. It was a seesawing contest between the two captains and their teams finding their way but was ultimately spoiled by events off the field. Civil unrest caused by the arrest of former Indian Prime Minister, Indira Gandhi, meant that the entire fifth day of the Test match was cancelled, leading to another drawn Test.

But for a bit more of a hurry up, India were tantalisingly close to winning the third Test in Calcutta. Gavaskar won the toss and batted, but slow batting by both teams in the first innings wasted valuable time. The skipper himself scored a century to assist India to 300 all out and a century to Basil Williams got the Windies to 327.

Gavaskar took the initiative in the second innings, with 187 not out, once again scoring twin centuries in a Test match and becoming the first man to do it thrice. Dilip Vengsarkar joined in on the party with 157 not out and Gavaskar declared at one wicket for 361, leaving West Indies to score 334 to win. The batting team started steadily, but when they lost Kallicharran at 133/3 things started to unravel. They finished the final day nine down for 197, bravely holding on for a draw and assisted by the bad light calling off play earlier. India were criticised for not getting through the overs more urgently. A victory slipped through their fingers.

The nervousness of the two young teams and their relatively novice captains meant that the fourth Test at Madras was another seesawing contest and both teams were in the hunt until the end. Had either been a more settled outfit then victory would have been less painful. As it turned out, the slightly more settled Indian team won by three wickets. Gavaskar failed in both innings, but his bowling attack of Ghavri and

Dev, along with Venkat, who was the main spinner – for the first time in twelve years there was no Bedi, Prasanna or Chandrasekhar – toiled hard. The Indian team fielded well and held on to their catches, while the Windies spilled several crucial chances. As is often the case with a low total to chase in the fourth innings, a couple of wickets and a bit of panic sets in, but India got there with three wickets to spare. India went one up in the six Test series.

Rain and slow scoring sentenced the fifth Test to a draw, but not before another century to the skipper and an attractive maiden century to the young allrounder, Kapil Dev. With seven hours lost to rain across days four and five, the Test petered to a draw. Rain and slow batting again marred the sixth Test which was also drawn, despite being extended to six days. Out of six Test matches between the two teams only one ended with a result, giving India a series victory 1-0.

Gavaskar attracted some criticism for defensive captaincy, but the defensive style of Kallicharran's captaincy was also a factor in the lifeless series. That said, the new skipper had won his first Test series as captain.

It then makes it a curiosity that he was stripped of the role for the 1979 tour of England. The official reason was that Venkat, a previous captain but for only one Test as a stand-in, had a better knowledge of English conditions. This is a bit hard to understand given that Gavaskar had twice toured England in the past. Perhaps a more potent reason was that there was speculation circling that Gavaskar was on the verge of signing with World Series Cricket. The truth is unknown, but after having captained India to a series win in his first outing, he was dumped.

Perhaps it was a blessing in disguise, England disposing of India 1-0, but Gavaskar himself had an excellent series and nearly singlehandedly crafted an unlikely victory in the fourth Test, with 221 runs from his bat in the second innings. India were set the seemingly impossible target of 438 for victory and India were nine runs shy with two wickets in hand when play ended. Gavaskar finished an excellent series with 542 runs at 77.42.

Venkat was relieved of the captaincy for the final time and Sunny returned to the role for a huge 1979/80 season with six Tests scheduled against Australia and another six against Pakistan, both at home.

Australia, under the captaincy of Kim Hughes, had been through a process of rebuilding following the WSC defections two years earlier and were a much stronger outfit than the last time these two sides met. However, Hughes, along with a vast number of the team had never played in India. Paceman Rodney Hogg, leg spinner Jim Higgs, keeper Kevin Wright, batsmen Graeme Wood, Graeme Yallop, Andrew Hilditch, Dav Whatmore, Alan Border, among others, made their Test debut in India in the first Test at Madras.

Hughes won the toss and batted, scoring an even hundred on debut against India and Border 162. Apart from those two, there was not much else, all out for 390, Dilip Doshi picking up six wickets in his debut. Plenty of starts and plenty of runs for India, with Kapil Dev top scoring with 83 in a team total of 425. Higgs picked up seven wickets. Dropped catches by both teams and rain interruptions meant that the Test match tapered off into a draw.

Rain won again in the second Test at Bangalore, although India had the upper hand. Gavaskar won the toss in the third Test, at Eden Gardens, Calcutta and immediately set about scoring a 114 run opening stand with Chetan Chauhan after electing to bat. Good bowling by Hogg and Dymock restricted the score to 271. Australia used spinner Bruce Yardley to open the batting in the absence of Rick Darling, injured while fielding. Yallop top scored with 89 before he trod on his stumps, and Darling came in at number eight and made 59, Australia all out 304.

Bright batting led by the blade of Chauhan with 84 took India's second innings to 311, leaving Australia a victory target of 278. They were never in the hunt and crumbled against the sharp pace of Kapil Dev and the off spin of Shivlal Yadav to be all out for 125, India winning the Test by 153 runs.

Centuries to Gavaskar, Viswanath and Sharma helped India to 510 after the skipper won the toss at Delhi. Australia were forced to follow on, skittled for 298 on the back of Kapil Dev's five wickets. They proved more stubborn in the second innings and the match ended in another draw.

Hughes won the toss and Australia batted in the fifth Test at Eden Gardens and on a slow wicket piled on 442 runs, with Yallop scoring

CAPTAINS FILE: INDIA

162. India responded with 347 and in an effort to try and provoke a result Hughes and his men, down one nil in the series, went after quick runs and were lucky not to get themselves in a heap of trouble. They lost wickets regularly before Hughes declared at 151/8, setting India a target of 256. The match ended drawn, India 200/4 when play stopped on day five.

Five Tests and only one result. Someone had to take charge. Gavaskar won the toss in the sixth Test and batted, making 123 out of a total of 458. Australia collapsed against the spin of Yadav and Doshi to be all out for 160. They fared little better in the second innings, despite a brave knock of 80 from Kim Hughes, all out for 198 and victory to India by an innings and 100 runs, giving them the series 2-0. Two full series by Gavaskar, two series wins.

A series victory against Australia is one thing, and not to be taken for granted, but there was immediately a more pressing assignment and one of far greater import: a six Test series against Pakistan, and an opportunity for revenge after losing the last series 2-0. Pakistan captain Asif Iqbal, whose uncle Ghulam Ahmed had been the 7th captain of India, brought a powerful unit to India. Names such as Imran Khan, Zaheer Abbas, Javed Miandad, Abdul Qadir, Majid Khan and Mudassar Nazar.

Asif won the toss at Bangalore, site of the first Test and batted, Pakistan making 431. Gavaskar led the way with 88 in India's reply 416, but the Test was consigned to a draw, the slow batting from both teams destroying any chance of victory. Like two old prize fighters, they were just circling each other in the ring, sizing up their opponent.

Seesawing fortunes in the second match produced an exciting Test match at Delhi, albeit another draw. Iqbal won the toss and batted, Pakistan making 273, Wasin Raja with 97, and another day at the office for Kapil Dev with yet another bag of five wickets.

Gavaskar top scored with 31 in India's disastrous reply of 126, destroyed by paceman Sikander Bakht who took eight wickets. Batting a second time, Pakistan made 242, leaving India the mammoth task of either holding out for a draw or scoring 390 for victory. They began the final day at 117/2, the overnight score, needing 273 more for victory. They finished just shy, six wickets down for 364, thanks mainly to 146 not out from Dilip Vengsarkar. Oh so close.

At Wankhede Stadium, Bombay for the third Test, Gavaskar won the toss and batted, but India lost both openers quickly, 31/2. They rallied through Vengsarkar and Viswanath, and later from some lower order runs from Kapil Dev, to make a respectable 334. The spin from India's tweakers crashed through Pakistan who were all out for 173. India were then crippled by the spin of Iqbal Qasim and they themselves were out for a low score, 160, leaving Pakistan to negotiate a tough target of 321. It was to prove far too much and they were bundled out for 190, giving India a lead in the series, 1-0.

At Green Park Kanpur for the fourth Test, a green park it certainly was, with wickets tumbling quickly on the first day. Gavaskar won the toss and batted, but probably wished he hadn't as they were lucky to make 162 against a pace attack that didn't include Imran Khan. Wasim Raja again the mainstay of the Pakistani batting, with 94, as they too struggled on the pacey pitch, all out for 249 with Dev taking six. Batting got a little easier in the second innings for India, but rain was the eventual winner and the Test was drawn.

Asif won the toss for Pakistan in the fifth Test, at Madras, and batted. Many batsmen got starts but they squandered opportunities and were bowled out for an under par 272. Gavaskar then batted for just under 10 hours, the longest innings ever by an Indian, as he made 166. Lower order fireworks from Kapil Dev and Roger Binny progressed the total to 430. Kapil Dev then did the job with the ball, knocking over seven Pakistani batsmen for 56 as they collapsed to be all out for 233, leaving India a small target which they easily reached for no loss. India ahead 2-0.

Fortunes fluctuated in the sixth Test which ended in a draw with India taking the series. It looks a comfortable series win in hindsight, but the Pakistan team were a powerful unit and a number of the Tests were in the balance.

Gavaskar did not captain the final Test match. Along with his team mates he was about to play the twelfth Test at home during that season. The board had hurriedly organised a quick tour to the West Indies following the Pakistan series. Gavaskar didn't want to go. Viswanath was given the captaincy to allow him to settle into the role in preparation for the tour. Viswanath captained the next Test, a one off against England, in which Gavaskar also played. In the end, The West Indies didn't want an Indian team touring without the drawcard of

Gavaskar, so it was cancelled altogether and the captaincy reverted to Sunny.

Reinstated for the tour to Australia and New Zealand, Gavaskar's own form let him down, but against an Australian team back to its full strength after the WSC split, India did well to square the series, winning the third Test in Melbourne after being one down. The Test was marred by a controversial move by Gavaskar. Unimpressed at being given out LBW when he indicated that the ball had hit his bat, and reacting to the chirping of the delighted Aussies, he took the extraordinary step of attempting to take his fellow opener, Chetan Chauhan from the field in protest. Gavaskar, who had walked when out during the series was struck by what he felt was an injustice and the noise from the Aussies, particularly Dennis Lillee who had gone up to the batsman after the decision and pointed at his pads.

Fortunately wiser heads prevailed. SK Durani, the team manager, averted a full blown crisis by ushering Sunny up the stairs and Chauhan back onto the field. Second innings heroics from Kapil Dev won the match for India.

If the series in Australia had its disappointments, it got worse in New Zealand. It was a less than impressive performance opposite the Kiwis, against whom India lost a Test series for the very first time. Gavaskar's own form was poor, but the advent of one day internationals extended each and every tour and a certain tiredness and staleness had to be a factor.

Six more Tests, against England at home in 1981/82 nearly didn't go ahead, once again for reasons unrelated to cricket and it involved Prime Minister, Mrs Indira Ghandi. Geoff Boycott and Geoff Cook, having been involved in a tour in South Africa, were deemed unfit to tour by the government. A stand-off occurred until ultimately the two players were permitted to tour. It was a dull and lifeless series, plagued by unresponsive wickets, and India won the series 1-0.

England gained revenge in the immediate tour to their shores by India in 1982. Like the previous series, it was won by a margin of 1-0. It was a lean tour for the captain, but two future captains, Kapil Dev and Ian Botham, kept the series interesting for the spectators.

In the one off Test against Sri Lanka at Madras, the first encounter between the two nations, Gavaskar scored 155 in a welcome return to form, but India could not put their novice opponents away, the Test ending in a draw. It wouldn't get much better for India over a hapless summer.

In fact, it got worse. Playing a six Test series away to Pakistan, India were well and truly outplayed by a strong Pakistan team, losing 3-0. It resulted in a change of captaincy, and Gavaskar's first period as captain was over, replaced by the enigmatic allrounder, Kapil Dev. Once again a bad result against Pakistan led to a change in captain.

Without the added burden of captaincy, Sunny continued his march to mow down batting records, but returned to captaincy against Pakistan in 1984/85 with the only two Tests of the series ending in draws.

England arrived in India for the 1984/85 tour only to find the sad news that Mrs Indira Ghandi had been assassinated. Just before the first Test, the deputy British High Commissioner, was shot dead. Again events outside of cricket impacted a tour of India. The English team were understandably nervous and there was some contemplation of cancelling the tour, but it is to their credit that they pressed on.

David Gower won the toss at Wankhede Stadium, Bombay, for the first Test and chose to bat. Leg spinner Laxman Sivaramakrishnan weaved a spell over the English and took six wickets as they were trundled out for just 195. It could have been worse but for lower order resistance from wicket keeper Paul Downton and spin bowler Phil Edmonds.

A big century to Ravi Shastri batting at six and another to Syed Kirmani, the keeper, batting at nine, helped India amass 465. Mike Gatting's debut Test century and some more help from Downton with 62 helped England to scrape to 317 but it was not enough to create a difficult target and India easily made the 51 runs required for victory, by eight wickets. It was understandable that England might not have been at their best, given the political unrest. For India, it broke a 31 game streak without victory. It was a welcome, if brief respite.

England fought back magnificently to win the second Test by eight wickets, on the back of 160 by Tim Robinson and solid work with the ball by Edmonds, Richard Ellison and Pat Pocock. They had levelled the series against all odds and now the home team was on the back foot.

The third Test at Eden Gardens was a pointless and bizarre draw which occurred days after a selection impasse. Chairman of selectors, Chandu Borde, would not budge. Kapil Dev was to be dropped following an indiscreet shot leading to his wicket in the second Test loss. Further, Sandeep Patil was also to be dropped, replaced by debutant Mohammed Azharuddin.

The home team elected to bat on and on, despite time lost due to inclement weather and incited the crowd to jeer their own team as Gavaskar curiously chose to bat the first innings well into day four. The captain was jeered and booed by a section of the crowd. Some pelted fruit when he eventually led the team onto the field.

The only bright spot was a century on debut for Azharuddin. It was cricket at snail's pace and a Test best forgotten. However it does highlight the simmering tension between the BBCI, the selectors, and the captain.

Gavaskar won the toss at Madras for the fourth Test and chose to bat. It must have seemed like T20 pace after the previous Test as India made 272 from 67.5 overs. Double centuries each to Fowler and Gatting, supported by dropped catches and defensive fielding tactics helped England to amass 652/7. A second century in only his second Test, Azharuddin, along with Mohinder Amarnath gave some respectability to India's second innings, but ultimately England only had to chase 34 runs for victory, doing so with only one wicket down.

Gavaskar and his team did their utmost to win the fifth Test, at Kanpur, and indeed played exciting cricket on the final day to try and manufacture a result but the Test ended in a draw, England winning the series 2-1. Azharuddin scored his third successive century.

Gavaskar, who had a poor series, resigned from the captaincy. He continued on as a player, before retiring in 1987, in the fifth Test of the series against Pakistan. He went agonisingly close to scoring a century in his final innings, out for 96.

That he is one of the finest opening batsmen to ever pick up a blade is undeniable. His statistics prove it and his courage under fire is well documented. He could be aggressive and equally could knuckle down and weather the storm. A similar personality was brought to his captaincy. He could be aggressive, trying to manufacture a win, such as the fifth Test against England in 1984, but equally he could be extremely defensive as displayed in the third Test of the same series.

The highlights must not be forgotten: he won his first Test as captain, he won his first three series as captain. He followed the path of some of his predecessors, to the commentary box, but he has also written several books and has been a match referee for the ICC.

He's won several awards, both during and post career: Indian Cricket Cricketer of the Year in 1971, Arjuna Award in 1975, Wisden Cricketer of the Year in 1980, the Padma Bhushan in the same year and the CK Nayudu Lifetime Achievement Award in 2012.

Captaincy Record	Tests	W	L	D	%
New Zealand 1975/76 (NZ)*	1	1	0	0	100%
West Indies 1978/79 (India)	6	1	0	5	17%
Australia 1979/80 (India)	6	2	0	4	33%
Pakistan 1979/80 (India)*	5	2	0	3	40%
Australia 1980/81 (Australia)	3	1	1	1	33%
New Zealand 1980/81 (NZ)	3	0	1	2	0%
England 1981/82 (India)	6	1	0	5	17%
England 1982 (England)	3	0	1	2	0%
Sri Lanka 1982/83 (India)	1	0	0	1	0%
Pakistan 1982/83 (Pakistan)	6	0	3	3	0%
Pakistan 1984/85 (Pakistan)	2	0	0	2	0%
England 1984/85 (India)	5	1	2	2	20%
Total	**47**	**9**	**8**	**30**	**19%**

Not captain for full series

19

BISHAN SINGH "BISH" BEDI

A colourful cricketer, from the patka's he wore during his playing days, to his quiet and deadly approach to the wicket, seemingly innocuous at times, but then so too is a cobra before it unleashes. His slow, left-arm orthodox bowling caused havoc among opposition Test batsmen from 1966 to 1979 and during that period teamed up with three others, Prasanna, Chandrasekhar and Venkat to form the deadliest quartet of spin bowlers in the history of the game. While each of the four brought different qualities, Bedi's flighting of the ball was his most potent quality.

His frank and sometimes outspoken views are sometimes controversial, but while one might not always agree, the opinions come from a sharp mind, the mind of a man who captained his country for 22 Tests. His views are often delivered with wit and absurdity and are frequently entertaining, refreshing from a sportsman in this day of sanitised media performances.

He made his debut in first class cricket at the age of fifteen for Northern Punjab, and his Test debut at age twenty, in the second Test against the West Indies in the 1966/67 season, at Eden Gardens, Calcutta, under the captaincy of Tiger Pataudi. He bowled alongside Venkat and Chandrasekhar. It was an innocuous debut, although the two wickets he picked up, Basil Butcher and Clive Hubert Lloyd, were no slouches with the bat. In the third Test at Madras he picked up four second innings wickets and this time bowled alongside Prasanna and

Chandrasekhar. From the moment he'd been introduced to Test cricket the group had been formed.

He toured England with the India team in the disastrous three nil drubbing of 1967, the most notable aspect being the third Test, where for the first time the entire quartet of spinners played in a Test match together.

He played only a minor role in the series in Australia in 1967/68, playing just two Tests, but the tour that followed in New Zealand, he played in the entire series. He picked up his best haul in Test cricket thus far, 6-127 in the second Test at Christchurch and finished the Test series with 16 wickets at 23.18.

In the return series at home in India in 1969/70 he collected 15 wickets at 20.53 in the three Tests. Against the touring Australians in the same season, he picked up 21 wickets at 20.57 over the five matches and had his best Test figures to date of 7-98. Two average series away to West Indies and England in 1970/71 but back to his brilliant best at home against the touring English in 1972/73 with 25 wickets at 25.28.

Tiger Pataudi was once again removed as captain at the end of the West Indies series in 1974/75 and a new skipper appointed for a tour to New Zealand in 1975/76. Bishan Singh Bedi was to become the 18th captain of India, but an injury prior to the first Test delayed his captaincy debut. Sunil Gavaskar captained the first Test, Bedi returning for the second and third and thus became the 19th Indian Test captain.

The Captaincy

In the second Test of that series at Lancaster Park, Christchurch, Bedi called correctly when Glenn Turner tossed the coin, and chose to bat on a lively pitch. Pace man Richard Collinge caused no small amount of damage, taking 6 wickets for 63 while RJ Hadlee was wayward.

India made their way to 270 runs, largely held together by Viswanath's 83. The spin trio of Bedi, Prasanna and Chandrasekhar were largely ineffective, with nine of the Kiwi's ten wickets falling to Madan Lal and Amarnath – Bedi taking the only wicket for the spinners.

Was that a first during this period, nine wickets to the quicks? Normally they weren't even given nine overs, let alone take nine wickets. New Zealand helped themselves to 403, Turner with 117, however it was at quite a slow pace. The slow batting, compounded by rain intervention on days three and four consigned the match to a draw.

The third Test at Wellington saw Bedi win the toss and bat, but the previously wayward (now Sir) Richard Hadlee, considered lucky to get a guernsey again, bowled like a champion, as part of a four pronged pace attack. India all out for 220, Hadlee getting four wickets while Brijesh Patel anchored the innings with 81. The Kiwis ground out 334 runs in reply, 114 runs in front with Bedi, Chandrasekhar and Madan Lal each taking three wickets.

In the second innings, Richard Hadlee wasn't the first bowler used. In fact, he wasn't the first Hadlee used, his brother Dayle opening the bowling, but his seven wickets annihilated India, taking 7-23 as India were cleaned up for 81 runs. It was New Zealand's first victory in a Test match by an innings. It should be noted that Gavaskar was unable to bat because of an injury to his cheek, courtesy of a pull from Lance Cairns while fielding at short leg. Would it have made a difference? Probably not. Hadlee was on fire. Our new skipper finished his first series squared at one all, but he'd not even played in the winning Test match.

Bedi's next assignment was a tour of the West Indies in 1976 with his band of merry spinners. Unfortunately there was a band of merry pacemen awaiting who had just had the pace of Lillee and Thompson give them a template for the next twenty years.

The first Test was at Barbados, not a happy hunting ground for India. (Ask Nari Contractor.) Bedi won the toss and batted on a fast wicket, and true to their growing reputations, Andy Roberts and Michael Holding inflicted early damage, but it was actually the spin of Holford that brought India undone, albeit through some untidy shot selection, all out 177. Bedi and his two spinning sidekicks also bowled well, but India were struck down by their Achilles heel: poor catching. Clive Lloyd and (now Sir) Vivian Richards took full toll, sometimes in brutal fashion and both scored centuries taking the team total to 488. India capitulated in the second dig to lose by an innings.

Bedi won the toss at Port of Spain for the second Test, which lost the entire first day to rain. Water still lurking on the pitch he sent the Windies in to bat and his decision vindicated when he had the home team all out for 241, 130 of them from the blade of Richards. The captain led from the front taking five wickets.

Despite being 35/2, India settled in through Gavaskar, and the little opener batted patiently for 156 while at the other end Patel found his way to his first Test ton and India had a commanding lead having scored 402. Bedi went thought the motions, giving Madan Lal and Amarnath just seven overs before bringing himself, Chandrasekhar and Venkat into the attack. And attack they did, but were defied once again through sloppy catching. Had his team been able to hold on to the chances, India would have squared the series immediately. The Windies were able to hold out for a draw and India went into the next Test match still one down.

The third Test, also at Port of Spain, was history in the making, India achieving what no team ever had done before. Clive Lloyd won the toss and elected to bat. IVA Richards continued his role as Indian nemesis scoring 177 from a team total of 359. There was no stopping this man apparently. Bedi picked up four and Chandrasekhar six. India buckled against Michael "Whispering Death" Holding as he picked up 6-65, rattling the visitors out for 228, a deficit of 131 runs.

The Indian spinners were again amongst the wickets, but the first innings lead gave Lloyd and his men the opportunity of scoring fast runs, and he declared at 271/6, setting India the task of scoring 406 to win. He would have done that confidently. Only Sir Donald Bradman's *Invincibles* had scored over 400 to win a Test match but then, they didn't have to face Andy Roberts and Michael Holding. It was to prove a costly misjudgement by Lloyd.

Roberts and Holding were fast, but ineffective and they didn't count on the stubbornness of Gavaskar, nor the resistance shown by the rest of the batting line-up. Gavaskar, 102, Amarnath, 85 and top score Viswanath, 112, saw India home in the greatest run chase of all time to date. They had gone one better than Bradman's Invincibles and at the same time, humbled the West Indies much heralded pace attack, squaring the series. How Bedi must have rued those dropped catches in the second Test, for he and his men would be one up instead of even.

The fourth Test was a bad advertisement for cricket and if there was any justice the match would have been awarded to India by default. A debacle of this kind should never have been allowed to continue and in this day and age of match referees and media scrutiny such a Test match may have been declared null and void. Flamboyant local umpire Douglas Sang Hue did not present his finest hour.

It was a fine cricket contest from the outset, to be sure. West Indies won the toss at Sabina Park, Kingston and sent India in to bat, Holding opening the bowling with debutant Wayne Daniel. The first innings stand of 136 between Gavaskar and Gaekwad (son of former skipper, DK Gaekwad) belied the vagaries of the wicket. The bounce at either end was alarmingly unpredictable and with the pace of the Windies bowlers must have been frightening to face. There was a surplus of short pitched bowling which should have captured the umpires' attention but they did nothing to intervene.

The bowling was nothing short of intimidatory and the fourth and fifth wickets to fall were out, retired hurt. That India managed 306 is a miracle and Bedi declaring at six down was a case of protecting his bowlers rather than strategy. India of course did not have the same weaponry to unleash on the West Indies batting. Just spinners. Lloyd's men made 391 and then the match descended into farce in the second innings.

Gavaskar went early, 5/1. A partnership between Vengsarkar and Amarnath took the score to 68. Madan Lal, the pace bowler, batting at four, came and went. Venkat, the spinner, batted at five. Five! Out for a duck. When he was out, at 97/5, the innings was over. Bedi hadn't declared, he just didn't have any fit batsmen. The next five were recorded in the scorebook as absent injured and the West Indies had no trouble scoring the twelve runs for victory. India didn't need an airplane to leave the Caribbean, they needed an ambulance.

Back at home and on more friendly pitches, India hosted New Zealand for a three Test series in 1976/77. It's true that the Kiwis were missing a few old stalwarts, players such as Congdon, Howarth and Wadsworth who knew the conditions but even so they were utterly unprepared for the spin onslaught that hit them.

Bishan Bedi won the toss at Wankhede Stadium, Bombay, the scene of the first Test, and elected to bat. He'd get first use of the wicket and then let his spinners loose on the Kiwis who would be batting last. Gavaskar scored a century and there was a plucky 88 by Syed Kirmani, the wicket keeper, batting at number eight. India fell one run short of 400. No demons in the wicket for captain Turner (65) or John Parker (104) who was run out, but the rest of the batting struggled against Bedi and his spinning mates and the Kiwis were all out for 298, 101 runs in arrears. The run rate of 1.94 only emphasised the batting team's struggle to play the spinners confidently.

Bedi had his batsmen looking for runs and he provocatively declared 202/4, a lead of just 303, knowing it would be a big ask for New Zealand on a day five pitch. He declared just in time, for the Kiwis, while never in the hunt, clung on for dear life, but were eventually prised away from the wicket for 141, the skipper leading from the front with 5-27. India now led the series 1-0.

Bedi won the toss for the second time in succession and on a flat wicket at Green Park, Kanpur, chose to bat. So flat was the wicket that everyone got runs, but there were no centurions. Bedi himself scored his first Test match 50, batting at number ten. The Indians were all out 524.

A century to Turner and half centuries to Burgess and Roberts took the Kiwis to 350, but the signs were ominous, each of the three spinners picking up 3 wickets. Quick runs in the second innings and a polished century to Viswanath helped India to 202, but bad light foiled Bedi's ability to declare and that delayed declaration until the fifth day allowed the Kiwis to escape with a draw.

A hat trick of tosses to the Indian skipper meant they batted first once again, this time at Madras, but they wouldn't see any cricket until the second morning – the entire first day was lost to rain. Lance Cairns struck early, picking up both openers, but the rescue mission started with Viswanath (87), then Kirmani (44), and the highest Test score by one of our earlier subjects, spin bowler Venkat (64), all contributed to a reasonable 298. New Zealand had to put up with constant rain interruptions during their innings and that, combined with the guile and flight of Bishan Bedi and company, had them all out for 140, the captain again bagging another five wickets.

India started their second innings steadily then put the foot on the gas, allowing Bedi to make the declaration 201/5 leaving New Zealand

359 to get, but it was never going to happen. Spun out again, this time for 143, marginally better than their first effort and India took the Test match and the series 2-0. It was good to be back on the winner's dais after the defeat in the Caribbean.

The Vaseline Series

The team was jaded. Barely a fortnight after New Zealand had moved on, a powerful English outfit arrived under the captaincy of the charismatic Tony Greig. Tired after having just finished a series, India's key players were strangely out of form and they were comprehensively outplayed and outmanoeuvred by Greig and his squad.

Greig won the toss in the first Test, at Delhi, and batted, but things didn't start well for them. Bedi unleashed his spinners and soon England were 65/4 with Mike Brearley, Graham Barlow, Bob Woolmer and Keith Fletcher all back in the sheds. A stubborn knock of 179 from Denis Amiss, aided by the doughty Alan Knott (75) and a half century to bowler John Lever and all of a sudden 65/4 became a highly competitive 381. They were assisted by poor fielding and dropped catches. Again.

Greig came to India with no intent of trying to match the Indian spinning squad and hit them with pace and he hit them hard. Chris Old, Bob Willis and John Lever were his main weapons and it was the latter, fresh from his batting heroics who picked up seven Indian wickets as they were blasted out for 122. Four ducks in the humiliating capitulation and India were forced to follow on, and lost by an innings, all out for 234. England had rocked India to take a 1-0 lead in the series.

The second Test was just as disastrous, England winning by 10 wickets and by the time the third Test was over, England had an unassailable 3-0 lead in the series. Greig and his Englishmen had walloped the home team in a way no English team had done before and he'd done it with his pace attack on Indian pitches.

There were howls of discontent from fans and the media. "Bedi should be sacked", his head being made to roll for the debacle. Yet the third Test produced what has become known as the "Vaseline Affair" and then there were howls of a different kind.

Fast bowlers John Lever and Bob Willis had been complaining of sweat getting in their eyes in the Indian heat. An old boxer's trick to remedy the situation was to put Vaseline above the eyes to channel the sweat away. Team Physio Bernard Thomas reportedly supplied them with gauze strips, coated with Vaseline to put on their foreheads. Willis discarded his early on in the piece, near the boundary line, as it was falling off. Lever became annoyed with the strip while bowling and he removed it too, but near the stumps. This was discovered and reported by umpire Reuben who believed the Vaseline strip contravened Law 46, or ball tampering. Bedi was batting at the time and at the tea break Reuben reported the matter to the authorities.

Little wonder then, according to the Indian skipper, the fans and the media, that Lever was taking all these wickets. Lever, Greig and the English management saw it differently, that if they were ball tampering they wouldn't have made it so obvious. The spot fire quickly burned out of control. The BCCI had the gauze strips and the ball sent to a laboratory where both contained traces of Vaseline.

Was it an innocent mistake or was England trying to gain an unfair advantage? Ultimately there was no official sanction and the English would have no part of the allegation that Lever was tampering with the ball. Their contention was that it was sour grapes, and that as Bedi was taking a hammering in the media this was his way out. Following the series Bedi is reported to have tried to patch things up with Lever, suggesting that the BCCI were guilty of inflaming the situation.

India fought back superbly in the fourth Test at Bangalore. Tensions were understandably high as the two captains went to the middle for the toss which Bedi won. India batted and made 253, this time humbled by the pace of Bob Willis who took six wickets. Chandrasekhar found his old form returning and picked up six English wickets as they crumbed to 195. India replied with 259 in their second dig, with half centuries to Viswanath and Gavaskar, leaving England a victory target of 317. England were skittled for 177, courtesy of six wickets to Bedi; a typically stubborn innings from wicket keeper Alan Knott of 81 prevented it from being worse. Lever picked up only one wicket in each innings.

By the time the fifth Test was underway at Bombay, both the media and the fans were at fever pitch, still angry about the Vaseline Affair. The fans had banners adorning the stands with anti-Lever and anti-

England statements. In front of all of this was actually a very exciting Test match. Bedi won the toss and batted, Gavaskar scored a century and India made 338. England were nearly on par, with 317. Underwood bowled superbly in India's second innings and they folded to be all out for 192, leaving England with a target of 214 runs to get on the final day. The final day seesawed from one side to the next, England batting for the win then after wickets fell, played for time. Play finished at a tantalising 152/7. Were it not for Keith Fletcher's dogged 58 not out in three hours, England probably would have lost. The final Test drawn, England winning the series easily, 3-1.

To the aftermath. In what should have hailed as England's finest tour of India, in the opinions of the English players, fans and media, was marred by what they saw as a huge over-reaction from Bedi, the BCCI, the Indian media and the fans. They had their honour questioned and their glorious quest sullied by what they felt were false allegations. Had they wanted to cheat, they would have been far more subtle. It is an entirely reasonable perspective. It was disappointing for Tony Greig, in his finest hour. The series was his final glory for England, for within months his decision to join Kerry Packer's World Series Cricket would see him lose the England captaincy.

And what about Lever? He'd broken the idea that pace couldn't take wickets in India by his crushing spells in the first Test and was understandably upset by the accusations. It is easy to point the finger at Bedi who would have taken any port in a storm after being rattled by the English, the fans and the press.

However there are some legitimate questions that arise. Lever took 19 wickets at 11.36 runs per wicket in the first three Tests, before the incident occurred. In the final two, he took 7 wickets at 23.42. In his next 16 Tests, he took 47 wickets at 33.42. In itself it doesn't say anything specific, and there have been plenty of swing bowlers who have been magicians one day and trundlers the next. The numbers certainly add to the intrigue. Lever also had a habit of using the sweat from his brow, legitimately; could it have been a completely inadvertent thing?

That the England captain, manager Ken Barrington, the players, the MCC and the English media backed Lever is obviously natural, the same way that the BCCI, Indian media and fans backed Bedi. Either way, there are enough unanswered questions to provide continual intrigue. Ball tampering is a serious issue and there is no way that the umpires could have ignored it, nor the opposition captain.

One Heck of a Series

As stated earlier, Tony Greig's decision to join World Series Cricket resulted in his dismissal as captain of England. He would be joined by a number of other English players. Australia, on the other hand, lost an entire team to World Series Cricket. If there were ructions in India over Vaseline, the Australian cricket community was sorely in need of it to lubricate the divide between the establishment and Kerry Packer's outfit. It was into this turmoil that Bishan Bedi led his team on their next tour: Australia 1977/78.

This promised to be, and ultimately delivered, an absorbing and exciting series. India, winless on the faster Australian pitches where their main strength, spin bowling, generally took a back seat, were keen to change the record. Australia was a tough place to tour for any team, but particularly so for India. It wasn't just the cricket. It was the crowds, it was the media. In fact the first opponents a touring team faces in Australia is the hostile media.

Australia was ripe for the picking. No Lillee, Marsh or Chappell. No Walters, no Walker. In fact the only player of proven Test quality India would face was Jeff Thompson. No other bowler had ever been heard of. If ever there was a chance to beat Australia at home, this was it.

Under the captaincy of 41 year old Bobby Simpson, 10 years retired, was a bunch of young guns ready to make names for themselves. It set up a Test series with two teams hunting victory from the first ball and the crowds voted overwhelmingly with their feet. The Packer Super Tests had the superstars, but all of the intrigue that Test cricket has to offer was with the Australia/India Test series.

India had good preparation going into the first Test having beaten every state side they'd played. As Simpson was the elder statesman of Australia, his team fielding no fewer than six debutants, Bedi was for India, and led from the front with his flighty explosives.

Bobby Simpson won the toss at Brisbane and had no hesitation in opting to bat. Openers Paul Hibbert and Gary Cosier were given the task of negotiating Amarnath and Madan Lal, but pretty soon Cosier was back in the pavilion, followed soon after by David Ogilvie and Craig Serjeant. Then Simpson. Then Hibbert. What Amarnath had started, Bedi continued. NSW batsman Peter Toohey, gave the only resistance, scoring 82 in his first Test, in a team total of 166. Simpson's team had failed to take advantage of first use of the wicket. Bedi bamboozled the batsmen, taking 5-55.

India's stronger batting line-up of Gavaskar, Vengsarkar, Viswanath et al could have been expected to knock off the 166 on their own and then go to town, but they didn't reckon on Jeff Thompson and Wayne Clark who ripped through the Indian batting line-up. Amazingly they were trundled out for 153, 13 runs behind.

Hibbert, Cosier and Serjeant were early victims in the second innings, as Madan Lal and Amarnath looked to repeat the efforts of the Australian quicks, and at 7/3, Australia looked like folding again. However first Ogilvie (46), then Simpson (89) and Toohey again (57) pulled Australia back from the brink and the icing on the cake a 50 run tenth wicket partnership between Thompson and Alan Hurst took Australia to an excellent 327, leaving India to score 341 for victory.

With Gavaskar holding fort, anything can happen and his century was the foundation for a magnificent second innings from India as they took up the challenge to score the runs. Ultimately wickets again to Thompson and Clark, four each, India fell agonisingly short in a finish that went down to the wire. Australia won by just 16 runs. It was an incredible advertisement for the Test cricket establishment.

If the first Test was a heart stopper, then the second Test in Perth was a recipe for cardiac arrest. With both teams providing the same bright cricket as the first Test another tight finish was on the cards. This kind of cricket was the essence of the game itself.

Bishan Bedi won the toss and elected to bat, and India lost Gavaskar early, but half centuries to Chauhan and Amarnath, combined with good support right down the order, left India with a commanding first innings total of 402. Australia were in strife early, but Bobby Simpson saved the day with a six hour stay compiling 176 runs, putting his stamp on the series and helping Australia attain a score of 394. Bedi too, put his stamp on the series taking five wickets, no mean feat for a spin bowler at the pace friendly WACA.

Centuries to Gavaskar and Amarnath helped Bedi declare at 330/9, leaving Australia the daunting task of chasing 339 for victory. They lost an early wicket before the close and sent in night watchman, spin bowler Tony Mann, to see them safely home to stumps. Mann did the unthinkable the following day and scored an unlikely century.

Even when Ogilvie went for 47, at 195/4 Australia dared to dream with Simpson and Toohey at the crease and they were still there when the last hour began. However Simpson was soon runout and Kim Hughes fell immediately afterwards and panic began to set in, when the score was approaching 300. With only nine to win, Bedi deceived Toohey and the game was in the balance. When Bedi trapped the keeper, Rixon, LBW, he could sniff victory. In a nail biter Clark and Thompson saw Australia home, victors by two wickets, but not before Bedi had taken five wickets, and for the first time in his career, ten for the match.

What else did this series have to offer?

For the New Year's Test in Melbourne, all Simpson and his men needed to do was win or draw and the series was either squared or won. Bedi had other plans however. He won the toss and batted, which immediately appeared a regrettable decision as the openers were back in the sheds, both scoring ducks. However the middle order fired, first through Viswanath and Amarnath, then Vengsarkar and Mankad, and India rallied to make it to 256. Chandrasekhar then weaved his magic with the support of his skipper and the young Aussie outfit were skittled for 213, 43 behind.

Gavaskar then fired for his skipper and held the Indian second innings together with a silken 118, his third ton in the series, and India forged ahead with 343, leaving Australia the huge job of making 387. Despite their heroics in Perth, this total proved to be a bridge too far, and they crumbled against Chandrasekhar (12 wickets for the match) and Bedi, to lose by 222 runs. India pegged one back, but still down 2-1.

Bobby Simpson won the toss for the Sydney Test match and batted. The Australian novices batted like novices and were dismissed for a dismal 131. No centuries to India but a solid reply gave them 396, a whopping lead, leaving Australia to scramble for a draw. Their response a little better in the second innings but India's spinners took advantage of the SCG pitch and cleaned up the Aussies, winning by an innings and two runs. Not only had they squared the series 2-2 after being 2-0 down, they now had the Aussies on the run and potentially their first series win on Australian soil. The series, with India in the ascent, was well set up for the fifth and final Test at Adelaide Oval.

Often, Adelaide can produce an epic encounter. The city of churches, one of the most picturesque grounds in the world and a pitch that has something for every player: pace, spin, batsman. Probably the most perfect cricket pitch in the world in terms of generosity to all disciplines. Bobby Simpson won the toss and elected to bat and for once the young Aussie guns fired, albeit on a good batting track.

A solid start by openers Graeme Wood and Rick Darling laid the foundation for centuries to Graham Yallop and Simpson, with good support from Toohey. Although the lower order failed to add much, the Australians posted a commanding total of 505, Chandrasekhar the main destroyer with five wickets. A big blow to Australia losing paceman Jeff Thompson to a hamstring injury and he was only able to bowl 3.3 overs, however he managed two decisive blows himself. In the short time he was able to bowl he knocked over Gavaskar and Amarnath.

Led by Viswanath, India's middle order got things back on track, but it was well short of Australia's total, all out for 269. Simpson, mindful of Thompson's inability to bowl declined to enforce the follow-on. Both teams were looking to be positive, given that there was a series on the line. Simpson wanted quick runs and Bedi wanted quick wickets. Half centuries to Darling and Simpson were the main contributions in Australia's total of 256.

India began the climb up the mountain, 493 runs to win. It would need to be the highest run chase in Test cricket history. They had a couple of advantages however. There would be plenty of time and no Jeff Thompson, the latter being a massive blow to Australia. Gavaskar and Chauhan started solidly enough and if India were to make the total they'd need every cell in Gavaskar's body to reach the total. Unfortunately Gavaskar fell for 29 and not long after Chauhan joined him in the sheds, leaving India 79/2. However, the middle order, led by Amarnath (86), Viswanath (73), and Vengsarkar (78) produced a remarkable fightback and they were well served by the lower order as well.

They came awfully close, falling just short at 445. It was a marathon effort and the highest fourth innings total in a losing Test to date. (Overtaken by New Zealand with 451 against England in 2002) It was cruel to have one team on the losing side after such a hard fought series, but the crowds, players and media celebrated one of the most entertaining series ever between India and Australia.

Back to Pakistan

War between India and Pakistan meant that Test cricket was shelved between 1961 and 1978, but the time had come and India would head to Pakistan in 1978/79 for a three Test tour. Not one of Bedi's team had played a Test match against Pakistan. His opposite number Mushtaq Mohammad was the only player in his own line-up who had ever played a Test against India. The two teams must have looked like two prize fighters, circling each other, probing for weaknesses in the first Test at Faisalabad.

Mushtaq won the toss and batted, his brother Sadiq along with Majid Khan, opening the batting against Mohinder Amarnath and Test debutant Kapildev Ramlal Nikhanj, better known as Kapil Dev. It was a steady start, but three quick wickets fell, the openers and the captain, Mushtaq, two of them to Bishan Bedi. That brought together Zaheer Abbas and Javed Minadad and 255 runs later, there was another wicket, Zaheer out for 176. Having hit the 500 mark, Mushtaq declared, leaving Miandad not out on 154.

Gavaskar and Chauhan made a solid start against the pace of Imran Khan and Sarfraz Narwaz, taking the score to 64 without loss at the end of day two, but not before some controversy. Gavaskar, objecting to a barrage of short pitched bowling from Sarfraz, called Bedi to the pitch to register his complaint. Mushtaq, to his credit, immediately replaced Sarfraz thus dousing the flames with cold water.

The openers took the score to 97 before losing Chauhan, but Gavaskar soldiered on to record 89. The hero of the batting however was Viswanath who scored a splendid 145, his highest score and with it came the distinction of being the first Indian to score a Test century against every nation. Curiously Mushtaq's captaincy was very defensive, given the large total he had in the bank. Imran and Sarfraz continued to pepper the batsmen with bouncers, while Mushtaq directed most of his own bowling outside leg stump. India managed to get close with 462 and they were assisted by the Pakistanis with 40 extras, including 34 no balls.

There was little time for a second innings, given that it had taken nearly four days to complete the first, and the Test drifted to a draw. Pakistan declared four down for 264, with Asif Iqbal recording a century and Zaheer unlucky to miss one, out for 96. Of note for India, Kapil Dev took his first wicket in Test cricket, Sadiq caught by Gavaskar. India 0/43 when the stumps were drawn.

Mushtaq won the toss at Gaddafi Stadium, Lahore, scene of the second Test and decided to field first after inspecting the wicket and noticing it would suit his quick bowlers. It turned out to be a wise decision. Gavaskar, ever the lynchpin, went early and Imran and Sarfraz each picked up four wickets as India were rolled for 199, Vengsarkar the best with 76.

When Mushtaq declared at 539/8, India would have well been sick of the sight of Zaheer Abbas who was again amongst the runs with 235 not out and giving Pakistan a healthy lead of 340 runs.

India, through Gavaskar and Chauhan, started the long slow haul and both were very unlucky to be dismissed shy of their centuries. India continued to dig deep, with Viswanath making 83 and Kapil Dev 43, but the key was keeping wickets intact and eventually they could hold out no longer, but finished with 465 but still some 100 minutes left to play. Needing 126 to win, Pakistan attacked with gusto and won the match with eight wickets in hand.

Bedi finally won a toss and batted first in the last Test at Karachi. A win would square the series and Gavaskar's century helped India to get a healthy first innings of 344, with an entertaining 59 from Kapil Dev, batting at number nine. On the pacey wicket, Bedi, as he had done all series, struggled to make much of an impact, so too Chandrasekhar. Another century to Miandad and Mushtaq declared the Pakistani innings closed at 481/9. Another century to Gavaskar was the bedrock of India's second innings but they struggled against the pace of Imran and Sarfraz and finished with only 300.

There was little time left for Pakistan to score the required 164 runs for victory, but they did just that. Buoyed from their run chase in the second Test, they came at India harder this time and won the Test by eight wickets again, giving them the series 2-0.

While there was some justifiable criticism of Bedi's leadership during the series, it was probably more a measure of Pakistan's superiority than anything else. Their batting held enormous strength and Bedi had no answers, nor the firepower to match the pace of Imran and Sarfraz. The young Dev was still at the beginning of his career and would have his time in the sun in the future. India looked tired and ragged in the field, Kirmani's keeping wasn't the best and India returned home, soundly beaten. It was Bishan Bedi's last Test match as captain.

Bedi went on two more tours; the West Indies in 1978/79 under Gavaskar and England 1979 under his old spinning mate, Venkat. He has since been a coach of the Indian team and has been an outspoken critic of modern cricket, everything from bats to T20 and also of bowling actions. It signals is a man whose heart lies in the purity of cricket.

This celebrated captain of India won Indian Cricket Cricketer of the Year in 1967, Arjuna Award in 1969, Padma Shri in 1970 and the CK Nayudu Lifetime Achievement Award in 2004. In 2015 Bishan Singh Bedi was inducted into the Wisden India Hall of Fame.

Captaincy Record	Tests	W	L	D	%
New Zealand 1975/76 (NZ)*	2	0	1	1	0%
West Indies 1975/76 (WI)	4	1	2	1	25%
New Zealand 1976/77 (India)	3	2	0	1	67%
England 1976/77 (India)	5	1	3	1	20%
Australia 1977/78 (Australia)	5	2	3	0	40%
Pakistan 1978/79 (Pakistan)	3	0	2	1	0%
Total	**22**	**6**	**11**	**5**	**27%**

* *Not captain for full series*

20

GUNDAPPA "VISHY" VISWANATH

With his supple wrists and exquisite timing, Gundappa Viswanath, "Vishy", was one of India's finest Test batsmen and with Sunil Gavaskar the bedrock of India's batting in the 1970's. Sunny at the top of the order and Vishy holding the middle together. They were so well connected to each other that Vishy married Gavaskar's sister.

With 91 Tests to his name, he scored 6080 runs at 41.93 with fourteen centuries and a highest score of 222. It wasn't just the way Vishy scored his runs, but the importance of his time at the crease. It seemed that when Gavaskar failed, Vishy was the one to hold the innings together. Some of his most important innings were on difficult pitches when runs were hard to come by.

He debuted against Australia at Kanpur in 1969 and scored a century in his first Test in the second innings after scoring a duck in the first.

When Vishy scored a century, India never lost a Test. His 139 against the West Indies at Calcutta in 1974/75 helped lay the foundation for an Indian victory after they'd lost the first two. In the next Test of the same series, arguably his finest knock, was just shy of a century, with 97, and again it was the foundation for an Indian victory.

Perhaps his most celebrated knock was in cahoots with Gavaskar, again against the West Indies, when both scored centuries in India's famous victory run chase of 406 in 1975/76.

Vishy was the 20th Test captain of India, but only captained two Tests, both times filling for his brother-in-law, the sixth Test against Pakistan in 1978/79 and the one off Jubilee Test in England in 1980. He was being groomed for the captaincy because of the unavailability of Gavaskar for a tour to the West Indies which was ultimately cancelled. Vishy got the two Tests as leader and then normal service resumed.

The Pakistan series already won, the sixth Test could have been an exercise in going through the motions but both teams fought keenly. It was off to a good start for Vishy as he won the toss at Eden Gardens, Calcutta and batted first. India negotiated the speed of Imran as they worked their way to 331. Pakistan captain, Asif Iqbal, made a bold and courageous declaration, 272/4, 59 runs behind, as he tried to engineer a result. It was going well for him when he had India 95/6, but Kapil Dev and Ghavri saved the situation, India all out 205, leaving Pakistan 264 for victory. They made a bright start but it began to unravel when wickets started falling, a couple of those through run-outs, they played for time ending up 179/6 and the Test finished in a draw.

Wankhede Stadium, Bombay was the appropriate setting for the Golden Jubilee Test between India and England in 1980. Or, to put it more correctly, India versus (now Sir) Ian Botham, for the England allrounder dominated the match. The only thing he didn't do was take a catch, but there weren't many to take after England wicket keeper Bob Taylor had picked up a world record ten on his own.

Vishy won the toss and elected to bat, and there were plenty of starts, but not much else. Given that this was the thirteenth Test match of the season (six against Australia, six against Pakistan) the players could have been forgiven for being a little jaded. Or maybe it was just Botham, for he took 6-58 as India stumbled their way to 242.

Ghavri picked up five English wickets and Kapil Dev three. Things looked good for Vishy and India when the opposition had been reduced to 58/5. Then Ian Botham belted 17 fours on his way to 114, with solid support from Taylor and the tail, and England scrambled to a 54 run lead, all out for 296.

At this point it might have been nice for India if Botham had a bit of a rest, but unfortunately, he was raring to go and with the new ball in his hand, continued to act as a wrecking ball, taking 7-48 as India were rattled for for 149. Kapil Dev's 45 not out the only real resistance. Boycott and Gooch easily knocked off the 96 runs for victory and England, or Botham, had won the Jubilee Test.

Thus ends the captaincy of Vishy, as Gavaskar returned to the job, however in truth he was only a part time skipper, but would have been honoured to fill the role, albeit for a brief time. Vishy's chief claim to fame was being India's main man for a crisis and the glue that held the Indian middle order together for thirteen years.

Post his Test career, Vishy served as an ICC Match Referee and was at one time Chairman of Selectors. He was Indian Cricket Cricketer of the Year in 1970, awarded the Padma Shri in 1971, the Arjuna Award in 1977/78 and the CK Nayudu Lifetime Achievement Award in 2008.

Captaincy Record	Tests	W	L	D	%
Pakistan 1979/80 (India)*	1	0	0	1	0%
England 1979/80 (India)	1	0	1	0	0%
Total	2	0	1	1	0%

Not captain for full series

21

KAPILDEV RAMLAL NIKHANJ – KAPIL DEV

A genuinely quick bowler with subtle variations, and an explosive batsman whose instinct to fight saved India on many an occasion. By the time this man had retired from Test cricket, it seemed as though he had ticked every box and climbed every mountain. He was at the time, the greatest wicket taker in the history of Test cricket with 434 wickets, taking over from Kiwi great, Sir Richard Hadlee. He was India's greatest wicket taker in both Tests and ODI's. He was the only man in history to have taken over 400 wickets and score more than 5000 runs in Tests. He stood proudly next to his contemporaries, some of the greatest allrounders in Test cricket: Sir Ian Botham, Sir Richard Hadlee and the great Imran Khan. That's some heady company. Some say Kapil Dev was the best of the lot.

He debuted in Test cricket on the toughest tour of all, against neighbours Pakistan in 1978/79 and took one solitary wicket in the first Test of that series, a bat-a-thon in Faisalabad. He was given an opportunity up the order in the second Test, and made 43 runs, batting at number five. He scored an explosive 59 and took three wickets in the third Test. India had lost the series but they had unearthed a talented new allrounder.

Dev started to find his feet in Test cricket in the following series against the West Indies at home in 1978/79. He formed a good opening bowling partnership with Karsan Ghavri and for the first time in a while, India had opening bowlers that bowled more than a few token overs with the new ball. He begun to shine with the bat and his captain, Gavaskar, used the young allrounder in various positions. Dev was proving to be very adaptable. He could bat anywhere and was comfortable against either pace or spin. He repaid Gavaskar's faith by scoring 126 not out in the fifth Test in Delhi and finished the series with 329 runs at 65.80, a century and two half centuries. He picked up 17 wickets at 33.00. If he'd announced himself as a new talent against Pakistan, he was thumping on the table after the series against West Indies.

As he played on through the early 1980's he was becoming the game's premier allrounder. He didn't always fire with bat and ball, but like any top allrounder, he was never out of the game. If he failed with the bat, he picked up wickets. If the wickets ran dry, he scored runs. Oh, and how he scored runs! He was out of the same bludgeoning mold as Botham and Hadlee. He plundered runs like they did and at a strike rate that was ahead of the times. One Day Internationals had by now become a part of any Test tour and Dev didn't seem to care in which format he played. He scored at a cracking rate.

First Term

Following the 3-0 loss to Pakistan in 1982/83, Gavaskar was replaced as captain, and the enigmatic allrounder, Kapil Dev, at age 22 was announced as the new skipper, ready to take on the West Indies in the Caribbean. Mixed throughout the Test series, three ODI's, a formula that has since been changed. Forcing the players to jump from Tests to ODI's and back again through a tour is very difficult, and more so for the touring team who have less resources on which to call. Is this the reason Kapil Dev and his team lost the five Test series to the West Indies two nil? No. India were up against one of the most potent cricket teams of all time, but the scheduling would not have helped. (Different cricket administrations around the world were guilty of the same sin during that period. No-one had really encountered the issue before. The One Day International was the 1980's version of T20.) That India were even competitive against this team just goes to show how truly strong India was during this era. Dev had brought a new dynamic to this team. Now he was in charge of it.

Clive Lloyd won the toss at Sabina Park, Kingston, scene of the first Test and elected to field. Why not? A fast wicket and a couple of handy bowlers. How's this for a line-up? Roberts, Holding, Garner, Marshall.

A half century to Sharma was all the top order could muster, but the real hero was Sandhu, batting at number nine, with 68 valuable runs that took the score to a half decent 251. The aforementioned battalion of battery shared the wickets between them, Roberts with four.

Without the same artillery, and against a batting line-up as follows: Greenidge, Haynes to open, followed by Richards, Gomes, Logie and Lloyd, backed by keeper/batsman Dujon, this is a first class batting line-up in any era. That they only managed three more runs than India is testimony to the inspired bowling performance by the skipper, who picked up four wickets and was assisted by the spin of Ravi Shastri, who also picked up four.

Holding took one ball to remove Gavaskar. Marshall helped him dissect the top order and then Roberts completely obliterated the lower order, all out 174, leaving the West Indies to score 172 for victory from 26 overs. The batsmen, particularly Richards, went berserk and scoring at an amazing 6.82 runs per over, they won by four wickets with four balls to spare.

The West Indies then won the first ODI.

Two days later, the second Test at Queen's Park Oval, Port of Spain, Lloyd won the toss and once again sent the opposition in to bat. As if there weren't enough troubles with the West Indies bowling line-up, Gaekwad was runout when the score was one. It went downhill from there. Amarnath's 58 and Shastri's 42 were the only bright spots in an innings of 175, Marshall picking up five wickets and Roberts three.

But India would not lay down. Sandhu found the outside edge of Haynes, caught by Kirmani for a duck and then bowled Greenidge for the same score. The captain, bowling from the other end then took out Richards. West Indies, three down for one run. Gomes and Lloyd then spoiled the party and both scored big centuries as the West Indies amassed 394, a lead of 219 runs. The best India could do was bat out time, which they did, courtesy of a century to Amarnath and a not out even hundred to the Indian captain.

Two days after the second ODI, the third Test, this time at Bourda, Georgetown, Guyana, rain was the winner, with the first innings unfinished when play stopped on day five. Rain delayed the start of the fourth Test also, nearly wiping out the entire first day. Lloyd won the toss and sent India in and the pace quartet peppered the Indian batsmen with short pitched deliveries from the outset. Roberts, Holding, Garner, Marshall, one by one. As one tired another was ready to go again. The frequency of bouncers led the Indian manager, Hanumant Singh, along with captain Kapil Dev, to lodge a complaint about intimidatory bowling. By the time the complaint went anywhere, the damage had been done. The Indian batting capitulated against the onslaught, and only a heroic innings from Mohinder Amarnath saved them from complete humiliation. His 91 runs the only reason India was able to score 203. The West Indies responded with a dominant 486 with half centuries to Greenidge, Haynes and Richards, and a century to Logie.

Needing to bat for a day and a half to save the match, 277 runs behind, only Amarnath and Gaekwad showed any resistance in the top order, and some fight by Kirmani and Dev in the lower order, but it was too big a task against this bowling attack. West Indies needing 1 run for victory, they received a no-ball from wicket keeper Syed Kirmani and won by ten wickets.

The fifth Test was a batting festival for both teams and finished in a draw. Of note, the debut of leg spinner, Laxman Shivaramakrishnan, centuries to Shastri and Amarnath and a 98 to the skipper. Kapil Dev lost his first full Test series 2-0 but it was a tough initiation for the new skipper, against one of the most powerful teams of all time. (The size of the task compares to the first series of Lala Amarnath as captain, in 1947/48, against Australia's "Invincibles".) It was not surprising that Mohinder Amarnath topped the batting for India, but also scored the most runs of any batsman for the series, with 598 at 66.44, but second in the averages was Kapil Dev, with 254 runs at 42.33. He also took the most wickets (17) at 24.94. Both of those averages, batting and bowling are better than his career averages. Captaincy seemed to agree with the young man and it clearly wasn't having any effect on his own performance.

On a happy note, Kapil Dev and his Indian team, largely made up of the Test team, extracted some heady revenge on the West Indies a few months later in England, June 1983 in the Prudential World Cup. Rolled for 183, Dev took the crucial catch to dismiss Vivian Richards and the Windies collapsed. Not only were Clive Lloyd and his men shocked by the defeat, so too the rest of the world. India had won the

World Cup.

From the sublime to the ridiculous. The home series of three Tests against Pakistan was an abysmal advertisement for Test cricket. Constant rain interruptions and dull cricket conspired to return three drawn Test matches. Little wonder they attracted small crowds.

Brighter cricket was expected between India and the touring West Indies later that summer for a six Test and five ODI series. The visitors took no trouble in extracting their own revenge for the World Cup loss and won the ODI series 5-0. They were in no mood to take prisoners in the Test series either, which they won 3-0. India's batting was again left to Gavaskar, but one innings of 236 not out, in which he broke Sir Donald Bradman's record for Test centuries, accounted for over fifty percent of his 550 runs. The most consistent batsman was Vengsarkar who averaged 53.12. The captain also struggled for runs, but the biggest surprise was the total meltdown of Mohinder Amarnath who scored just one run from six innings. Dev's biggest problem however, was that while he continued to spearhead the attack taking 29 wickets, he did so with little support from the other end. It seemed that Kapil could inspire himself, but not his team mates. That said, of the fourteen Tests he'd been at the helm, eleven were against one of the best teams of all time.

Justifiably, given his workload, and the series of unflattering results – the final Test against the West Indies was the 29th consecutive Test without a victory - Dev was relieved of the captaincy for the 1984/85 tour to Pakistan and Gavaskar chosen in his place. Gavaskar also retained the captaincy for the 1985 tour to India by England.

Second Term

Dev returned to the captaincy for the tour to Sri Lanka in 1985, a hastily put together programme of three Tests sandwiched between three ODIs. The team had had little preparation and precious little cricket before the first Test and this showed up in the results. Gavaskar had chosen to move down the batting order, but this left a glaring gap up the top. Without some determined batting by Gavaskar and Vengsarkar, and some fortuitous rain, Sri Lanka would have won the first Test and indeed, won their maiden Test match. India were outplayed by an enthusiastic home team. They wouldn't have to wait long to break open the champagne.

Duleep Mendis won the toss in the second Test at P.Saravanamuttu Stadium, Colombo and elected to bat. Despite slow going, Sri Lanka inched their way over the 300 mark, via a century to Amal Silva and 95 to Roy Dias, and ended their first innings with 385. As in the first Test, there was trouble at the top of the order, at one stage 3/3, then 79/4 when Kris Srikanth was dismissed for 64. Batting at six, Gavaskar partnered with Mohinder Amarnath and steadied the innings, both scoring half centuries, but India fell short on the first innings with only 244.

Mendis declared three down for 206 and set India a target of 348 to win on the final day. The Sri Lankan quicks were too good for India once again, where it must be said on the same wicket the Indian pace bowlers failed to deliver much at all. Without a defiant 78 from the skipper, India would have been far worse off, but the total of 198 well short of the victory target. Sri Lanka won their first ever Test match and Kapil Dev was the unfortunate captain on the receiving end. Sri Lanka was in the mood to celebrate and the following day was made a public holiday.

The best that Dev and his team could do was to try and save face by squaring the series in the third Test at Kandy. Dev won the toss and batted, and again his team struggled against the Sri Lankan swing bowling. A change at the top saw Ravi Shastri opening the batting, and despite several starts, only Vengsarkar passed the half century mark with India all out for another below par first innings score of 249. The Indian quicks then returned to normal service and rolled Sri Lanka for 198. Likewise the Indian batting in the second innings improved and built on the foundation of a century to Amarnath giving them 343 and setting the Sri Lankans the huge task of scoring 377. Centuries to Dias and Mendis took the attack right up to India, and for a while it looked as though an improbable victory was at hand, but a late collapse and bad light sent the match to a draw. Sri Lanka had won their first Test series at the expense of Kapil Dev and his men.

Against a considerably weakened Australian team that had just lost to New Zealand, Kapil Dev must have liked his chances in the three Test tour Downunder, and the opportunity to break his own duck of Test match victories must have seemed possible, but India's preparation was severely limited due to bad weather. There was little or no chance to become accustomed to the Australian conditions before the Test series because they spent most of their available practise time under umbrellas.

The two teams were nervous and it showed in their inability to find a way to win. The Australians struggled and were lucky to hold India to a three Test draw. A bit more urgency and India could have pressed for a victory in Melbourne and likewise in Sydney. It was probably India's best chance in five tours to the country to put Australia to the sword. As was becoming increasingly apparent, Kapil Dev saved his best performances when captain and was rewarded with the Man of the Series, however the skipper was yet to record his first win.

To England in a soggy May in 1986, things begun well for the tourists, due to play two ODIs and three Test matches, and they picked up some much needed practice in the middle against several county sides. The first Test was at the home of cricket, Lords, and Dev had no hesitation inviting David Gower's England to bat first on an overcast day. Initially it looked like a wrong move, but India clawed back after a strong start by openers Gooch and Robinson. After a wicket finally fell at 66, three more were taken in the 90's. Gooch was solid, registering a century, while Pringle scored a half century, and England's first innings was a score of 294. India's quick bowlers, particularly Chetan Sharma, did the damage. On the back of Vengsarkar's century, India replied with 341, a valuable lead of 47.

Rain delays and tumbling wickets saw England's second innings as dreary as the weather. Leading from the front, Kapil Dev picked up four wickets and after the Indians had bowled 96.4 overs, England was all out for a painstaking 180, leaving India a shot at victory, needing 134 to win. They began shakily, losing steady wickets until Kapil Dev joined Ravi Shastri, and between them they guided India home. Kapil Dev was named Man of the Match, but it would have seemed of no significance next to the real prize, that of having won his first Test as captain of India. It was only the second Test India had ever won in England in 54 years of touring.

England were down and ready for the knockout blow and they hastened proceedings by giving their captain one. Going into that first Test Gower and his men had lost the preceding five Test matches. Enough was enough, and Chairman of Selectors, Peter May, himself a successful former captain, sacked Gower and replaced him with Vice-captain Mike Gatting.

Dev won the toss at Headingley and batted first against an England team smarting from the first Test loss, a new captain and minus a couple of stars, namely Ian Botham and David Gower. The home side seemed to have shaken it off however, when they bundled India out for 272, Vengsarkar top scoring with 61 and some useful lower order runs from wicket keeper Kiran More and Madan Lal, the latter having been brought in at the last minute to replace Sharma.

Madan Lal picked up opener Wilf Slack for a duck and the rot set in early for England, who never recovered. Roger Binny was the pick of the quicks with five wickets as England were humbled for only 102 runs giving India an excellent advantage of 170 runs on the first innings.

Vengsarkar once again was the rock of the Indian innings, scoring a not out century in a total of 237. The second best score in the game was his first innings effort of 61. No other player came close as India's bowlers repeated the dose in the second innings, cleaning England up for 128 runs, giving India victory by 279 runs and Vengsarkar rightly was named Man of the Match.

Not long after having one his first Test as captain, Kapil Dev had won his second, along with his first series win as India took an unassailable lead going into the third Test which was ultimately drawn. Kapil Dev had finally removed the monkey from his back.

Fresh from his series victory against England, Kapil Dev and his team prepared for a tour by Australia to India. Perhaps in home conditions they could beat Alan Border and his men, something they couldn't do in the previous series in Australia. However, the series produced no decisive results, Australia having rebuilt since their nadir and not as wobbly with the bat. Border and his men were a far more formidable outfit than they were a year earlier.

One could muse that a Test series with no result would be three dull draws, however there were only two, for the first Test in this series was the famous tied Test at Madras, giving both these two teams their own place in Test cricket history. Dean Jones' marathon innings of courage and exhaustion, Kapil Dev's own swashbuckling century, the unlikely spin heroes Matthews and Bright. For only the second time in the history of Test cricket, this was truly a remarkable event. Jones and

Dev were joint winners of the Man of the Match award. That the two teams could not be separated made them both winners.

The second Test was washed out and the third a tame draw. Perhaps fitting that neither side won the series.

Hosting Sri Lanka at home in 1986/87, Kapil Dev and his team were able to exact revenge on their embarrassing defeat two years earlier. The Sri Lankan batsmen struggled with the spinning ball and India had no trouble winning the series, and it marked Dev's maiden series win at home.

Following the Sri Lankans was a tour of India by Pakistan, for a five Test series. Like so many series before, this was a war of attrition. Batting friendly tracks where after four Tests there had been no result. It took until the fifth Test, at Bangalore, for the deadlock to be broken and Pakistan won the series by winning that single Test match, by 16 runs. It was Kapil Dev's final match as captain of India.

He continued to play on for many seasons, but as a player only, and his prodigious talent an ace in the pack for the Indian Test team, be it with bat or ball. He finished his glittering career in New Zealand in 1994, having begun some 15 years earlier. He had been a faithful servant to India and one of the most successful allrounders in the history of Test cricket.

As a captain his first stint at 22 years of age was premature. That said, he led from the front and his form did not suffer from the burden of captaincy. It is worth repeating that in his first term as captain, eleven of the fourteen Tests were played against one of the most powerful units ever assembled, Clive Lloyd's West Indians. It would not have mattered who captained.

He suffered the embarrassment of losing a series to (then) minnows, Sri Lanka, but bounced back to inflict the best ever series victory in England, then the magnificence of the tied Test, revenge against the Lankans and then the dull series loss to Imran Khan's Pakistanis.

On balance, Dev occupied both penthouse and cellar as a Test captain. Could he have pressed harder when victory was on offer? Most certainly, but that is a comment you could easily say of other captains. The long and dull drawn Tests against Pakistan – well, that is hardly Dev's fault alone. Captains of both teams have found themselves in that position and it probably says more about the Boards than the captains.

On balance, while he was clearly a better performer for himself than for other captains, he was probably a better asset for India without the burden. One will also never forget his crowning achievement, victory in the 1983 World Cup.

In retirement he did a term as national coach and held the position of Chairman of the National Cricket Academy. In 2002 he was announced as one of the finalists for Wisden Indian Cricketer of the century and won the award, beating such players as Tendulkar and Gavaskar.

Captaincy Record	Tests	W	L	D	%
West Indies 1982/83 (WI)	5	0	2	3	0%
Pakistan 1983/84 (India)	3	0	0	3	0%
West Indies 1983/84 (India)	6	0	3	3	0%
Sri Lanka 1985 (Sri Lanka)	3	0	1	2	0%
Australia 1985/86 (Australia)	3	0	0	3	0%
England 1986 (England)	3	2	0	1	67%
Australia 1986/87 (India)**	3	0	0	2	0%
Sri Lanka 1986/87 (India)	3	2	0	1	67%
Pakistan 1986/87 (India)	5	0	1	4	0%
Total	**34**	**4**	**7**	**23**	**12%**

** *Includes Tied Test*

22

DILIP BALWANT VENGSARKAR

Nicknamed the "Colonel" for his similarity to CK Nayudu, as one of the mainstays of the Indian batting order during the 1980's Vengsarkar was one of the few batsmen to get on top of the fearsome West Indian pace quartet, although it's doubtful they would have fed him too many deliveries for his signature stroke, the drive. He took over the captaincy from Kapil Dev for the series against the West Indies in 1987/88 and lost the captaincy after his third series, also against the West Indies in 1988/89 after an acrimonious relationship with the Board.

A talented teenager, he was blossoming in the Ranji Trophy when snapped up to play for India and opened the batting against New Zealand for his debut Test at the age of 19. In and out of the team for a couple of seasons, he didn't cement a spot until the 1977/78 tour of Australia under Bishan Bedi, but even then his returns were a rather modest 320 runs at 35.55. It was in the second Test of that series where he was moved down the order, away from opening the batting. It would be a successful relocation for many years to come.

During a purple patch in the mid-eighties, he was one of the leading batsmen in the world. He'd rescued India time and again with stubborn innings when all around him had crumbled. The sort of man you might like as captain.

He took over the captaincy for the home series against the all-powerful West Indies in 1987/88, for a four Test series, although he missed the fourth through injury.

At Delhi for the first Test, he won the toss against (now Sir) Vivian

Richards and taking a gamble, batted first on a tough wicket. He probably rued that decision when the West Indies bowled India out for 75, and was one of only three players to make double figures against the pace of Patrick Patterson and Winston Davis. However he had pace at his disposal too, and former captain Kapil Dev with Chetan Sharma gave as good as they got and removed the West Indies for 127. Both totals, incidentally, were the lowest each of the teams had scored against each other.

Batting was easier in the second dig, the captain forged the way with a century and ably assisted by Dev and More, India posting a far more healthy 327. The basis for Vengsarkar's gamble at the toss was that West Indies would be batting last on this wicket and would have to front up to his spinners.

Chasing 276, the Windies safely negotiated their way to victory, the spinners not enjoying the assistance they might have otherwise received. Richards scored a century, so both skippers led from the front in the second innings.

The second Test lost the entire second day to the weather and as a result ended in a draw, although the West Indies had the upper hand. A dull, lifeless wicket at Eden Gardens in Calcutta, for the third Test led to a dull and lifeless draw. Another century to Vengsarkar, but a cruel blow. He fractured his hand and not only had to retire hurt, he was not able to play in the fourth Test, which turned out to be a victory for India.

A seemingly easier assignment hosting John Wright's New Zealanders in 1988/89, spearheaded by the aging warrior, (Sir) Richard Hadlee, who more than left his mark on the series. (Post career Wright went on to be a very successful coach of the Indian Test team.) Hadlee broke the record for the most wickets in Test cricket in the first Test match and of course playing opposite was the man who would take it from him later on, Kapil Dev.

Vengsarkar won the toss at Bangalore and opted to bat, and while Hadlee made his presence felt immediately, there were runs at the top for Navjot Sidhu with a century and 75 for the skipper, along with valuable contributions lower down by Shastri, Dev and More. Hadlee picked up 5-65 as India made a solid 384. A mix of spin and speed accounted for New Zealand who folded for just 189 at the snail pace of 1.54 runs per over. Folded is an appropriate description, for the Kiwis were folded over from a mystery virus which effected a number of the team, so their slow scoring should also be seen in that context. In fact, Richard Hadlee was so ill he did not bowl in India's second innings. Searching for quick runs, Srikanth, Arun Lal and Sidhu scored at just over five runs per over, allowing Vengsarkar to declare at 141/1, leaving New Zealand to chase 337. Wright made a fighting 58, but New Zealand capitulated to be rolled for 164, India winning the Test by the comfortable margin of 172 runs.

A tremendous comeback to health and subsequently cricket form for New Zealand in the second Test, winning by 136 runs. Hadlee was the star of the show, with ten wickets, but John Bracewell's eight wickets and a belligerent half century won him man of the match. Significantly, Vengsarkar scored 25 and a duck, for once not being the main man.

John Wright called correctly at Hyderabad for the deciding third Test and opted to bat. They stumbled early but fighting and patient knocks to Mark Greatbach and wicket keeper Ian Smith held the innings together to give a fair first innings total of 254.

The Kiwi quicks took all of the Indian wickets to fall, but not before they'd helped themselves to 358 runs at good clip, with Mohammad Azharuddin top scoring with 81 giving India a sizeable lead of 104 runs. It was almost enough, as New Zealand, save for John Wright and Richard Hadlee, were trundled out quickly for a measly 124 and India's openers batted T20 style and knocked off the 22 runs in two overs and one ball, giving India and her captain a series victory, 2-1.

Vengsarkar could be forgiven for saying, "didn't we just play the West Indies?" for they were about to embark on a tour to the Caribbean straight after the New Zealand series. It was not a happy tour, nor was the aftermath and it was Vengsarkar's last series as captain. Perhaps he felt it before the tour but he certainly knew by the end. It was one of the least successful tours ever undertaken by an Indian team abroad, not winning a single match.

It was the West Indies who could be forgiven for being flat and disinterested. They'd just been on tours to both England and Australia and when you are the best in the world, every team, be it international or provincial, comes at you hard, but they were a professional outfit and when India arrived the Windies were ready from ball one.

Vengsarkar was having issues with the Board. He was wanting to participate in some non-core promotional matches in the United States after the series, but it was not sanctioned. By the end of the tour, the Indian skipper had lost the captaincy along with his place in the team. Was this on Vengsarkar's mind during the tour? It had to have a bearing. His own batting was lacklustre by his lofty standards and this mood seemed to permeate through the team and effect everyone else's. India lost the series 3-0.

You don't leave a player of Vengsarkar's class out of the side for long, but by the time he returned to the team for the New Zealand tour in 1989/90, the captaincy had already gone through two other sets of hands.

Whether it was lack of hunger or a sign that his days were numbered Vengsarkar could not achieve in the early 1990's the brilliance of his earlier batting. He finished 116 Tests with 6868 runs at 42.13 a true giant in world batting during the 1980's. A somewhat reluctant captain, his value to the team was his ability to guide his team through a crisis. During easier times, an exquisite driver of the ball.

Post retirement he has been involved in administration and in 2006 was appointed Chairman of Selectors.

He was Indian Cricket Cricketer of the Year in 1976 and won the Arjuna Award in 1981. He was a Wisden Cricketer of the Year in 1987 and was awarded the Padma Shri in 1987. In 2014 he received the CK Nayudu Award.

Captaincy Record	Tests	W	L	D	%
West Indies 1987/88 (India)	3	0	1	2	0%
New Zealand 1988/89 (India)	3	2	1	0	67%
West Indies 1988/89 (West Indies)	4	0	3	1	0%
Total	**10**	**2**	**5**	**3**	**20%**

23

RAVISHANKAR JAYADRITHA "RAVI" SHASTRI

Ravi Shastri was potentially a long term captain of India, which makes it puzzling just how little he did captain the team. He was the long term deputy so was always in the mix, but in fact, he served the minimum: one Test. The good news about that is that he captained a winning team and thus has 100% record with Test wins as captain. With that sort of record, who knows, maybe they offered him the captaincy again but he turned it down?

Like many other examples in Test cricket, Shastri started his Test career as a spin bowler, but graduated into being a very useful allrounder for the team and India became more reliant on his steady batting as his career progressed. He was called upon to open the batting quite regularly, such was the calm nature of his style at the crease. (He nearly achieved the same feat as Vinoo Mankad in terms of positions he batted in. The only spot he never batted in Test matches was number 11.) What did stand out during his long career, was that while he wasn't blessed with the talent of a Vengsarkar, or Viswanath, he had an appetite for hard work, and it was that work ethic that helped him rise higher through the ranks than talent alone.

There were plenty of highs, but mixed with some lesser performances and that inconsistency is perhaps one of the reasons he never got the captaincy full time. Untimely injuries also did not make his path any easier. Among the highs, he equalled Sir Gary Sobers record for hitting 6 sixes in an over during a first class match; he was Shane Warne's first Test match wicket, but only after he'd made his highest Test score of 206, many of which came from the young leg spinner. A shrewd tactician, he won the only Test he captained.

Regular captain, Dilip Vengsarkar, upon scoring a ton in the third Test at Calcutta in December 1987 had his hand broken while batting against West Indies quick, Winston Davis, meaning he was out of the Test match to follow in Madras. The Windies had won one Test already and the other two were drawn. The fourth Test was the opportunity to square the series and Ravi Shastri was selected as India's 23rd Test cricket captain.

The stand in skipper was not only up against the might and power of the West Indies, but he was also minus the team's best batsman in Vengsarkar, the man he replaced as captain. Topping that off, he had three debutants: Woorkeri Raman and Ajay Sharma, both batsmen, and a leg spinner from Uttar Pradesh, Narendra Hirwani.

He had one advantage: the pitch was underprepared and was going to turn from day one. When he won the toss, Ravi Shastri had no hesitation in batting first, knowing the West Indies would be batting last on a pitch that was likely to get better by the day for his spinners.

Srikanth got off to a flyer, as was his style, but he was out when the score was 30 and a couple more went with him shortly afterwards, Amarnath and the debutant Raman. Arun Lal and Azharuddin steadied the ship, and then the lower order stayed with Kapil Dev, who hit a princely 109 in very good time. It gave India a very competitive first innings total of 382. Ominously, Richards and Hooper picked up three wickets between them bowling their spin.

Kapil Dev quickly accounted for West Indies debutant opener, Phil Simmons, caught and bowled, but it wasn't long before Shastri introduced spin. Rather than put the 19 year old Hirwani into the firing line straight away, he shrewdly chose to bowl himself and Arshad Ayub first. It brought an immediate benefit, with the skipper picking up Desmond Haynes. And that was the last wicket anyone else, apart from Hirwani, took in that innings. Shastri brought the young leggie on, and with good flight and savage turn he picked up eight West Indies wickets for 61, the tourists bundled out for 184. The Windies narrowly avoided the follow-on but were 198 behind on the first innings.

Courtney Walsh came hard at the Indians in the second innings, and picked up three quick wickets, but the debutant Raman scored a patient 89 and along with Azharuddin, helped put the innings back on track. It wasn't to stay that way and India were cleaned up for 217, leaving West Indies to chase down 416.

It was Bob Massie at Lords in 1972 who picked up 16 wickets in his debut Test, eight in each innings for Australia versus England. Nearly sixteen years later, Narendra Hirwani equalled the feat, taking eight West Indies wickets for 75 runs as they were routed for 160. Deceived by Hirwani'a flight, four of the batsmen were stumped by wicket keeper Kiran More (who also got another stumping from Raman's bowling – plus one in the first innings, a total of six and a record.) India had won by 255 runs, a glorious way to square the series after having been on the back foot. Shastri guided the team well without having contributed a whole lot himself, but his handling of the young spinner was smart, and his reading of the pitch and conditions spot on.

Although it remained as his only Test captaincy, Shastri continued to play through the 1980s and was a regular in the side until his final match against South Africa at Port Elizabeth in 1992 at only 30 years of age, a knee injury forcing him out of the team and he never returned.

Post cricket Shastri has been a television commentator since 1995 and for a brief moment coached the Indian team in 2007 and then again from 2017 to 2019 onwards.

Away from cricket, he's also been a Goodwill Ambassador for UNICEF and had the honour of being a celebrity torch bearer for the 2008 Summer Olympic Games.

Captaincy Record	Tests	W	L	D	%
West Indies 1987/88 (India)*	1	1	0	0	100%
Total	**1**	**1**	**0**	**0**	**100%**

Not captain for full series

24

KRISHNAMACHARI SRIKKANTH

The swashbuckling opener was a revelation in the 1980's. In fact you could suggest that he invented an entirely new mindset for opening the batting in Test cricket. Sure, there had been attacking openers before Srikanth, but not like this. He was a forerunner to the likes of Virender Sehwag or Australia's David Warner. He went at it from ball one, and in doing so, was both a crowd pleaser and a disappointment. The inconsistent results due to his flamboyant aggression, mean that he was in and out of the team throughout his career. His career average also points to his on one day, off the next, approach to batting.

However, his aggressive style was most suitable in the one day game and it was there that he was a major force for India and indeed top scored in the final of the World Cup when India were victorious in 1983.

Following the sacking of Vengsarkar after the West Indies tour of 1988/89, in which Srikanth didn't even play, he was appointed as captain for the away series to Pakistan in 1989/90 season, which seems rather odd. The next long term captain would be Azharuddin, who played in the series, but wasn't assured of his place initially. Given that the captain is quite often replaced after a series against Pakistan, was Srikanth given a poisoned chalice, keeping the seat warm for Azharuddin for the next series?

It was definitely a heavyweight showdown: two of cricket's greatest allrounders, Imran Khan and Kapil Dev against each other. One very good pace attack, one outstanding, both with solid batting line-ups. It ought to have been a fight to the death but unfortunately the contest proved to be four drawn Tests. No winner, yet it was lauded as a success on both sides. There were some great moments and some big landmarks. For the first time between these two nations, they had neutral umpires. Already some of the potential blow-ups had been nullified.

In the first Test at Karachi, Kapil Dev and Prabhakar caused all sorts of trouble to the Pakistani batsmen after they'd made a pretty good start, but the captain, Imran Khan stood defiant and made 109 not out to guide his team to an excellent 409. India were in all sorts against one of the great opening bowling pairs of all time, Waqar Younis and Wasim Akram, with an excellent first change bowler in Imran. Coming in at 41/4, facing a fired up Waqar Younis, a young fellow, just sixteen years of age, made his Test debut. SR Tendulkar, made 15 runs before being bowled by Waqar who coincidentally was also playing his debut Test match. India were all out for 262.

Pakistan went looking for quick runs and a solid lead and set India 453 for victory. Sanjay Manjrekar (son of Indian great, Vijay Manjrekar) batted for nearly six hours to save the match. It would not be the only key innings from that man during what was a watershed series for him. During the Test, Kapil Dev, played his 100th Test (and becoming the first bowler to do so) and took his 350th wicket in Test cricket.

The second Test at Faisalabad Pakistan again had the better of things, and aside from two gutsy half centuries to Manjrekar, the Man of the Match, there was also the first in what would be a very long line of Test half centuries to the young Tendulkar.

At Lahore, the third Test was a run fest and ended before the first innings was completed by both sides. For India, Manjrekar continued to put his stamp on the series with 218, especially important as they'd lost two early wickets. For Pakistan, Javed Miandad scored 145 in his 100th Test. Records tumbled but results didn't. The fourth and final Test, another day, another draw.

While Manjrekar and Azharuddin were the mainstays of the batting, the captain Srikanth was at the bad end of the averages. He made just 97 runs for the series at 13.85. In a season where runs were aplenty, the captain had failed with the bat. He was dropped as captain and

CAPTAINS FILE: INDIA

dropped from the team. It would be two years before he got another game, on the tour to Australia in 1991/92. In his last Test he passed his 2000th run in Test cricket, at the WACA ground in Perth.

After cricket he spent some time as coach of India A team and various commentary roles. In 2008 he was appointed Chief Selector of the Indian cricket team, a post he held for four years.

Captaincy Record	Tests	W	L	D	%
Pakistan 1989/90 (Pakistan)	4	0	0	4	0%
Total	4	0	0	4	0%

25

MOHAMMAD AZHARUDDIN

He announced himself to the Test cricket arena both in style and substance. Mohammad "Azhar" Azharuddin scored a century in each of his first three Test matches, the only player in Test cricket history to do so. The tall and elegant right hand handed batsman was a joy to watch as he plundered the leg side in his early career and then added silky offside play as his career progressed, equally elegant off front or back foot, always immaculate looking with his trademark long sleeves.

He scored a century in his last Test match, his 99th, and enjoyed a wonderful and celebrated career in between. He was, to that point, India's most successful Test captain.

And then the career was not only over, it virtually vanished, for he was a figure in one of the darkest days of cricket history. He was implicated and ultimately banned from the game for life by the ICC in the match fixing scandal that embroiled former South African captain Hanse Cronje. In more recent years, the BCCI lifted the ban in 2006 and after a decade of appeals, in and out of the courts, a Divisional Bench consisting of Justice Ashutosh Mohanta and Justice Krishna Mohan Reddy of the Andhra Pradesh High Court in 2012 dismissed the ban.

> "It was a long drawn out legal case and it was painful. We fought in the court for 11 years. There were lots of adjournments, changes in the case. But, finally, the verdict has come and I am happy that the ban has been lifted by the court." Azharuddin press conference following the decision.

It all could have been so different.

When he batted at home in India, he was completely unstoppable. Dominant. Yet, he also had his weaknesses. His record overseas is patchy and his record against high quality pace is likewise less than perfect. He looked so damned good at times and others, all at sea. His Test career was a series of ups and downs for this enigmatic batsman. Flawed genius is an overused term but it sits easily with Mohammad Azharuddin.

He debuted in 1984/85 in the home series against David Gower's England team, under the captaincy of Sunil Gavaskar in the third Test, at Eden Gardens, Calcutta. He scored his maiden century with Ravi Shastri scoring one at the other end. He scored a century at Madras in a losing side in the fourth Test, and in the drawn fifth Test, promoted to number three, another century. No player before or since has reached those heights.

The "away" anomaly hit in his second series, the humiliating loss in 1984/85 against Sri Lanka, under Kapil Dev. Azhar averaged just 18.66 after his stellar first series. Ordinary returns in Australia in 1985/86 and in England in 1986, then back to his stellar best at home in 1986/87 where he averaged 58.18 across nine Test matches with three centuries, one of those being his highest score of 199.

He continued to be a mainstay of the middle order through the late 1980's and but for his occasional lapses might have actually captained the team against Pakistan in 1989/90, but perhaps missing out on that honour was a blessing in disguise. He was rewarded with the captaincy after the sacking of Srikanth, and took the helm in the away series to New Zealand in 1989/90 and thus became India's 25th Test cricket captain. Former captain Bishan Bedi was tour manager and together they proposed to play positive and entertaining cricket.

At Lancaster Park, Christchurch for the first Test, Kiwi captain John Wright won the toss and batted. And batted. The skipper helped himself to 185 of a total of 459. If India's stated intent on arrival in New Zealand was to play attacking cricket they got a little carried away and suffered badly for it in their first innings reply. Loose shots against the tight bowling of Hadlee and Morrison were principally to blame for their capitulation to 160 all out. Attractive batting, but all too brief. They followed on and performed marginally better with 296, but it was far too little to save the match and the new skipper lost his first Test by ten wickets.

Lousy weather completely ruined the second Test at Napier, meaning the best Azhar could do was to square the series in the third Test. If they needed some exciting cricket, they got it.

Humid conditions at Auckland helped Azharuddin make the choice to field first when he won the toss and it paid immediate dividends. At 7/131 New Zealand was on the ropes, until Richard Hadlee launched a counter attack with 87 and then wicket keeper Ian Smith joined in with a stunning knock of 173 from 136 balls. Aided by Snedden, the two scored the highest ninth wicket partnership in Test history by New Zealand, 136 runs. Smith's innings was the highest by a Kiwi 'keeper in Tests and the highest in all Tests by a number nine batsman. New Zealand made it to 391 and after the start they had it was an excellent result.

Away from home and against pace had been the Achilles heel of Azharuddin, but in this Test he shone and once again fell short of a double century, scoring 192 in India's reply of 482. However there were many more runs to be had in this wicket. Centuries by Andrew Jones and Martin Crowe ensured that New Zealand would not lose as they amassed one more than the Indian first Innings total, 483. There was insufficient time for India to chase down the 393 for victory and thus Azharuddin lost his first series as captain 1-0.

Things didn't get much better for the new skipper when they toured England in 1990.

Often a Test match can be impacted by a toss, many times not, however at Lords for the first Test, Azharuddin won the toss and sent the opposition in. Next thing you know, Graham Gooch has been bowled by Manoj Prabhakar, but not before scoring 333. Centuries to Allan Lamb and Robin Smith gave Gooch the luxury to declare at 4 down for 653. The captain's decision at the toss was a costly mistake.

Shastri got a ton, Azhar got a ton, Kapil Dev was 77 not out and the Indian first innings was a single run past the follow-on, with 454 runs. Both teams had scored at, or about four runs per over in the first innings so there was plenty of time. Gooch however put his foot on the gas pedal and England scored at over five runs per over in the second innings, the captain helping himself to another century. Left with 472 to win, India folded for 272. Fittingly the final wicket involved Gooch who caused the run out of Sanjeev Sharma. Suffice it to say he was Man of the Match.

The second Test at Old Trafford marked the debut of twenty year old leg break bowler, Anil Kumble. He picked up three wickets in England's first innings. Another Test match of runs, runs, runs, Gooch and fellow opener Michael Atherton put on over 200 for the first wicket, after Gooch won the toss and batted. Centuries to Gooch, Atherton and Robin Smith helped England amass 519.

Just as the Indian skipper scored three figures in the first Test, Azharuddin performed again, with 179, ably supported by the seventeen year old wunderkind, Sachin Tendulkar and India's reply was 432. Both teams scored at a good clip in the first innings England did the same in the second and with a century to Lamb, Gooch declared four down for 320, leaving India a whopping target of 408. They were in trouble at 183/6, but the youngest member of the team batted for 224 minutes, wearing a pair of Sunil Gavaskar's pads, and scored his maiden Test century, guiding India to the safety of stumps and saving the Test match.

The third Test at the Oval was another run fest. Has there ever been more runs scored in a three Test series? Azharuddin won the toss and batted. Shastri scored 187 at the top of the order, Kapil Dev helped himself to 110, Azharuddin 78 and wicket keeper Kiran More 61 not out batting at number nine. Nine declared for 606. England failed to repeat their earlier feats, scored only 340 and were made to follow on. David Gower's not out 157 the centrepiece of England's second innings of 477, but time was the enemy and the Test was drawn, England winning the series 1-0.

Finally there was a Test match victory for the still novice captain when India played a one off Test against Sri Lanka in November 1990. Winning the toss Azhar opted to bat and India made a modest 288. Sri Lanka buckled against the spin of SLV Raju and were rolled for a mere 82. Raju's figures of 6-12 were his peak in Test bowling. Following-on Sri Lanka did little better with 198 and Azharuddin finally opened his account of Test victories.

From the penthouse to the cellar. A tour of Australia is tough at the best of times and Azharuddin and his men were greeted with a very strong Australian team heading for their own run of greatness when the Indians toured in 1991/92. India had not toured Australia since Kapil Dev's team in 1985/86. With a ridiculously small lead-in – just the one match against the ACB Chairman's XI at Lilac Hill in Perth, more of a hit and giggle than a serious encounter – India went into the first Test in Brisbane hopelessly underprepared. Moreover, Azharuddin didn't play in the warm-up match. India fell victim to the pace and bounce of the Brisbane wicket which Craig McDermott and Merv Hughes exploited as well as any Australian quick bowler would. It's bread and butter for them. Australia won by ten wickets.

To add insult to injury the teams swapped white clothes for coloured ones and begun the first half of the ODI tri-series which also included West Indies. Between the first and second Tests they played five ODIs against two different teams. Hardly the best programme for sorting out your batting issues in the Test matches.

To Melbourne for the Boxing Day Test, it was more of the same, although India did show a little more fight with the bat and a little more bite with the ball through Kapil Dev and Manoj Prabhakar. Still, it was a loss by eight wickets.

On the spin friendly SCG India had the best of a drawn Test match – this being Ravi Shastri's 206 run demolition of Test debutant Shane Warne, aided and abetted by the young Tendulkar who produced a blemish-free 148 not out.

A break for five more ODI's and then to Adelaide for the fourth Test and as is often the case, the best Test match of the series. After winning the toss, Azharuddin sent Australia in to bat. Dev and Prabhakar got terrific movement in the air and with the help of the spin of Raju and Tendulkar, Australia collapsed in four and half hours for just 145. McDermott, Hughes and Michael Whitney returned fire and at one stage India was 70/6 but a fightback from the lower order, headed by a half century to Dev and India had a lead of eighty after scoring 225.

Australia through Mark Taylor and David Boon then ground out the deficit and went about setting up a total, both scoring centuries. Alan Border and Ian Healy also added runs and Australia finished far better than their first innings effort with 451, setting India the task of chasing down 373. Miraculously, they nearly did it, and from the blade of the captain, Azharuddin, finally scoring some runs with a timely century. India went for the target and were helped by Border's attacking fields. It was a close and exciting run to the finish. But for some unfortunate LBW decisions, they might have got there but as it was they finished short, losing by 38 runs.

Teams visiting Perth are generally unaccustomed to the fast bouncy WACA wicket which is of great benefit to the quick bowlers if they use it properly. Some bowlers get excited by the extra bounce and end up bowling too short. It is a very unique wicket and can be very tough to bat on if you are not used to it however it is generally a very good wicket on which to bat once the batsman is settled. The other peculiarity of Perth is the "Fremantle Doctor". It's a stiff breeze that comes in the mid to late afternoon and helps swing bowlers. Local bowlers Terry Alderman and Bob Massie were both brilliant when working with the Doctor during their careers.

Alan Border won the toss for the fifth and final Test and had no hesitation in batting. Prabhakar and Dev used the conditions to their advantage and it was slow going for the Aussies, but they eventually scored 346. In reply, the Indian batsmen struggled. Hughes and McDermott were quick while Whitney used the conditions to pick up four wickets. India were predictably rolled on this wicket, and were all out for 272, but one young man stood up and showed that an Indian batsman could indeed handle the pace, the extra bounce. Tendulkar scored 114.

The Aussies piled on the runs in the second innings, Border declaring 367/6 leaving India 442 to chase. They crumbled in the face of an onslaught by Whitney, who took seven wickets, and lost by 300 runs. It might have been nice to fly home at that stage, but the ODI Word Cup was getting underway. Drop the whites and return to the coloured clothing. India failed to make the semis but the one saving grace was beating eventual winners Pakistan in a pool match.

Tour of Zimbabwe and South Africa 1992/93

Next stop, the continent of Africa for a maiden Test versus Zimbabwe and a debut Test series against South Africa, so the tour was a historic occasion, if nothing else. And it really was little else for the cricket was dull. The leading benefit of the tour was the team's success as ambassadors, visiting townships and interacting with communities.

Azharuddin goes down as the first Indian to captain a Test against Zimbabwe. David Houghton won the toss at Harare, Zimbabwe batted and immediately set about ensuring they would not lose, which is probably fair enough for a new team on the Test circuit but it doesn't make it fun to watch. On a batting track, they painstakingly made their way to 456 and Houghton celebrated with a century of his own. If not for Sanjay Manjrekar's century and, need it be said, salvation in the lower order courtesy Kapil Dev, India struggled and were fortunate to make 307. Zimbabwe held the upper hand. AJ Traicos picked up five wickets, but the one he will never forget is getting Tendulkar, caught and bowled for a duck. There was little time for a second innings and the match petered out to a draw.

Heading southwards to South Africa, it should have been far more exciting on the pitch, but it was more of the same again. The first Test at Durban, despite losing a day to rain, would still have not finished any differently, a lifeless draw.

Nelson Mandela attended the second Test at Johannesburg. Tendulkar got a ton. Another draw. After seven ODIs the third Test got underway in Port Elizabeth and perhaps influenced by the limited overs cricket, which by its nature forces a result, there was finally a result in a Test match.

Kepler Wessels won the toss and surprisingly sent India in to bat, but his decision was to be proven correct as India struggled against the hostility of Alan "White Lightening" Donald who took five wickets. Azharuddin, who had been criticised previously for his lack of runs against genuine quick bowling, played a heroic captain's knock, top scoring with 60 in the team total of 212. Without a century to Hanse Cronje, crafted over eight and a half hours, South Africa would have fallen well short of the Indian total. His was the last wicket to fall, South Africa all out for 275, a lead of 63.

Two incredible performances highlighted the Indian second innings. White Lightning was back at his frightful best and he picked up seven wickets in a hostile display of fast bowling. When opener Ravi Shastri was dismissed, India were 31/6. It was a stellar performance of fast bowling. And who would lead any sort of fightback from the lower order? Of course it was Kapil Dev belting 129. It was an extraordinary innings of the highest calibre. He received good support from Prabhakar, More and Anil Kumble, all of whom scored exactly 17 runs each. India all out for 215. Wessels guided his team home with 93 not out as SA won by nine wickets.

The fourth Test at Cape Town, the less said the better. Looking back on it over 25 years later and one feels sorry for those forced to watch it. The run rate during the course of the Test was 1.83 runs per over. Unsurprisingly it was a draw. Lucky it was not a timeless Test or they might still be playing it today. South Africa won the series 1-0.

Four full series and two one-off Tests and just a solitary victory against Sri Lanka. It hardly says "retain the captain". The record was abysmal. Azhar needed to turn it around.

England toured India in 1992/93 and they were going through some growing pains themselves. Azharuddin needed to take advantage and put his own decisive stamp on the series. He started the trend by winning the toss in the first Test at Eden Gardens, Calcutta and chose to bat. And bat he did. The captain led the way with 182 and India had a solid start to the series with 371. The formidable batting line-up of Graham Gooch and his England team scored less than Azharuddin did himself, collapsing for 163. Following on, they made India bat again, but it was a small chase of 82 runs and India won by seven wickets, going one up in the three Test series.

Azharuddin continued his luck with the coin and won the toss in the second Test, this time at Madras, against stand in England skipper Alec Stewart. Centuries to Navjot Sidhu and Tendulkar enabled Azharuddin to declare at the imposing first innings of 560/6. England rolled over for 286 and were forced to follow on. They did worse in the second innings and India won by an innings. Azharuddin had finally won his first Test series.

Gooch was back for the dead rubber, won the toss and batted. Graeme Hick made 178 in a good total of 347. Vinod Kambli's 224 helped India score a huge 591. The English were demoralised and displayed little resistance as they were knocked over for 229, giving India victory by an innings. India had taken the series 3-0. England were the first side to have such a result inflicted upon them in India.

Zimbabwe popped in for a Test match in 1993 and were beaten by an innings. The only real significance was that one of the umpires was S Venkataraghavan, AKA Venkat. Welcome back skipper.

Back to back series against Sri Lanka, both home and away for a series win each and after that it falls away considerably. Azharuddin captained another twenty Tests for 5 wins, 7 losses and 8 draws at a win percentage of 25%. His overall percentage was 30% so the second half of his captaincy just drifted. In 1996, he was replaced by the young understudy, Sachin Tendulkar. The first half of the new captain's tenure didn't work out so well and the Board returned to Azharuddin, but lack of wins, form and other pressing issues put an end to his career.

As a batsman, easy on the eye. As a skipper, shrewd but leaning towards the defensive line that has often thwarted India.

Post cricket he has been a politician, but it is easy to see that cricket is his greatest love. He spent a decade fighting his ban and has been welcomed back into the arms of Indian cricket. One can take any number of attitudes towards Azharuddin the cricketer. One can look through the prism of the match fixing affair, but as grubby as that episode was, the ban was lifted by the High Court. Better to celebrate a wonderfully talented batsman and at the end of his captaincy, the one with the most number of wins.

Captaincy Record	Tests	W	L	D	%
New Zealand 1989/90 (New Zealand)	3	0	1	2	0%
England 1990 (England)	3	0	1	2	0%
Sri Lanka 1990/91 (India)	1	1	0	0	100%
Australia 1991/92 (Australia)	5	0	4	1	0%
Zimbabwe 1991/92 (Zimbabwe)	1	0	0	1	0%
South Africa 1992 (South Africa)	4	0	1	3	0%
England 1992/93 (India)	3	3	0	0	100%
Zimbabwe 1992/93 (India)	1	1	0	0	100%
Sri Lanka 1993 (Sri Lanka)	3	1	0	2	33%
Sri Lanka 1993/94 (India)	3	3	0	0	100%

Captaincy Record continued	Tests	W	L	D	%
New Zealand 1993/94 (New Zealand)	1	0	0	1	0%
West Indies 1994/95 (India)	3	1	1	1	33%
New Zealand 1995/96 (India)	3	1	0	2	33%
England 1996 (England)	3	0	1	2	0%
Australia 1997/98 (India)	3	2	1	0	67%
Zimbabwe 1998/99 (Zimbabwe)	1	0	1	0	0%
New Zealand 1998/99 (New Zealand)	2	0	1	1	0%
Pakistan 1998/99 (India)	2	1	1	0	50%
Pakistan 1998/99 (India)	1	0	1	0	0%
Sri Lanka 1998/99 (Sri Lanka)	1	0	0	1	0%
Total	**47**	**14**	**14**	**19**	**30%**

26

SACHIN RAMESH TENDULKAR

Arguably the greatest batsman ever to play the game. Many would say Sir Donald Bradman was but even Bradman himself said that of all the players, the one who played most like himself was Sachin Ramesh Tendulkar. There are kilometres of paragraphs dedicated to the mastery of his skill as a batsman. As an Indian batsman, his ability to bat anywhere in the world is not something many of his fellow countrymen can boast. His name will forever be etched in the history books, the statistics themselves defying belief.

Two hundred Test matches. Just a tad under 16,000 runs. One of his heroes was Sunil Gavaskar, the first man to pass 10,000 runs in Test cricket, the one who broke Bradman's record for Test centuries and Polly Umrigar's Indian batting records, but Tendulkar took it so much further. Fifty-one Test centuries. 51! Over those 200 Test matches he averaged 53.78 with a high score of 248 not out. His tidy little off-breaks earned him 46 Test wickets. Never before had there been such a cricketer who had reached such lofty heights.

If playing 200 Test matches doesn't make you feel a bit tired, how about 483 ODI matches with 18,426 runs and a further 49 centuries, giving him total of 100 centuries at international level. That's 683 international matches with over 34,000 runs. In anyone's language it is a colossal performance and many would say it cannot be repeated.

His Test debut at age 16 in Pakistan against the might of Wasim, Waqar and Imran was a young man thrown to a pack of hungry, quality bowlers. He made just 15 from 24 balls, bowled by Waqar, also making his debut, but it took him only one more innings to pass the half century and from then on it was an avalanche of runs from his blade for the next 24 years.

However, we are not here to marvel in Sachin Tendulkar's wonderful career as a batsman. We are specifically here to look at his Test captaincy record. In keeping with the Board's template of making the best player the captain, it was only a matter of time before Sachin was given the keys.

Australia arrived in India, after an absence of ten years, for a one-off Test in 1996, the inaugural Border-Gavaskar Trophy, named after two of both country's greatest players. It was perhaps fitting that Sachin Tendulkar would have this particular Test match for his debut as leader, the 26th Test captain India.

Australia's Mark Taylor won the toss and chose to bat on a Delhi wicket that looked like it was going to take spin right from the outset and in fact the Australian players were most concerned about the wicket. It showed in their batting.

The only one not falling to the spin of Anil Kumble, Sunil Joshi and Aashish Kapoor was Taylor himself, and the Australians collapsed to be 173 all out. It was no less difficult a pitch for the Indian batsmen, but a patient 152 by 'keeper and opener Nayan Mongia, with good support from Sourav Ganguly and Rahul Dravid, guided India to a good first innings of 361.

Stubborn resistance from Stephen Waugh was the only thing between India and an innings victory, his 67 not out showed that with patience, there was opportunity. Australia finished with 234, Kumble picking up five more wickets, leaving a small target of 56 runs.

McGrath and Reiffel gave a bit of a scare, but 21 not out from Ganguly helped India home. The new captain? Bowled by McGrath for a duck, but the victory was his and India's as they took home the Border-Gavaskar Trophy for the first time. Like his idol Sunil Gavaskar, Tendulkar won his first Test in his captaincy debut.

Following the one off Test, there was a tri series of ODIs between India, Australia and the South Africans and then a three Test series against the South Africans. With the victory in the Test against Australia followed a victory over their rivals in the ODI series. It seemed that Sachin was warming to the captaincy.

South Africa's Test team was beginning to find its feet on the world stage after their long absence. Keppler Wessels had retired and a shrewd new captain, Hanse Cronje, was leading a team on the rise. Batsmen such as Gary Kirsten, Darryl Cullinan, Jonty Rhodes, an allrounder in Brian McMillan and a good bowling attack that centred around Alan Donald. It was a well-balanced outfit and they had come close to winning the ODI series just completed.

Tendulkar won the toss for the first Test Ahmedabad, and given the state of the pitch, there was only decision. Bat first and then unleash his spinners on South Africa. However it was the South African bowlers unleashed, all contributing, but it was Donald who starred along with a fielding exhibition by Jonty Rhodes. India were all out for 223, the captain top scoring with 42.

The spin of Kumble, Joshi and Narendra Hirwani did the damage for India when South Africa batted and but for a fighting and patient knock from Fanie deVilliers of 67 not out, they would have finished behind. As it was, they made 244 and secured an invaluable lead.

Cronje let Donald out of the cage again and he quickly had both Indian openers accounted for. Debutant VVS Laxman was top scorer with 51 as India collapsed for 190. Set 170 to win, now it was Indian paceman Javagal Srinath's turn to fire. He got Hudson and Cullinan for ducks in quick succession. South Africa rallied through Cronje, but his was a lone hand. Srinath picked up six wickets and South Africa were humbled for just 105, India winners by 64 runs and a lead of 1-0 in the series. This captaincy thing was going well.

South Africa came back hard in the second Test, at Eden Gardens, Calcutta, all guns blazing. They had two debutants, Herschelle Gibbs and Lance Klusener. Cronje won the toss and batted, and with centuries each to the two openers, Hudson and Kirsten, South Africa notched up 428 runs.

India started well in reply, but fell away through some ordinary running between the wickets. Azharuddin, the former skipper, retired hurt after sustaining an injury to his elbow. It wasn't looking good, but when Azharuddin returned at 161/7, he found an unlikely partner in Anil Kumble. They steadied the innings and then Azharuddin cut loose. He scored his century from just 74 balls, back to his vintage form. Kumble meanwhile, a study in patience and measured aggression, made his best Test score to date of 88 and the two shared a record eighth wicket partnership for India of 161. However it was really only a short reprieve. India were all out for 329, ninety nine runs in arrears.

Cronje and South Africa pressed home the advantage. Kirsten added to his first innings century and Cullinan made 153 not out. Cronje declared at 367/3, leaving India to chase 467. They were never even in the hunt. Klusener, in his debut Test, demolished India on his own, taking 8-64, the best in a debut by a South African. India were humbled for a mere 137, victory by a whopping 329 to South Africa, who had now levelled the series. Tendulkar had now tasted the bitterness of defeat as a captain.

For two teams that have had a disproportionate share of draws in their time, this was one exciting series and it drew crowds at a time when Test cricket was struggling against ODIs in terms of crowd support. Now these two teams, with a victory apiece were set for a showdown at Green Park, Kanpur.

Tendulkar won the toss and batted and while the top four got starts, no-one really went on with it, although 61 for Tendulkar was his first half century as skipper and that score is hardly a failure. But after the fourth wicket at 185, India collapsed to be al out for 227. It was the "frog in a blender" bowler, Paul Adams, who picked up six wickets.

It was an almost identical tale for South Africa. The top five got to double figures and then they too collapsed. Four down for 121, all out for 177. India now had a lead of fifty and in the context of both match and series, a handy one.

Despite an early hiccup, India came back strongly and no-one more so than former skipper Azharuddin with a brisk 163. Tendulkar declared at 400/7, leaving South Africa to face the ominous task of scoring 461 to win the series. It was too tough an ask and they never really got close, India winning by 280 runs and taking the series 2-1. It was a heady start for the new captain.

India in South Africa 1996/97

South Africa on their own turf are a formidable opposition. They travel about as well as any team but at home, they are a different proposition altogether and Tendulkar and his team found this out the hard way and no more so than the preparation. They had little practice in South Africa's unique conditions before being thrust into the thick of things. The FIFO method – fly in fly out – is a major cause for teams struggling away from home as it takes a few matches to truly acclimatise.

At Durban, India was skittled for 100 and 66. They had no resistance for the frightful pace of Alan Donald. In the second Test at Newlands, Cape Town, South Africa amassed 529 and a spirited fightback from Tendulkar and Azharuddin saved India from further humiliation. Their dashing centuries out of character with the state of the match when they came together at 58/5, helping India to 359 but it was not enough. South Africa again won easily after rolling India for 144 in the second innings.

The third and final Test ended in a draw. Tendulkar contends that India could have won, but for the rain on the final day. It's a moot point, although 2-1 sounds an awful lot better than 2-0. Tendulkar had tasted his first series defeat as a captain.

India in West Indies 1996/97

Another away series beckoned, this time a trip to the Caribbean in 1996/97 and despite being on the wane, the West Indies were still a very powerful force in world cricket, especially in their own back yard. As India had not won in the West Indies since Ajit Wadekar's team in 1971 Tendulkar and his team looked forward to the challenge.

Both teams had lost their previous series, West Indies to Australia and India to South Africa, so Sachin Tendulkar, and Courtney Walsh the West Indies captain, were both keen to get their respective teams on the positive side of the ledger. Unfortunately bad weather and dull wickets hindered the tour. Both the first two Tests were drawn which prompted both captains to request more lively wickets. In Barbados for the third Test, they got their wish.

On a wicket with far more grass on it than the first two Tests it was a paradise for fast bowlers, yet West Indies captain Courtney Walsh, himself a fast bowler, would miss the Test due to injury. Brian Lara filled in. Sachin won the toss and invited the West Indies to bat. Although wickets fell steadily, West Indies still managed to score 298. It was a similar tail for India who were all out for 319. The second innings however, had wickets falling steadily but for much fewer runs.

Lara top scored with 45 as his team were bowled out for 140. Fast bowlers Venkatesh Prasad, Abey Kuruvilla and Dodda Ganesh took all the wickets. Spinner Anil Kumble didn't even bowl a single ball. (When was the last time a spin bowler didn't get a run for India?)

Against the West Indies and their pace battery, India had played themselves into a winning position. They needed just 120 to win but they were bowled out on the last day for just 81. VVS Laxman top scored with 19. Extras was second top score. It was a low point for Tendulkar in his short captaincy career.

The last two Test matches were destroyed by the weather, which meant that West Indies won the series 1-0. Had India not collapsed so badly in Barbados, the Test and the series would have been a triumph instead of a misery, but the Indians went home having suffered two series defeats back to back.

Two draws from two Tests away in Sri Lanka and then three more draws at home against the same opposition. Tendulkar had gone through four series without winning a Test match and it was taking its toll. Not only that, but India were struggling in the one day format too, which was the format people were more focussed on at the time.

The media circus that once fawned over the man were now calling for his head. And they got it. The BCCI sacked Tendulkar as captain and the media knew before he did. Tendulkar wasn't the first captain to learn of his dismissal via the media and he probably won't be the last. His hiatus from the captaincy sharpened his resolve to become an even better batsman. Mohammed Azharuddin took over for the next two years.

Return to the Captaincy

In December of 1999, Tendulkar was back at the helm, leading India against the visiting New Zealanders. It was a very different team. Form had eluded Azharuddin and he was no longer in the squad. The core of the batting centred on the middle order, Tendulkar, Rahul

Dravid and Sourav Ganguly. It would remain that way for many years, one of the most dynamic and prolific middle orders of all time. The bowling was Srinath and Prasad as the quicks and Kumble the main spinner. It was a good unit at the time, perhaps minus a good opening batting pair, but a good unit nonetheless.

Stephen Fleming's New Zealand team, while not world beaters, were certainly not minnows either. They possessed a brilliant and shrewd captain in Fleming, an explosive allrounder in Chris Cairns, solid middle order batsmen such as Nathan Astle and Craig McMillan and a bowler who ought to enjoy travelling to the spin friendly world of India in Daniel Vettori.

However it was a bloke called Dion Nash who went through the heralded Indian line-up in the first Test, after Fleming put the opposition in, taking 6-27 as India were embarrassed for 83 runs. New Zealand started poorly, recovered and then collapsed themselves, but not before scoring a handy lead, all out for 215. Javagal Srinath the destroyer with six wickets.

Then the wicket which was full of demons in the first innings flattened out into a road. Tendulkar, after centuries to himself and Dravid, declared at 505/3, leaving New Zealand 374 for victory. Time was the winner, New Zealand seven down when the match ended.

Fleming won the toss at Green Park, Kanpur and batted, but the visitors squandered the opportunity with poor batting and ended up with only 215 for their efforts. India started well but they too wasted the opportunity, falling apart against the spin of Vettori, all out for 330. Kumble's six wickets ensured there wouldn't be much of a run chase as New Zealand's second innings finished with only 155. India lost only two wickets in the chase winning the Test easily. It would be Tendulkar's last Test match victory as captain. The third Test ended in a draw, the most notable feature a double ton to the skipper, India winning the series 1-0.

India in West Indies 1996/97

What followed was five Tests against two strong teams and five straight losses. Touring Australia for three Test matches against Steve Waugh's team, in the middle of their record run of 16 straight wins, luck was not with India, and despite Tendulkar's own form being good, the Australians were simply too strong, especially in their own back yard.

After that series Tendulkar communicated to the BCCI that he no longer wanted to be captain, and that his deputy, Sourav Ganguly was ready for the job. They agreed, but only if Tendulkar would lead the team one more time against South Africa, at home, in order to make a smooth transition for Ganguly. That South Africa managed to win the series two nil, while its captain, Hanse Cronje and four of his team mates were under investigation for match fixing is quite extraordinary, but it was Tendulkar's final series as skipper and sadly for him lost both Test matches.

He continued to play on, a glorious career that ended with his 200th Test match in Mumbai in November 2013. He batted only once and made 74. India won. A true legend of the game had retired. There were no more mountains to climb.

Having broken so many records and been the premier batsman of not just his own, but many generations, Sachin Tendulkar had no equal as a batsman, Bradman aside.

As a captain, his career is less of a celebration. In 25 Test matches as captain, he had four victories and three of those in the first four Test matches, which meant he captained India in 21 further Tests for one solitary victory. His winning percentage overall is a low 16% and ought to have been higher when one considers the personnel at his disposal during his time as skipper.

To be fair, he was reluctant to stay in the role. As a craftsman, he knew his own limitations. He changed his style to conquer Shane Warne. He could do that as a batsman. But what he could not do was change his players. He did not have the capacity to influence his players in a way that inspired them to achieve greater results.

Loved around the world for his batting, but also for his grace and humility. He was awarded Padma Shri in 1999 and Padma Vibhushan 2008. In 2010 he won the Sir Garfield Sobers Trophy for cricketer of the year and Wisden Leading Cricketer in the World. In 2012, in Australia, he was named an Honorary Member of the Order of Australia.

Captaincy Record	Tests	W	L	D	%
Australia 1996/97 (India)	1	1	0	0	100%
South Africa 1996/97 (India)	3	2	1	0	67%
South Africa 1996/97 (South Africa)	3	0	2	1	0%
West Indies 1996/97 (West Indies)	5	0	1	4	0%
Sri Lanka 1997 (Sri Lanka)	2	0	0	2	0%
Sri Lanka 1997/98 (India)	3	0	0	3	0%
New Zealand 1999/00 (India)	3	1	0	2	33%
Australia 1999/00 (Australia)	3	0	3	0	0%
South Africa 1999/00 (India)	2	0	2	0	0%
Total	**25**	**4**	**9**	**12**	**16%**

27

SOURAV CHANDIDAS GANGULY

Affectionately known as Dada (elder brother), Sourav Ganguly was the Prince of Eden Gardens in Kolkata. His regal airs made him a polarising figure. Loved at home in India, loathed in some places overseas. Sometimes it looked to some as though he was above the game. He wasn't an enthusiastic fielder and left the field for long periods in Test cricket for no apparent reason. He was unceremoniously removed from the captaincy during his public brawling with India coach Greg Chappell and made a triumphant return in time for the World Cup in 2007.

Whichever side of the fence you sit with Ganguly, he was undeniably an aesthetically pleasing left handed batsman, his exquisite off side strokes legendary, and the simple fact remains, that he had so garnered a fractured and losing Indian Test cricket team he became India's most successful captain to date. Aggressive and shrewd, he also used that polarising aspect as part of his armoury. He was an astute and clever captain of cricket. If one accepts that a captain puts his own mark on a team, then Sourav Ganguly is the template.

Born in Calcutta (now Kolkata), in West Bengal, the youngest son of a wealthy businessman, he grew up in relative luxury and earned the nickname Maharaja. His father was involved with the CAB (Cricket Association of Bengal) and Sourav spent much of his youth at Eden Gardens, watching cricket.

Initially a right hander, borrowing his brother's equipment he became a left handed batsman! A gym and indoor wicket were built at home so the brothers could practice. Watching old video footage of cricket matches Sourav became an admirer of graceful left handed Englishman, David Gower. It was suggested (and refuted) that he refused to do the duties of twelfth man, such as carrying drinks, as this was beneath his station. He was born to be a leader, not a drinks waiter.

He made his first class debut for Bengal in season 1989/90. Following a good season in the Ranji Trophy in 1991/92 he toured with the Indian team to Australia and played in two tour games. He made his ODI debut against the West Indies on the same tour and was reportedly dropped for his arrogant attitude, a claim Ganguly denies. He languished in domestic cricket for several seasons until he was selected for the tour of England in 1996. He made 46 in the only ODI he played in and wasn't going to play in the Test series, however ill feeling between captain Mohammed Azharuddin and Navjot Sidhu had the latter leave the tour, and so Ganguly was selected to make his debut in the second Test at Lords. Batting at number three, Ganguly scored 131, and thus a century on debut at Lords, a rare feat. For good measure, he scored 136 in the next Test match at Old Trafford, becoming only the third batsman in history to score a century in each of his first two Test innings.

Sourav continued to consolidate his position in the middle order, often in the pivotal number three position. He grew with the team and the younger players around him under first Azharuddin and then Tendulkar, the nucleus of a side that also included Rahul Dravid, Anil Kumble, Javagal Srinath, Harbhajan Singh. Azharuddin had been the most Test successful captain of India, with 14 wins, but form saw the captaincy shift to Tendulkar, but given the talent on offer India were still not performing to expectations in Test cricket.

By 2000, Tendulkar had had enough and Azharuddin was implicated in the match fixing scandal. Tendulkar put Ganguly's name forward and in Bangladesh in November 2000, Sourav Ganguly became India's 27th Test captain. It was a one off Test, in Dhaka, Ganguly lost the toss but India won the game and so he opened his account with a win immediately. Not a bad feat when you consider that the stench of match fixing was very much in the air at the time and India was front and centre of that scandal through the local bookmakers.

Two home Tests against Zimbabwe gave one win and one drawn

Test, but the match fixing scandal continued to dominate headlines over the cricket. It needed something special to get the focus back on the sport itself.

The Epic Encounter

Australia was due for a three Test series and by the time it was over, cricket again was dominating the headlines but for good reason. It has been labelled as one of the best series of all time. It was certainly an absolute cracker. The Australian team, under Stephen Waugh had conquered all before them, including India, as they had recorded a record feat of fifteen consecutive Test match victories. No other side had ever reached such a lofty height and they had taken the mantle from the powerful West Indies outfit of the 1980's. Even Bradman's Invincibles had not achieved such a streak of Test wins.

Waugh's team was full of superstars; Waugh himself, brother Mark, Matthew Hayden, Adam Gilchrist, Ricky Ponting, Justin Langer, Michael Slater, Jason Gillespie, Shane Warne and Glen McGrath. Little wonder they had won fifteen consecutive Tests.

That said, Australia had a history of struggling in India, often bemoaning the food, the accommodation, the pitches and the umpires. It had not been a happy hunting ground since WM Lawry's team visited in 1969/70.

While the Australian team was without doubt one of the greatest ever assembled, Ganguly in the short time since he had taken over the captaincy had put a new spring into the step of the Indian team. Now they had a better performing machine, ready to take on these champions from Downunder. Under Tendulkar the team was mauled by the Australians in their home conditions the last time these two teams met. This new team wasn't ready to rollover, despite what happened in the first Test. For the Australians, it was the billed as "the final frontier".

In only his fourth Test match as captain, Sourav Ganguly went out to toss the coin at Wankhede Stadium, Mumbai against the iconic Stephen Waugh. The Australian won the toss and sent India in to bat. That in itself was an aggressive move by the Australian captain and a rarity – they almost always bat first.

McGrath, Gillespie and Fleming did their bit before leg spinner Shane Warne came in to clean up, India all out for a mere 176. With ducks to Ponting and Mark Waugh, Australia were in a precarious position at 99/5 before Gilchrist joined Hayden. Both left handers nullified the spin of Harbhajan "Bhajji" Singh by constantly sweeping. It worked. Gilchrist in particular was savage. His 122 came from 112 balls. Hayden more laid back with 119 from 172, but the damage had been done and Australia finished with 349. India's second innings didn't fare much better and they were rolled for 219. Australia chased down the 47 runs required without losing a wicket. In doing so they had reached new heights – sixteen consecutive victories. They were unstoppable.

The second Test was at Ganguly's home ground, his turf, Eden Gardens, Kolkata. It seemed to make no difference. Waugh once again won the toss and the Australians were dominant. Hayden missed his second century of the tour by three runs, eventually succumbing to Harbhajan, but Stephen Waugh found some form and scored 110, Australia with a formidable total of 445. It would get worse. The Australians bowled superbly, caught brilliantly and India were reeling, save for a half century to Laxman, and were humiliated for 171 runs. Australia enforced the follow-on and were licking their lips in anticipation at victory number seventeen.

The openers toiled hard but were both gone by 97 and then Tendulkar, the great Tendulkar, was out for 10 and the score was 115/3. With him gone, so was the match. Ganguly hung around with Laxman for 48 and then the man known as The Wall, Rahul Dravid, joined Laxman in a partnership that has gone down as one of the greatest in the history of Test cricket. Certainly it must be the greatest fightback of all time. VVS Laxman was outstanding. Dravid, immovable. Between them they not only saved the Test match, they set it up for victory. And how. Records tumbled. Laxman's 281 was the highest ever score by an Indian in Test cricket to that time. His partnership with Dravid of 376 was also a record, the highest fifth wicket partnership in Indian Test cricket. After being down on the canvas, ready to throw in the towel, Ganguly now found his team with a massive total of 657 and he declared, setting the Australians 384 for victory. After being down and out, they now had the world champions on the ropes.

Slater and Hayden began well, but once Ganguly handed Harbhajan the ball, Australia were crippled. The turbaned tweaker had picked up India's first ever hat-trick in Test cricket in the first innings with seven Aussie victims, and he created just as much havoc in the second, claiming six more wickets to give him 13 for the match. Against all odds, Ganguly's team had knocked off the world champions in one of the greatest Test matches ever. It was compared with the 1981 English victory over Australia at Headingley.

Fittingly, the final and deciding Test in this magnificent series, was also a nail biter. At MA Chidambaram Stadium, Chepauk, Chennai, Stephen Waugh won the toss for the third time in the series and batted. It was the Hayden and Harbhajan show yet again. As if he hadn't scored enough already, the big left hander belted a double century. As if Harbhajan hadn't already inflicted enough pain, he picked up seven more wickets. It was as though no-one else was playing. Except maybe Stephen Waugh, who became only the sixth batsman in Test history to be given out Handled the Ball. Shane Warne broke a record too. His duck was his 23rd, an Australian record. Despite the chaos and confusion, Australia managed a good first innings total of 391.

It was tough going for the Australians in the field, as Shiv Sunder Das, Sadagoppan Ramesh and Laxman each scored half centuries and Tendulkar stamped his own authority with 126. The runs flowed and India was eventually all out for 501, a lead of 110.

Harbhajan then stepped it up a notch. In 41.5 overs, the spinner took eight Australian wickets to fall for 84 runs, giving him an incredible 15 for the match. Australia were all out for 164, leaving India a modest chase of 155. It was going along smoothly until Australia engineered their own collapse and in a tight finish India just fell over the line with two wickets to spare. Fittingly one of the not out batsman was Harbhajan. Ganguly and his team had knocked off the world champions in an epic Test series, one of the greatest of all time. Unsurprisingly, Harbhajan was named the Man of the Series and Dada's captaincy had reached new heights. And it put cricket right back where it belonged.

The Chappell Saga

Things began to flounder and the old monkey on India's back of not being able to win away from home, came back to bite. A drawn series with minnows Zimbabwe and losses to Sri Lanka and South Africa put the glory of the victory over the Australians in the background.

England and Zimbabwe visited in 2001/02 and naturally, at home, victory was assured. Five Tests away to West Indies in 2001/02 and India lost 2-1. This was the very thing Tiger Pataudi spoke of all those years ago and nothing had changed. India continued to dominate at home and were losing abroad.

A win at home against the West Indies in 2002/03 then a loss away to New Zealand. A draw at home to New Zealand and then the ultimate insult: loss at home to the Adam Gilchrist led Australians in the place of regular captain Ricky Ponting. Now India was starting to lose at home.

Ganguly's back injury prevented him from playing full series against Australia and Pakistan in 2003/04 and 04/05 respectively. Something had to change and it did. India got a new coach, former Australian captain Greg Chappell.

Chappell was a successful captain for Australia during a period of dominance for that country. He finished his Test career with 7110 runs, the most by an Australian when he retired, at the world class average of 53.86. Yet as a coach his resume wasn't flattering. He'd coached South Australia for five seasons without success. Still, he had an excellent cricket brain and Ganguly welcomed the new coach initially. Then things started to unravel.

Chappell, who played things with a straight bat, became increasingly frustrated with Ganguly who he thought was creating a divide within the team. Was it that or was Chappell simply not aware of how Indian cricket tweaked? Kiran More, former Test wicket keeper and now Chief Selector, sided with Chappell and had Ganguly replaced as captain. It's not hard to see why. Dada had built this team into a formidable line-up, yet the results were not commensurate with either the talent within the team nor the expectations.

India was clearly underperforming, Chappell started pointing fingers and something had to give. Both coach and captain had been formidable players on the international circuit and both were used to getting their own way. It caused a rift like no other in Indian cricket and the country was torn in two. The underperforming superstars were being tested by an outsider. They didn't like it.

The period of Greg Chappell's tenure as coach was an unhappy one for India. They were fractured and underperforming before he arrived and despite the turmoil he did manage to turn around the results in ODIs. However, just as Ganguly was a polarising figure in world cricket, so Chappell was a polarising one for Indian cricket. With Ganguly's sacking as captain came his sacking from the team. His last Test match as captain was against Zimbabwe in 2005/06.

In 2007, Chappell's contract was not renewed, India having unceremoniously missed the finals of the 2007 World Cup. By then, Ganguly had returned to the team. He'd outlasted Chappell, but never returned to the captaincy.

Like so many others, Sourav Ganguly's time as captain started on a positive note and then tapered off. His galvanising effect on the team took an underperforming bunch and turned them into a team which believed in themselves and it is not hard to draw a parallel with Pataudi's captaincy. To hell with what everyone else says, we are India and we will do it our way.

By the time he retired in 2008/09, against his old nemesis, Australia, Ganguly had chalked up more wins than any other captain of India and his win percentage of 43% was far better than any previous long serving Indian captain. He had rewritten the record books and statistics wise he was the best captain India ever had to date.

As a way of saluting his old captain, MS Dhoni, India's captain in Ganguly's final Test, gave the reins to Dada in the last session of the match.

After his retirement he has played in the IPL with Kolkata Knight Riders and been on the speaking circuit and has also been a popular television commentator.

Among his awards, he was Indian Cricket Cricketer of the Year in 1996 and picked up the Padma Shri Award in 2004.

Captaincy Record	Tests	W	L	D	%
Bangladesh 2000/01 (Bangladesh)	1	1	0	0	100%
Zimbabwe 2000/01 (India)	2	1	0	1	50%
Australia 2000/01 (India)	3	2	1	0	67%
Zimbabwe 2001 (Zimbabwe)	2	1	1	0	50%
Sri Lanka 2001 (Sri Lanka)	3	1	2	0	33%
South Africa 2001/02 (South Africa)	2	0	1	1	0%
England 2001/02 (India)	3	1	0	2	33%
Zimbabwe 2001/02 (India)	2	2	0	0	100%
West Indies 2001/02 (West Indies)	5	1	2	2	20%
England 2002 (England)	4	1	1	2	25%
West Indies 2002/03 (India)	3	2	0	1	67%
New Zealand 2002/03 (New Zealand)	2	0	2	0	0%
New Zealand 2003/04 (India)*	1	0	0	1	0%
Australia 2003/04 (Australia)	4	1	1	2	25%
Pakistan 2003/04 (Pakistan)*	1	1	0	0	100%
Australia 2004/05 (India)*	2	0	1	1	0%
South Africa 2004/05 (India)	2	1	0	1	50%
Bangladesh 2004/05 (Bangladesh)	2	2	0	0	100%
Pakistan 2004/05 (India)	3	1	1	1	33%
Zimbabwe 2005/06 (Zimbabwe)	2	2	0	0	100%
Total	**49**	**21**	**13**	**15**	**43%**

Not captain for full series

28

RAHUL SHARAD DRAVID

Cricket's Mr Nice Guy, Rahul Dravid, with his imposing Test batting record was not such a nice guy to opposition bowlers. Nicknamed "The Wall" for his brick wall like defence which at times seemed impenetrable for oppositions to find a way through. His impeccable technique, combined with his impressive temperament, made him one of the finest batsmen of his generation. Together with Tendulkar, Ganguly and Laxman he was part of one of the most imposing middle orders of all time.

Born in Indore, his family moved to Bangalore, Karnataka, where he grew up. He began to play cricket at the age of 12 and represented Karnataka from Under 15's onwards.

He made his first class debut in 1990/91 where he made 82 in a quarter final for the Ranji Trophy for Karnataka, batting alongside future Test team mate Anil Kumble who made 111 not out. He made a century in his second match, against Bengal, which featured the Ganguly brothers, Sourav and Snehasish. His was not a meteoric rise to the top however, but a slow and methodical push, which in many regards is how he approached batting.

His Test match debut was in 1996, in the second Test in the series against England in the same match that Sourav Ganguly made his Test debut. Unlike Ganguly, he was just shy of a debut century, agonisingly close at 95. In his second match, again falling short with 84. Still, not a bad entry into Test cricket.

Rahul Dravid had played 70 Test matches under Azharuddin,

Tendulkar and Ganguly before he was asked to fill in for the injured Ganguly in the second Test against New Zealand at Mohali in 2000/01 becoming the 28th Test captain of India. The Test was drawn. He was called upon once more in the away series against Pakistan in 2003/04, again in place of Ganguly and he won the first Test, but lost the second. India took the series 2-0 upon Ganguly's return for the third Test.

Called upon again to fill in against another fill-in, Adam Gilchrist in the Australian tour of 2003/04, he lost against Gilchrist but won against Ponting, however India lost the series 2-1.

Full Time Captain

The Chappell coaching saga reached a crescendo in 2005 and led to the dismissal of Sourav Ganguly and the instalment of Rahul Dravid as the full time captain of India's Test cricket team for the 2005/06 series against Sri Lanka at home.

It was a slow start to the new captain's career and a most unusual one. Within his team he had two former captains in Tendulkar and Ganguly, and two future ones in Kumble and MS Dhoni. And for good measure a future stand-in, Virender Sehwag. That's five other leaders, apart from himself. Add in the tensions with the coach and thank goodness the first three days of his first Test as skipper were washed out. It would have given him some good thinking time.

The second Test, at Mohali, went for the full duration. Dravid won the toss and not only batted, but opened the batting. A century to Tendulkar and seven wickets to Muttiah Muralitharan saw India post a total of 290. Sri Lanka's reply was 230, six wickets to Kumble.

Irfan Pathan opened the batting in India's second innings and made 93. Dravid had dropped down to number five. He declared at 375/6 and Sri Lanka were well short of the 435 victory target. Dravid had won his first Test match as permanent captain and had shown he was prepared to mix things up in terms of the batting order.

No sooner had the celebration ended and Dravid was out of the third Test, injured, replaced by fill-in Virender Sehwag.

Dravid next led a tour to Pakistan, that graveyard for Indian skippers, in 2005/06 and a graveyard it continued to be as his team lost the Test series 1-0 to Inzamam-ul-Haq and his men.

At home against England in 2005/06, it would be a three Test showdown between two very strong teams. Against Dravid's Indians were Michael Vaughan's England team. It contained Andrew Strauss, Marcus Trescothick, Kevin Pietersen, Andrew Flintoff and a good bowling line-up that included Simon Jones, James Anderson, Ashley Giles. What ensued was a rather strange series. By the time the first Test had arrived England were in complete disarray. Michael Vaughan the captain had to return home due to an injury to his knee. Trescothick the vice-captain went home in a hurry in what were unusual circumstances. Simon Jones injured his knee. Ashley Giles, the main spinner, also had to leave due to injury.

Replacing the missing opening batsman they drafted in *England A* player Alastair Cook who was on tour with his mates in India at the time. That is how desperate England were. Given the horror start of losing two of their best batsmen, which included both captain and vice-captain, and two key bowlers, it is surprising that Dravid and his team did not win the series 3-0. However they didn't.

Stepping up as captain was the allrounder Andrew Flintoff. He won the toss and batted at the Vidarbha Cricket Association Ground, Nagpur. The debutant Cook opened up with 60 runs and Paul Collingwood anchored the innings in the middle with a fine 134 not out. England all out 393. In reply India struggled against the workman-like Matthew Hoggard who took six wickets, including three LBW's. It was also the debut of charismatic spin bowler Monty Panesar and he picked up two wickets. In reply, Mohammad Kaif top scored with 91 in a total of 323, India 70 runs behind.

England batted a second time and Cook scored a century, not out 104, supported by Pietersen and Collingwood. Flintoff declared at three down for 297 setting India a tough target of 368 runs to win. Despite a bit of a rush in the last session to try and make the runs India fell short and the match petered out to a draw. The hastily patched together England team had shown they had some fight, but it wouldn't last.

Flintoff won the toss at Mohali and chose to bat and while they struggled at the top of the order they scored 300 courtesy of half centuries to Pietersen, Flintoff and the wicket keeper, Geraint Jones.

Anil Kumble picked up 5-76. India replied with 338 runs in their first innings built around the captain's 95. Interestingly Dravid was bowled by his opposite number Flintoff, who collected four wickets.

England's 2nd innings was a disaster, all out for 181 struggling against the spin attack of India and once again Kumble amongst the wickets. Set 144 to win the captain was there at the end and India won by 9 wickets.

Things got off to a good start for Dravid in the third test at Mumbai by winning the toss. For some inexplicable reason he sent England into bat, later admitting that this was a mistake. It certainly was. A century to Strauss and half centuries to Owais Shah and the captain Flintoff helped them to 400 runs.

India's reply was a struggle against the swing bowling of Anderson, Flintoff and Hoggard, all out for 279 with MS Dhoni top scoring with 64 and Dravid 52.

England made 191 in the second innings setting India the target of 313 to win. They never even got close. Tendulkar top-scored with 34 and only two other players reached double figures as India were all out for 100. England won the third Test, squaring the series. This was an amazing turn around for a team that had lost four key players before the series even begun and it was England's first Test win in India for 21 years. It was not a happy series for the home captain and after the match presentation had been completed sections of the Mumbai crowd were shouting "bring back Sourav".

The next tour was to the West Indies and the first Test of the four match series was in Antigua, home of legend Sir Vivian Richards. Dravid won the toss and batted but it was a laboured innings and he himself stayed for 249 minutes to scratch out 49 and be the top scorer in a total of 241. The West Indies fared slightly better and off the back of half centuries to Chris Gayle, Ramnaresh Sarwan and Dwayne Bravo made 371. India's 2nd innings was all about Wasim Jaffer who made 212 and became the fourth Indian to score a Test double century. Dravid to declared 6 down for 521 giving the West Indies a target of 392. It ended up to be quite an exciting draw, the West Indies holding out with only one wicket to spare at 298/9.

The West Indies had the weather to thank for saving them in the second Test, a match dominated by the batting of Sehwag, Dravid and

Mohammad Kaif. The third Test was also drawn, neither side seemingly able to land the knockout blow.

The fourth Test was a low scoring affair at Sabina Park, Kingston. Dravid won the toss and batted, top scoring with 81 out of a total of 200, a dim effort after winning the toss, but a spell of 4.3 overs from Harbhajan Singh destroyed the West Indies. He took 5-13 as the Windies collapsed for 103. India also struggled in the second innings, all out for 171, leaving the West Indies to score 269 for victory. They fell short by 49 runs, this time crumbling against Kumble and India had won the Test and the series. It was the first series win away to the West Indies since Ajit Wadekar's team in 1971.

An away series to South Africa in 2006/07 beckoned and the chance to continue the form away from home, but Graeme Smith's outfit were strong, balanced and well lead. A superb batting line-up consisting of the captain Smith, Herschelle Gibbs, Hashim Amla, Jacques Kallis, Ashwell Prince and AB deVilliers, a world class keeper/batsman in Mark Boucher and a bowling attack of Makhaya Ntini, Shaun Pollock, Andre Nel and Dale Steyn.

The series began well with the first Test at New Wanderers Stadium, Johannesburg. Dravid won the toss and batted, but India struggled against the pace of Ntini and Pollock and were bundled out for 249, with Ganguly top scoring with 51 not out. In an inspired spell, S Sreesanth destroyed the much vaunted South African batting line-up, taking 5-40, supported ably by Zaheer Khan, and the home side was decimated for a mere 84 runs. India replied with another modest total of 236 leaving South Africa a huge fourth innings chase of 401. They were well short, bowled out for 278. The new skipper was relishing the new role and India the overseas success.

It didn't last. It never does with a team like South Africa. When they are down, they come back harder and they didn't disappoint on this occasion.

Graeme Smith won the toss at Kingsmead, Durban and batted, and a century by Prince helped them obtain 328 runs. South Africa's pace bowlers were fast, accurate and miserly and India were lucky to make 240. After South Africa made 265 in their second innings, India set a target of 353. They were never in the race and were bundled out for only 179, leaving South Africa victors by 174 runs.

It was all square going into the final Test at Newlands, Cape Town. This was make or break. Rahul Dravid won the toss and batted, a century to Jaffer and half centuries to Karthik, Tendulkar and Ganguly helped India to a solid 414. South Africa went close to matching that, making 393. The wheels fell off in the second innings however and India were rolled for just 169, their advantage in the match completely squandered. South Africa were far more settled in their second innings and made the target with five wickets to spare. But for that lousy second innings, Dravid and his men may well have posted a tougher target. As it was, India lost the series 2-1. The away from home hoodoo had returned.

A bit closer to home, but still away, India toured Bangladesh in 2006/07. Weather destroyed an otherwise absorbing contest in the first Test. Both teams were in the hunt but the weather was the ultimate winner.

In the second Test, Habibul Bashar won the toss for Bangladesh and sent India in to bat. If there was ever a more incorrect call in the history of Test cricket, please let me know. India's first four batsmen made centuries and Dravid, one of those, declared at 610/3. Bangladesh did not enjoy the conditions as much and were bowled out for 118, and then 253 after following on. India won by an innings and 239 runs. It was an elusive away series win, but how much value against such opposition, still finding their way on the world stage?

A different kettle of fish was England, where India toured in 2007. It would be Dravid's last series as captain, and it was thought at the time, also the last tour of England by Tendulkar, Ganguly and Kumble. It turned out to be a very exciting series against Michael Vaughan's England team.

Vaughan won the toss in the first Test at Lords and batted, Andrew Strauss unlucky to fall for 96, while all of India's bowlers chipped in to dismiss England for 298. Ryan Sidebottom and James Anderson caused great havoc with the Indian batsmen and they were dismissed for a below par score of just 201, 97 runs behind. Through a Kevin Petersen century, England then put on 282, leaving India a tough chase of 380 runs.

England had India on the ropes, but stubborn resistance from wicket keeper MS Dhoni and curious stoppages to arrange the field by

Vaughan, the game went down to the wire and to the last minute. At nine wickets down for 282, India managed to hang on and save the match.

In the second Test at Trent Bridge Dravid won the toss and sent England in to bat given the murky conditions and it paid immediate dividends. Zaheer Khan and S Sreesanth got the early breakthroughs with some incisive swing and England never really found their feet, Kumble knocking over the tail, all out for 198.

The Indian innings began in a hit and miss affair. Both openers Dinesh Karthik and Wasim Jaffer played and missed an awful lot but when they weren't missing they were hitting boundaries and the innings gradually built on their foundation, both scoring half centuries. Tendulkar, Laxman and Ganguly all followed on from the openers lead and also scored half centuries, Tendulkar top scoring with 91. India were all out for an impressive 481 and were now in the dominant position.

A curiosity occurred during their innings when Zaheer Khan came in to bat. He noticed two sweets – jelly beans – sitting near the stumps. He believed they were thrown at him and his finger, or rather his bat, was pointed at Kevin Petersen, fielding at gully. "Pick on the right bloke. It wasn't me," was Petersen's response. Suspicion fell on those closer to the bat. England captain Michael Vaughan insisted that the jelly beans were not thrown, but likely placed there and had no idea who might have done it. Either way, it was a childish prank and Zaheer was furious.

He was 10 not out when the innings finished and was fired up to bowl at his tormentors.

England fared much better in the second innings on the back of a captain's knock by Vaughan who scored 124, but the Indian bowlers had fire in their bellies and bowled with vigour. Even Sreesanth was seething and managed to step over the mark himself, bowling a beam ball at Petersen and in another incident shouldered Vaughan. He was reprimanded by both his captain Dravid, and later the Match Referee Ranjan Madugalle. Zaheer targeted his aggression in a more productive way and had excellent movement and control picking up five wickets in a match winning performance. England were all out for 355 and India won the Test by seven wickets.

All of the incidents during the match were scrutinised by the media, but none more so than what was to become "Jellybeangate".

Dravid won the toss for the third and final Test, played at the Oval, and India batted. And batted. Not one player failed to make double figures. Every single player got a start. There were five half centuries, six if you count the 54 extras, yet only one century – to spin bowler Anil Kumble batting at number eight. They racked up a massive total of 664, effectively batting England out of the match.

England replied with 345, but Dravid didn't enforce the follow on, instead choosing to prolong the agony. It nearly backfired with the English bowlers having India 11/3, but Ganguly and Laxman steadied the ship enabling Dravid to declare at 180/6, setting England an unlikely 500 run victory target. England gave it a mighty effort and when play ended on day five they were six down for 369. India had won the series 1-0 and Rahul Dravid became only the third Indian captain to win a series in England, behind Ajit Wadekar and Kapil Dev. Not a bad way to end your captaincy career, on a high note.

Unlike many of his predecessors, Dravid actually stepped down from the captaincy, citing personal reasons, but The Wall continued to play until 2012, first under Anil Kumble and later MS Dhoni. His last Test was in Australia at Adelaide, under stand-in skipper, Virender Sehwag, the subject of the next chapter.

His class and dedication as a batsman is well known. With Ganguly and Tendulkar the Indian middle order dominated for a decade. While he played 164 Test matches, he captained only 25 of those and was given the captaincy at a time of internal conflict within the Indian team structure. That he governed effectively during that time of turmoil was admirable.

He was criticised for losing the series against Pakistan in 2006, and more so against England at home in the same year when he invited the opposition to bat first. Those are the lowest points. He was unlucky against South Africa. His 1-0 series win over West Indies in 2005/06 and the same margin over England in 2007 undoubtedly the high points.

After his retirement from Test cricket he continued to play in the Indian Premier League until 2013. Unsurprisingly he is the recipient of many awards, including Indian Cricket Cricketer of the Year in 1997, the Arjuna Award in 1998, he was a Wisden Cricketer of the Year in 2000 and ICC Player of the Year in 2004. In 2004 he was awarded the Padma Shri.

Captaincy Record	Tests	W	L	D	%
New Zealand 2003/04 (India)*	1	0	0	1	0%
Pakistan 2003/04 (Pakistan)*	2	1	1	0	50%
Australia 2004/05 (India)*	2	1	1	0	50%
Sri Lanka 2005/06 (India)*	2	1	0	1	50%
Pakistan 2005/06 (Pakistan)	3	0	1	2	0%
England 2005/06 (India)	3	1	1	1	33%
West Indies 2005/06 (West Indies)	4	1	0	3	25%
South Africa 2006/07 (South Africa)	3	1	2	0	33%
Bangladesh 2007 (Bangladesh)	2	1	0	1	50%
England 2007 (England)	3	1	0	2	33%
Total	**25**	**8**	**6**	**11**	**32%**

* *Not captain for full series*

29

VIRENDER SEHWAG

The most explosive opening batsman in Test cricket history. If Kris Srikanth made the template then Virender Sehwag remodelled and fine-tuned to the point where fast bowlers feared him rather than the other way around. Like his batting, some of his statistics are breathtaking:

- The first Indian to score a triple century in Test cricket.
- Fastest Test triple century (278 balls)
- Highest ever Test score in history at a 100-plus strike rate 319
- Most triple centuries in Tests: 2 (jointly held with Sir Donald Bradman, Brian Lara & Chris Gayle)
- Highest ever Test batting strike rate among all the cricketers who have scored 2,000-plus Test runs (93.2)

There are many more, and even more still if you take his ODI career into account.

He idolised Sachin Tendulkar when growing up and wanted to bat like the little master himself and got the chance to bat with him in his debut Test match, in South Africa at Bloemfontein in 2001 where both players scored a century. 102 Tests later, he'd become a name to be reckoned with, an imposing and dominant opening batsman.

As a captain, he was another of our stand-ins, as a long time vice-captain. His four Test matches as skipper were across four different series, in four different countries over seven years.

At home against Sri Lanka in 2005, a three Test series, where he played the first, missed the second and deputised for Rahul Dravid in the third. He won the toss at Ahmedabad and chose to bat, but it wasn't the skipper who scored the runs. Sehwag was out for twenty and five Indian batsmen were back in the sheds before 100 had been scored. VVS Laxman came to his skipper's rescue and with a willing lower order, the number three helped himself to a century while the contributions of MS Dhoni (49), Irfan Pathan (82) were invaluable, getting the total to a solid 398.

Ajit Agarkar and Pathan probed without much luck or impact after Pathan had earlier got Upul Tharanga caught behind for two, and then the skipper introduced spin with Anil Kumble and Harbhajan Singh. The spin twins cleaned up the remaining Sri Lankans. Harbhajan was devastating and got a personal tally of 7-62, Sri Lanka all out for 206, giving Sehwag and his men a handy lead of 192.

The skipper got a first ball duck in the second innings, but let's assume he had other things on his mind! India were five down for 100 when again the lower order mounted a rescue mission, along with Yuvraj Singh who scored 75. Pathan, Agarkar, Kumble and Harbhajan scored 144 between them and allowed Sehwag to make the declaration at 316/9 leaving Sri Lanka to chase 509. The visitors were never in the hunt and Sehwag dispensed with convention and opened the bowling from one end with Harbhajan. The spinner took three more wickets to give him ten for the match and for that he gained Man of the Match. India were victors by 259 runs, and Sehwag had a 100% winning record as captain.

Just over three years later, in March of 2009, Sehwag was called upon once again, during an away series against New Zealand at Napier, this time for MS Dhoni who had injured his back. India had won the first Test in the series and Sehwag simply had to keep his hand on the tiller and keep things steady.

Daniel Vettori won the toss for New Zealand and batted first on what must have been a road. Early indications were rather the opposite as the Kiwis lost three early wickets for 23 runs. Then it was a run fest. Ross Taylor got a century, as did Brendon McCullum. Jessie Ryder scored 201. There was absolutely no joy for the Indian bowlers, Vettori declaring at 619/9, saving noted "rabbit" Chris Martin the trouble of padding up.

Where the Indians struggled for wickets, the Kiwis found a way and India struggled to make it to 305 all out, Dravid top scoring with 83. Vettori enforced the follow-on and the skipper tried to launch a counter attack but was out LBW to Patel after making 22 runs from 21 balls. One might have thought he'd have batted with a little more circumspection but that is the way Sehwag bats. You take the good with the bad. Fortunately the rest of the top order dropped anchor and made themselves at home, Gambir with a century and Dravid and Tendulkar with long and patient half centuries enabling Sehwag to make a cheeky declaration at 476/4. However time had run out for the Kiwis to even put on their pads and the match was a draw.

In January 2010, Sehwag was again called upon to fill in as skipper for MS Dhoni, against Bangladesh in the first Test at Chittagong. Bangladesh won the toss and sent India in to bat. The skipper batted like only he knows how and made a quick-fire 52 before being the first wicket down for 79 and then wickets continued to tumble. The rescue this time was in the form of Sachin Tendulkar who scored his 44th Test century aided by the tailend. India were humbled for 243, however the pacemen quickly struck back against the Bangladeshi batsmen. Zaheer Khan, Ishant Sharma and Sreesanth all picked up wickets before Mishra cleaned up the tail, all out 242. India had a lead of one run.

A solid start by Sehwag and Gautam Gambir, who went on to make a century, was broken when the skipper was out for 45. The leg spinner, Amit Mishra, came in as night watchman and after finishing the day untroubled, came out the next day and scored a half century. Many more starts but only one more half century, to Yuvraj, but the total pushed along and it gave Sehwag the opportunity to head for victory with a declaration at 413/8.

Despite a century to wicket keeper Mushfiqur Rahim, the Indian pace trio, followed by the spin of Mishra made the result inevitable and the Bangladeshis were dismissed for 301 giving India victory by 113 runs. For his careful, guiding century in the first innings, Sachin Tendulkar picked up the Man of the Match award.

In Australia for the final Test in a four Test series, Sehwag received his last call up as captain, once again for MS Dhoni, but this time not through injury, but suspension for a slow over rate in the previous Test at the WACA in Perth. It had not been a happy tour for India on the back end of some bad results, and as Sehwag went out for the toss with Michael Clarke at Adelaide Oval, he must have thought he'd been tossed a grenade. Clarke won the toss and had no hesitation in batting first.

This started well, with Shaun Marsh and David Warner back in the pavilion early, and once Ed Cowan had gone for 30, Australia were 94/3. That's about as good as it got for India. Clarke joined Ponting and it was a batting exhibition, both the captain and his predecessor enjoying double centuries in a stand of 386. Clarke declared Australia's innings closed at 604/7. The Test match was as good as over for India.

Peter Siddle picked up five scalps as India showed little resistance, save for Virat Kohli's century and made only 272. Clarke chose not to enforce the follow-on and declared at 167/5 in the second innings, leaving India to score 500 to win. The captain went down with the ship, top scoring with 62 in a total of 201. Australia won by 298 runs. Sehwag as captain had lost a Test match for the first time, the last in which he was in charge. In truth, the result was over before the coin was tossed. India were a beaten outfit and there was minimal impact Sehwag could have had as captain.

While Sehwag's career continued for three more series, he was not required to step up as captain again. Only ever needed as a stand in, he acquitted himself well, with 2 wins from four matches, a draw and one loss. He had no time to stamp his own authority on the team and one can only speculate just how he might have gone in the role in the longer term. It could never have happened however. He played in an era where there was a queue for the captaincy and at any one time there were ex-captains in the team with better credentials. He played when Ganguly, Dravid, Tendulkar, Kumble and MS Dhoni were captains.

It's nice to speculate though. He was a thoughtful cricketer, even if his explosive batting suggested a man in a hurry and one would have enjoyed watching him shape the Indian team in his own way.

Rightly he's been the recipient of a stack of awards. Indian Cricket Cricketer of the Year in 2000, the Arjuna Award in 2002, twice a Wisden Leading Cricketer in the World in 2008, 2009 and ICC Test Player of the Year in 2010.

Captaincy Record	Tests	W	L	D	%
Sri Lanka 2005/06 (India)*	1	1	0	0	100%
New Zealand 2009 (New Zealand)*	1	0	0	1	0%
Bangladesh 2007 (Bangladesh)*	1	1	0	0	100%
Australia 2012 (Australia)*	1	0	1	0	0%
Total	4	2	1	1	50%

* *Not full series*

30

ANIL KUMBLE

Nicknamed Jumbo, his relaxed but efficient amble to the crease belied the venom inside his fast leg spinners. One of only two Test cricketers in history to take 10 wickets in a Test match innings, this thoughtful cricketer was almost always going to be a Test cricket captain for India. What is surprising is that it was not as long and decorated a career as was his bowling.

With 619 Test scalps to his name, Kumble is the third highest wicket taker of all time, behind Muttiah Muralitharan and Shane Warne. Like Warne he was a leg spinner, but a vastly different one. Where Warne relied on drift and prodigious spin, Kumble's leg breaks were more in keeping with his fellow countryman, BS Chandrasekhar, quicker through the air and with subtle changes of pace, causing the ball to vary as it bounced.

Born in Bengaluru, Karnataka, he made his first class debut at 19, representing Karnataka in 1989/90 and it was not long before he attracted the eyes of the national selectors, picked to go on the England tour of 1990. He played just the one Test and picked up three first innings wickets, his first victim being Alan Lamb.

He didn't feature in the national side again until the 1992/93 tour to South Africa and Zimbabwe, where he played in the one off inaugural Test against Zimbabwe and all four of the Tests against South Africa. He shared the spin bowling duties with Ravi Shastri and in the second Test of the series, picked up his first bag, 6-53 from 44 overs, proving he could not only bowl but he also had endurance. It wouldn't be the most number of overs he'd bowl in an innings in Test cricket; he bowled 72 overs in the first Test against Sri Lanka in 1997.

He spent a career spanning eighteen years accumulating some lofty achievements, none more important than his ten wickets in an innings against Pakistan in 1999. His 10-74 from 26.3 overs helped India to a 212 run victory over their rivals. Legend has it that once he had got nine wickets his teammate Javagal Srinath started bowling wide outside the off stump, so that Kumble could take the tenth.

He'd proven his wicket taking ability, his strength and his stamina, but there was another layer too, his courage. In a Test match at Antigua in 2002 against the West Indies, he had his jaw broken while batting. He was booked to fly home and have surgery, but instead managed to convince the team doctor to allow him to bowl. Dressed all up in bandages around his head, Kumble bowled 14 overs for India, took Lara's wicket and *then* he decided to fly home. His commitment to the team had just jumped yet another notch higher: preparedness to keep playing even with a broken jaw!

Test Captaincy

After he'd played 118 Test matches, Kumble was rewarded with the captaincy, India's 30th Test cricket captain, taking over from Rahul Dravid, but it would not be a long stint as he was already 37 years old.

Kumble's first assignment was a tour of India by Pakistan in 2007/08 season. As we have seen in seasons past, the delicacy of navigating the team through such a series should not be underestimated. First there's the history and the political tension over the decades, then there's the expectations of the crowd, whichever team is at home and finally there's the administrators. One does not lose a series like this. Winning is fine, but losing is a disaster, so Kumble had been handed the toughest assignment to open this new chapter.

The administrators struck the first blow. They delivered three dead pitches for the series so that it would be impossible to lose. A drawn series is a good result to that way of thinking. They didn't however, count on the weather, nor a determined home captain.

Pakistan's skipper, Shoaib Malik won the toss at Delhi for the first Test and elected to bat. The conditions were hazy and there was fog about, but perhaps in the back of his mind was the corresponding Test match eight years earlier, where his opposite number took ten wickets in the second innings.

The decision backfired. Pakistan lost early wickets and then continued to do so at regular intervals. Only Misbah-ul-Haq showed any long term resistance, making 82, but Pakistan were all out for 231.

Pakistan immediately struck back, first through the lightening pace of Shoaib Aktar, the steadiness of Sohail Tanvir and the leg spin of Danish Kaneria. VVS Laxman, ever the man for a crisis, top scored with 72 not out as India fell away for 276. Still, in this low scoring match a 45 run lead is gold. The skipper added an invaluable 24 batting at number eight, in a partnership worth 54 with Laxman.

Pakistan fared better in the second innings, but you have to wonder, with all those starts, when all of the top eight reached double figures, why only Salman Butt managed a score in excess of fifty. They were all out for 247, the wickets spread among the bowlers, with Sourav Ganguly even contributing two of them with his medium pacers, setting India 203 for victory.

Shoaib removed Dinesh Karthik early, but solid knocks from Wasim Jaffer, Dravid, Tendulkar and Ganguly got India over the line and Kumble, like many of his predecessors, won his first Test as captain. To top it off, the new skipper picked up the award for Man of the Match.

The second Test was one for the administrators, although Kumble had tried to make a match of it, setting Pakistan 345 to win on the last day, but the lifeless pitch saw to it that it was drawn. A slightly higher target of 374 was set in the third Test, but in a Test where bat was so dominant over ball, there was never going to be a result. And so it was that India won the series, Kumble's first as captain, 1-0, and he was named Man of the Series for his twenty wickets.

Kumble's next series was another tough one: four Tests against Australia away. It turned out to be very tough indeed, for the affable captain was forced to put all of his best political skills together as the tour was nearly called off halfway through. The series was played with a certain amount of acrimony and there were some ugly moments. Much of it stemmed from the simmering tension between two players, Australia's Andrew Symonds and India's Harbhajan Singh. They'd had some previous encounters and it all came to a head during this tour. It all started so mildly before the wheels fell off.

Ricky Ponting won the toss for the first Test, an MCG Boxing Day affair in front of 68,000 fans. He chose to bat and a century stand between Matthew Hayden and Phil Jaques got Australia on to solid footing, but once Kumble had Jaques stumped for 66, the momentum changed for Australia's innings and it was only Hayden's century that held it together, all out 347.

The Australian attack of Brett Lee, Mitchell Johnson and Stuart Clark were relentless, hardly bowling a bad ball between them and India were bowled out for 196. Only Tendulkar (62) and Ganguly (43) showed any real resistance.

While there were many starts, none of Australia's batsmen could manage a big score, but half centuries to Jaques and Michael Clarke, combined with some useful cameos in the lower order, made it possible for Ponting to declare seven down for 351, setting India 499 to win. They didn't need anywhere near that as the visitors capitulated for 161, Australia winning the match by 337 runs.

Some big hundreds and an exciting finish in the second Test at Sydney were overshadowed by umpiring blunders, an allegation of racism, a complaint about over exuberant appealing and disputed catches. There were so many controversies in this Test match that it's surprising there was any time for cricket, let alone a result, Australia's 16th victory in succession, equaling their own record of consecutive victories previously achieved by Steve Waugh's team.

Ponting won the toss at the SCG and batted and India's bowlers toiled while Australia's batsmen made difficult work of a good batting strip, at one stage six wickets down for 134, but a rescue mission by Andrew Symonds who made 162 not out with help from the lower order saved them from embarrassment and they ended up with a more than respectable 463. Umpiring errors marred the innings for both teams with wrong decisions going against both, but the worst when Symonds was caught behind for 30 and given not out by umpire Steve Bucknor. To put it mildly, it was a howler and Symonds later admitted having hit the ball. Another was missed when he was 48, this time from the third umpire. Instead of having Australia out cheaply, the umpiring issues were very costly. Of less consequence, Symonds was given another umpiring reprieve on 148, again by Bucknor.

The Indians were seething, however they needed to let their bats do the talking, and talk they did. After losing Jaffer early, Dravid scored a patient half century before a century to Laxman and a chanceless not out century to Tendulkar – his average at the SCG just 221… - India kept on coming before a delightful cameo by Harbhajan Singh of 63 and India were seemingly safe having scored 532, a lead of 69 on the first innings.

Centuries to Hayden and Michael Hussey, the latter the recipient of two more contentious umpiring decisions allowed Ponting to declare at 401, leaving India a chase of 333 to win. The wheels had turned now and the Australians in their will to win forced the issue aggressively. It is how they play the game and a factor behind their impressive win/loss record. However their exuberant appealing, along with some more bad umpiring decisions left a bad taste in the mouth of some. That they won the match was completely overlooked because of the turmoil. Journalist Peter Roebuck called for Ponting's sacking. The Indian hierarchy demanded – and received – Bucknor's head. He would not umpire again in the series.

That the umpiring was atrocious goes without saying, but it also must be said that the last Indian wickets fell more to bad shot selection than bad umpiring or good bowling. Certainly the Australians were excitable in their appealing, but this is not uncommon for a side pushing for victory in the fourth innings. They weren't the first and they won't be the last and indeed they weren't the inventors of that style of play.

And then there was "Monkeygate". This episode nearly exploded into all out war and the cancellation of the rest of the tour. It had its genesis in India on a tour in 2006/07 where it was alleged that the some crowd members had called Symonds a monkey and this was termed as a racist taunt. It was alleged that Harbhajan used the same taunt and this led to mediation between the two players.

Fast track to the SCG Test and Symonds alleged that Harbhajan, while batting, had done the same thing again, calling Symonds a monkey. At least one other player, Matthew Hayden, claims he heard the taunt. Harbhajan's defence was that he was misheard, instead using a Hindi term that merely sounded like monkey. Ponting got involved,

Clarke got involved, Tendulkar got involved. What was the truth of the matter?

In a post-match hearing, Match Referee Mike Proctor handed Harbhajan a three match ban for racial abuse. The Indian camp was furious that their side of the story seemed to have been brushed aside and threatened to cancel the rest of the tour. In the aftermath, Harbhajan appealed and a neutral judge was summoned, New Zealand High Court judge Justice John Hansen, and the racism charge was dismissed, downgraded to the lesser charge of verbal abuse. Harbhajan was fined 50% of his match fee but was free to play.

You can imagine just how frustrated both teams were. It's one thing to have a battle on the pitch, but another to fight it out in the courts. Cricket wasn't meant to be this way. Opinions were divided and not just along national lines. But as quickly as it had escalated, it also calmed down. For the third Test in Perth, Bucknor was dropped. So too Harbhajan and Brad Hogg, but not for reasons of tension but for cricket - Perth is not a happy hunting ground for spinners.

The WACA is the home of fast bowling and Australia have long prospered on this famous ground. They had the pace attack and they knew the conditions like the back of their hand. Yet it was India who came out with all guns blazing. Kumble won the toss and elected to bat and a steady, if unremarkable first innings ensued, Dravid top scoring with 93 out of 330. Where Australia's pace bowlers had struggled, India's shone, bundling out the home team for just 212.

Batting for the second time, India pressed home the advantage after some early setbacks, Laxman top scoring with 79, all out 294, setting Australia 413 for victory.

Australia, it must be said, gave the target a great shake, then collapsed and then shone again, but this would be India's victory, by 72 runs. A spin bowler, Kumble, as captain of India, had engineered his team's first ever victory at the WACA. Given what had gone on in the lead-up, this must have been the sweetest victory of all.

The fourth Test at Adelaide was a tame draw after days of easy batting. It seemed an odd way to end the tour, the calm after the storm. Australia won the series 2-1 but India had gained a bigger set of teeth. No more would they lay down against the men from down under.

The next assignment was a home series in 2007/08 against South Africa who were captained by Graeme Smith. It must have been a welcome return to home conditions and a less controversial series for Kumble.

Smith won the toss for the first Test at Chennai and elected to bat on a flat track and South Africa racked up a pile of runs, all out 540. In reply, India scored 627. Virender Sehwag scored a triple hundred, his second, joining Bradman and Lara as the only ones to make two Test triple tons. (West Indies' Chris Gayle would join that elite group in 2010.) Suffice it to say, with all those runs, the Test ended in a draw.

At the second Test, at Ahmedabad, Kumble won the toss and batted on a wicket that had more than a little grass. He might have been better not winning the toss for Dale Steyn and Makaya Ntini shredded their way through India's batting, minus the injured Tendulkar. India were humiliated, all out for 76, Pathan's 21 not out the top score, followed by extras with 19.

Then it was the AB deVilliers show. 217 not out, along with 132 from Jacques Kallis. Smith declared at seven down for 494 runs, 418 in front. A more positive response from the Indian batsmen in the second innings, but they were simply too far behind the eight ball after being rolled for 76 in the first innings and lost by an innings and 90 runs.

India won the third Test and squared the series, but Kumble was injured and missed the party! MS Dhoni, subject of the next chapter, filled in for his injured skipper and won his first Test match as captain, squaring the series 1-1.

Back in charge again, Kumble led the team across the water to Sri Lanka for a three Test series. In the first Test at Sinhalese Sports Club Ground, Colombo, Mahela Jayawardene won the toss and batted and was one of four centurions in Sri Lanka's top five. He declared, six down for 600.

India saw off the pace bowlers but struggled against the spin of Ajantha Mendis and Muralitharan, falling well short with just 223. The second innings was even worse with just 138 runs and they lost the Test match in a comprehensive thrashing by an innings and 239 runs.

Kumble won the toss at Galle International Stadium, scene for the second Test and had no hesitation in batting. No hesitation was shown by Sehwag either, as the opener plundered 201 not out, out of 329! He shared an opening stand of 167 with Gambir, who made 56, and the only other Indian to reach double figures was Laxman with 39. It was simply another whirlwind performance from an opening batsman who made his own rules.

Kumble and Harbhajan restricted Sri Lanka to 292 in reply before Sehwag and Gambir put on another century opening stand. India made 269, leaving a target of 307, but the pitch was wearing fast and Kumble, together with Harbhajan, bowled India to victory by a comfortable 170 runs.

The third Test at P Saravanamuttu Stadium, Colombo, Kumble won the toss but that's about all. India were comprehensively outplayed by Sri Lanka and the series went down 2-1.

Swan Song

Australia toured in 2008/09 and it would be Kumble's swan song as both player and captain and it is fair to say he was struggling for form. In fact, he wouldn't see out the series. In the two Tests he played, the matches were drawn, but in the other two, the 2nd and the 4th, captained by stand-n MS Dhoni, Australia were beaten soundly. It is one of life's ironies that Kumble was not present in either of the two victories.

Kumble's bowling career for India is unmatched by any of his fellow countrymen. He proved he was not only capable, but downright unplayable at times. 619 Test match wickets means you are one heck of a bowler. Taking 10 wickets in an innings merely underlines the point. Bowling with a broken jaw, well, you could never question the man's courage or commitment.

As a captain, it was a less decorated career. A 21% win record over his 14 Tests is not a big endorsement, but there were two standout series. His first, against Pakistan, where the captain is on a hiding to nothing and he won that series 1-0, so that's a bigger plus than the actual numbers suggest. Against Australia, the man stood up for his team despite insurmountable things both out of his control and out of his favour. The 2-0 series victory against Australia in 2008/09 would have still been 2-0 if he'd been playing and thus his tally would look much better. Had he spent more time at the helm, he would have been more on the positive side of the ledger than the negative.

Of course he was well awarded, Indian Cricket Cricketer of the Year in1993, the Arjuna Award in 1995, Wisden Cricketer of the Year 1996, Padma Shri Award in 2005 and inducted into the Wisden India Hall of Fame in 2014.

Captaincy Record	Tests	W	L	D	%
Pakistan 2007 (India)	3	1	0	2	33%
Australia 2007/08 (Australia)	4	1	2	1	25%
South Africa 2008 (India)*	2	0	1	1	0%
Sri Lanka 2008 (Sri Lanka)	3	1	2	0	33%
Australia 2008 (India)*	2	0	0	2	0%
Total	**14**	**3**	**5**	**6**	**21%**

Not captain for full series

31

MAHENDRA SINGH "MS" DHONI

Mahendra Singh Dhoni introduced himself to the world stage as a swashbuckling long haired wicket keeper, first in the Indian ODI team in 2004 and then to Test cricket a year later. He was an instant smash hit in both formats. Wisden described him as rock star. There had never been anything like this produced in India before and unlikely we'll see another one again any time soon. He is the quintessential "once in a generation" player.

One of the most difficult assignments in world cricket is the position of India's wicket keeper, for there is a perpetual spin attack requiring first class skills and concentration to deal with the pressure of standing up to the stumps so often. That Dhoni had done it so expertly *and* performed as a captain for so long, across three different formats, makes him a truly remarkable player. No player in history has done this for any sustained period. His unflappable demeanour belies the immense difficulty in juggling his responsibilities.

MS Dhoni started life in an area not known for producing cricket players, born in Ranchi, Jharkhand and his technique, both batting and wicket-keeping, home grown. Dhoni's idols growing up were Sachin Tendulkar, Bollywood actor Amitabh Bachchan and singer Lata Mangeshkar. He admits to also being a fan of Adam Gilchrist, and given that the former Australian wicket-keeper also batted like he was holding a cutlass, it's not hard to see the influence.

Dhoni also played football and badminton when he was younger. Though he had not played cricket, Dhoni impressed with his wicket-keeping skills and became the regular wicketkeeper at the Commando Cricket Club (1995–1998). Based on his performance at club cricket, he was picked for the 1997/98 season Vinoo Mankad Trophy Under-16 Championship and he performed well.

He was recognised for his efforts in the 2003/04 season, especially in the ODI format and was picked for the India A squad for a tour of Zimbabwe and Kenya. In the tri-nation tournament involving Kenya, India A and Pakistan A, Dhoni helped India A chase down their target of 223 against Pakistan A with a half-century. Continuing his good performance, he scored back to back centuries – 120 and 119 not out – against the same team. Dhoni scored 362 runs in 6 innings at an average of 72.40 and his performance in the series received attention from the then Test captain, Sourav Ganguly.

India had a number of wicket keepers all pressing for selection and initially others were preferred to him, although he finally got selected for the Bangladesh tour in 2004/05 and made his ODI debut at Chittagong on 23rd December 2004. He made a first ball duck and took no catches or stumpings. It wasn't the most auspicious debut for one of the world's greatest players.

Twelve months later, following solid performances in ODIs, Dhoni replaced Dinesh Karthik as Indian Test wicket keeper in December 2005. His Test debut was in a rain effected match against Sri Lanka at Chennai where play was cancelled for the first three days. On a lively deck where India were bowled out for 167, Dhoni contributed 30, the only lower order batsman to give any meaningful contribution. He got a not out half century in the second Test and a 49 in the third. A reasonable if quiet start to his Test career.

In the second Test against Pakistan in the same season, he broke through with his maiden Test century against the fiery pace of Shoaib Aktar who was using the short ball as his main attack weapon.

On the England tour of 2006, he struggled with the bat until a half century in the third and final Test, and it was a similar story on his tour of the West Indies, where his top score was 69. Yet while he's playing Tests, he's also keeping wickets and scoring runs at a good clip for the ODI team, and it's a difficult job to get noticed as a batsman when three of the players ahead of you in the batting line-up are Tendulkar, Dravid and Ganguly.

In 2007 Dhoni was given the captaincy of the ODI team and also the captaincy of the new format, T20. He led India to victory in the final over arch rivals Pakistan in the inaugural T20 World Cup in September of that year.

He made his debut as Test captain of India during the third and final Test against South Africa in 2008, replacing the injured Anil Kumble and in doing so became the 31st Test captain of India.

In his first Test as captain, the third of the series, South Africa was leading the series 1-0. The young Dhoni had experience at his disposal, no fewer than two former captains in Rahul Dravid and Sourav Ganguly (it would have been three if Tendulkar was playing) plus a part time captain in Virender Sehwag. He'd already led India to a World Cup victory in the T20 and had been ODI captain for a year, so he was surrounded by seniors and had experienced already the enormity of captaining India.

Graeme Smith won the toss at the Modi Stadium, Kanpur and batted; South Africa scored 269. In a hint of the unorthodoxy that would become a trait of his captaincy, Dhoni had Harbhajan Singh bowling first change and also used Sehwag, who picked up a wicket. India's reply was 325, of which the captain made 32, embarrassingly stumped by his opposite number, Mark Boucher.

In the second innings, Dhoni pushed the envelope a little further and opened the bowling with Harbhajan. The off spinner picked up four wickets and South Africa collapsed for only 121. India scored the required runs to win by eight wickets and in doing so had squared the series. Like Kumble, Sehwag, Ganguly and Tendulkar before him, MS Dhoni won his first Test as captain.

It would not be long before he had the job full-time. The aging warrior, Anil Kumble, found himself injured in the third Test of the home series against Australia in 2008/09, having already missed the second Test, and retired immediately. Dhoni captained India in the second and fourth Test matches of the series and won both of them. He was now the full time captain and had won three from three.

2008 brought an unhappy event for India. Terrorist activity had caused tragedy and mayhem in Mumbai. From November 26th to 29th, members of Lashkar-e-Taiba, an Islamic militant organisation based in Pakistan, carried out a series of 12 coordinated shooting and bombing attacks, killing 164 and wounding in excess of 300.

Mumbai was sad, India was sad, the world was sad, but perhaps no-one more so than Mumbai's favourite son, Sachin Tendulkar.

England were in the middle of a tour of seven ODIs and two Test matches. Five of the ODIs had been played and the two remaining matches were cancelled. The England team flew home, understandably concerned about their security. That they returned to play the two Test matches was a mark of great courage and a stance against terrorism altering normal daily life. They were rightly and roundly congratulated for their actions.

Getting on with cricket was essential and the first Test scheduled at Chennai was heavily surrounded by security, which would have been a little unnerving for the players, especially the English. England captain Kevin Pietersen won the toss and elected to bat. A century to Andrew Strauss and half centuries to Alistair Cook and Matt Prior helped England to a reasonable total of 316.

India struggled against Graeme Swann, making his Test debut, along with the spin of Monty Panesar and the pace of Andrew Flintoff to be bundled out for 241, 75 runs in arrears.

Another century to Strauss, becoming the first Englishman to make a century in each innings of a Test match in India, and a century to Paul Collingwood, the only real scores, save for 33 from Prior as the rest of the English struggled against the reverse swing of Zaheer Khan, with the support of Ishant Sharma. Pietersen declared 311/9, setting India the huge target of 387 to win the match.

As India's run chase got underway, the crowd and India were treated to a Sehwag special. He belted 83 in 68 balls, including 11 fours and 4 sixes. He signalled the intent and India were full steam ahead to run down the target. Needing 256 to win on the final day, they were guided home, most appropriately, by Sachin Tendulkar's century. It was an emotional finish as India won by six wickets. Sehwag was named Man of the Match and the Indian skipper had now won four from four as captain. That changed in the second and final Test of the series which was drawn.

Series victories against New Zealand (away) and Sri Lanka (home) in 2009, plus Bangladesh (away) in 2010, meant that MS Dhoni had not lost a Test match or a Test series since taking over as captain. He had captained India in 11 (non-consecutive) Test matches without a single loss. That was about to change when South Africa toured for a two Test series in 2009/10 under Graeme Smith's leadership.

Dhoni's first taste of defeat came in the very first Test at Nagpur. Smith won the toss and batted. Well, Hashim Amla and Jacques Kallis batted, with 253 not out and 173 respectively. Smith declared late on the second day 558/5. An express train by the name of Dale Steyn went through the Indian line-up, taking 7-51 and they were all out for 233, Sehwag a lone hand with 109.

Batting for a second time, a little better but still short to make South Africa bat again. India lost the Test by an innings and six runs and Dhoni had tasted the bitterness of defeat as a captain for the very first time. The only thing you can do from there is to bounce right back, which Dhoni and India did at Eden Gardens, Kolkata. In fact they inflicted a bigger defeat on the South Africans and squared the series.

South Africa batted first and made 296 and then they were hit by a tsunami of centuries. Sehwag 165, Tendulkar 106, Laxman 143 not out and the captain, 132 not out. Dhoni declared at 643/6. He set Harbhajan Singh straight on to the South Africans, opening with the spinner as he'd done on previous occasions. Harbhajan bowled 48.3 overs and took 5-59. South Africa all out 290. India had bounced back in the most emphatic way, winning the Test by an innings and 57 runs. The series drawn 1-1.

A squared series away to Sri Lanka in 2010, and continued success against the touring Australians in the same year resulted in two victories from two Test matches. A series win (home) against New Zealand, a squared series against South Africa and a win against the West Indies (away) in 2011. MS Dhoni was unstoppable as skipper and so was his Indian team, in more ways than one. During that period, India under MS Dhoni, won the ODI World Cup, himself making 91 not out as his team overhauled Sri Lanka's 274. He had now led India to World Cups in both T20 and One Day Internationals. He had also taken India to the pinnacle of Test cricket, for under him, India were now the number one Test playing nation in the world. It couldn't last forever, and it didn't. The champagne stopped flowing in June.

Dhoni led India on a four Test series to England in June 2011. Not only would he record his first series loss, but also a whitewash 4-0, culminating in England taking the Test world crown from India. It was total capitulation and total humiliation. How could the number one team in the world across every format, lose so badly in one series?

It's the oldest story in the book. One team on the rise, another in decline. Tendulkar and Dravid were both 38 years old. In fact Dravid made his T20 debut in the series. Tendulkar was closing in on his 100th hundred. The crowd and the media were focussed on that and he was hailed everywhere he played, for this would be their last chance to see the great batsman, surely. Tendulkar had, by his own lofty standards, a poor tour. India was also hit by an untold number of injuries and players were coming and going. It was hardly the right environment for consistency in performance. And one must give credit to England. They had a sniff at the Test championship and threw everything at it. While England were young and hungry, India were old, tired and broken. The results across all formats were emphatic. India won nothing at all.

Had Dhoni and his Indian team peaked? It wouldn't seem so. The West Indies toured in 2011/12 season and were roundly beaten in both Test and ODIs, but there had been no refreshing of the team, no new blood. Players such as Virat Kohli were standing by, waiting for an opportunity, but the selectors stuck with the old brigade. Dravid continued on, Laxman continued on and Tendulkar was still looking for that elusive 100th century. That's hardly Dhoni's fault and the victories are on paper, however it was a severely weakened West Indies outfit that turned up to play. India could have recalled Gavaskar, Kapil Dev and Ravi Shastri, and would have still won. The real Test would be the next series.

India toured Australia in 2011/12, still smarting from the defeat in England, but refreshed after an easy victory at home over the West Indies. They sent some squad members early, to get some solid preparation, among them Tendulkar, and according to many pundits, this Indian team were favourites to win the Test series. After all, Australia had seen some hard times too and they themselves were in a rebuilding phase under captain Michael Clarke.

India were never in the series at all. As with the England tour, it was a whitewash, losing 4-0. Clarke was having a golden summer, and Ponting and Warner also dined out. The rebuilt Aussies sent India packing, the one bright spot being Tendulkar's 100th century. It was little consolation for the team however.

They slipped over to New Zealand after the Australian tour and they themselves whitewashed New Zealand 2-0. How would they bounce back against England, at home in India in 2012?

England arrived under new captain, Alistair Cook, and not without their own problems. There had been ructions within the team with the in-again and out-again Kevin Pietersen. He was in again. England had just lost a series against Pakistan in the UAE and had major issues with the Pakistani spinners. That said, every team has its issues and these boys were after all, number one in the world. India of course, had extra incentive: they wanted revenge on the 4-0 drubbing they received in England.

In the first Test at Sardar Patel Stadium, Motera, Ahmedabad, MS Dhoni won the toss and elected to bat. It was a new team of sorts. Dravid was no longer in the team and they found a pretty good replacement for his number three batting spot in Cheteshwar Pujara, who helped himself to 206 not out before Dhoni declared 571/8.

The Indian skipper had off spinner Ravi Ashwin open the bowling with Zaheer Khan and PP Ojha to come on at first change. As much as they'd thought they'd conquered the demons of spin in India, the English clearly hadn't and they were rolled for just 171. Dhoni enforced the follow-on and opened with Yadav and Ojha. This concept of opening with spin bowlers was not new, and certainly not new to Indian cricket, but Dhoni seemed to be more prepared to push it from the outset. For the second innings, while it worked to a degree, England fought back through captain Cook, who made a fighting 176 and once again wicket keeper Prior showed how valuable he was to England at number seven, with 91. However the England total of 406 all out was not enough to create a big enough target for India who chased down the 77 required for the loss of just one wicket. It was a comprehensive turnaround for Dhoni and his team.

And then it turned around again! Just as the Indian spinners had weaved a web of destruction in the first Test, so Panesar and Swann spun England to victory in the second, England victors by 10 wickets, an almost identical margin to the previous match. And in the Third Test at Eden Gardens, Kolkata, England again out batted and out spun

India. Heads rolled for the fourth Test which India needed to win to at least square the series.

England won the toss at Nagpur and elected to bat and did so at snail's pace. Clearly there was no inherent need for them to do otherwise and they sauntered their way to 330. India on the other hand, did need to get a move on, so why they didn't have their foot on the gas is a mystery. A century to Virat Kohli and an unlucky 99 run out for Dhoni, saw India make 326 at 2.27 runs per over. Their first innings finished on the fourth morning of the match. England then batted for the rest of the match, cruising along to 352/4 at 2.28 runs per over. It was Test cricket on Valium and it was thankfully called off just after tea on the final day, England winning the series 2-1.

The biggest issue facing India was one of transition. They had reached the top through world class performers in the old guard of Tendulkar, Dravid, Kumble and Ganguly and that was supplemented by the introduction of the Dhoni's and the Sehwags, but several of the retirements took away a vast amount of experience. It also brought the return of one of India's Achilles' heels: sloppy fielding. As the old adage goes, the sharpness of the fielding is a direct result of the wicket keeper. Was the job of captaincy wearing on Dhoni? He didn't have long to wait. Australia were next to visit India, right after the English.

If Dhoni and his team were struggling with transition, then Australia were likewise in the same position. Ricky Ponting and Michael Hussey, a very large chunk of their middle order for many years, had retired. They were still trying to find the optimum 1, 2 , 3 batting combination. Pugilistic wicket keeper Brad Haddin was overlooked for Matthew Wade. If Australia were to retain the Border-Gavaskar Trophy, it was probably not going to do so with this team, but the result dished out to them by Dhoni and his men was even more severe than even Indian cricket fans might have dreamed of.

Australia's own internal ructions, reports of disharmony between the captain Michael Clarke and one of the senior players, Shane Watson. Tensions also flared between South African born coach, Mickey Arthur and some of the players, culminating in the infamous "Homeworkgate" fiasco where four players were stood down for the third Test for having not doing a task set for them by the coach. It meant that this team was not only short of talent, they were in internal disarray.

Michael Clarke won the toss at MA Chidambaram Stadium, Chepauk, Chennai, and chose to bat. Despite Ravi Ashwin's 7-103, a Clarke ton and half centuries to Warner and Moses Henriques helped Australia score a good first innings total of 380 runs. James Pattinson, the young speed demon, bowled Vijay, Pujara and Sehwag, and spinner Nathan Lyon picked up Tendulkar, "cheaply" for just 81.

What happened next defies belief. A man came to the crease and played an innings so destructive, so damaging, particularly to Lyon, that not only did it change the course of the match, it so shook the Australians that they never recovered in this Test or the rest of the series.

MS Dhoni's wanton destruction took all by surprise, and if there was ever an innings that could shape a series, particularly by a captain, then this was it. His 200 came from just 231 deliveries, eventually falling for 224 from 265 deliveries. He hit 24 fours and 6 sixes. A positively subdued century, by comparison, at the other end from Virat Kohli and India stamped their authority on the match with 572 runs.

Australia barely had time to change and they were facing not one but two spin bowlers. Dhoni opened the bowling with Ravi Ashwin at one end and Harbhajan Singh at the other. India's spinners had caused trouble for Australia's world champions earlier in the decade, but this new breed were simply inept against the quality spin and were rumbled for 241. India made light work of the victory target and won by eight wickets, but it was way they constructed the victory that set the tone for the series and that was done first through the blade of the captain Dhoni, and frankly, simply the presence of Harbhajan Singh opening the bowling.

India won by an innings and 135 runs in the second Test, at Hyderabad, and by six wickets at Mohali for the third. Australia's captain Michael Clarke, reacting to his side's easy capitulation, in the first two Tests, vacated his number five batting spot and moved up the order to number three. He made a first ball duck. It spoke volumes about the different captains' fortunes in the series. One took the game by the scruff of the neck in the first Test and the other struggled to make any impact. And Michael Clarke was no mug as a captain.

By the time the fourth Test was won by India, it was a whitewash, 4-0. This was India's heaviest defeat of Australia, and their first whitewash in the history of India's success over Australia. Some had labelled his captaincy as "defensive". There was certainly nothing in the cricket, nothing in the scorebook and nothing in the strategy that could be called defensive by MS Dhoni or his Indian team in this series.

As if to underline their newfound confidence, MS Dhoni and his team beat the touring West Indies 2-0 and both matches by an innings, giving him six victories on the trot and now this team, having gone through the pains of renewal were now reaping the rewards, yet the coveted away series victories proved elusive.

On the tour of South Africa in 2013/14 against Graeme Smith's team, an exciting drawn first Test match which could have gone either way was followed by a victory to South Africa in the second, and thus a series loss of 1-0 for the abbreviated Test series. In New Zealand, for yet another short quest involving only two Test matches, India lost 1-0, after BB McCullum did to India what MS Dhoni did to Australia in the 2012/13 series, belting 224, making exactly the same statement of intent. In fact it was exactly the same score Dhoni made.

And it was a similar story in England for the Pataudi Trophy, a trophy not won by India since its inauguration in 2007. It began so well, after gaining a draw in the first Test, Dhoni's men won a decisive victory at Lords on the back of some outstanding bowling from Ishant Sharma. Then the wheels fell off completely. England squared the series in the third Test and put the result beyond doubt in the next two, winning the series 3-1. It was an excellent result from the beleaguered England captain, Alistair Cook, who had become the first captain since Bradman to win the last three Tests of a five Test series after being behind.

MS Dhoni's last tour of duty as Test captain, and perhaps the last frontier, was Australia in 2014/15. It would be a series of replacement captains for both teams and the retirement of one. The original captains of both teams never got a chance to face up.

The first Test, at the Adelaide Oval was a tribute to the tragic death of Australian cricketer Phillip Hughes. There was not a dry eye in the house as both teams mourned the fallen cricketer. Runs aplenty but Australian captain Michael Clarke would not have allowed anything but an Australian victory for his fallen mate. Sometimes emotions take over and dictate a result. Opposite him, not MS Dhoni, but stand in captain Virat Kohli, who could not have done much more to help his team's score from his own bat, with centuries in both innings. A torn hamstring put Michael Clarke out of the rest of the series, his replacement, Steven Smith.

With Dhoni back at the helm, Australia won the second Test at Brisbane and the rest of the series was a run feast, resulting in two drawn Tests and Australia regaining the Border-Gavaskar Trophy 2-0. The third Test was Dhoni's last Test, and he retired from Test cricket, handing the baton on to new skipper Virat Kohli.

He came on to the scene a long haired, rock star, cavalier cricketer and he still plays the shorter forms today, having only retired from Test cricket. As a Test player, he was a revelation and a revolution. He had turned on its head the notion that a wicket keeper could not captain a team. He became India's most winning Test captain, both in aggregate and percentage. From his vantage point behind the stumps he was in an excellent position to ring the changes. He was an innovator with both his field changes placements and bowling changes. His win percentage of 45% is India's best of all time to that date.

He came across as a thoughtful and humble commentator on his and his team's performance in press conferences after each day's play. Never before had there been such a cricketer. He was a one of a kind.

Captaincy Record	Tests	W	L	D	%
South Africa 2007/08 (India)*	1	1	0	0	100%
Australia 2008/09 (India)*	2	2	0	0	100%
England 2008 (India)	2	1	0	1	50%
New Zealand 08/2009 (NZ) *	2	1	0	1	50%
Sri Lanka 2009 (India)	3	2	0	1	67%
Bangladesh 2009/10 (Bangladesh)*	1	1	0	0	100%
South Africa 2010 (India)	2	1	1	0	50%
Sri Lanka 2010 (Sri Lanka)	3	1	1	1	33%
Australia 2010 (India)	2	2	0	0	100%

CAPTAINS FILE: INDIA

Captaincy Record continued	Tests	W	L	D	%
New Zealand 2010 (India)	3	1	0	2	33%
South Africa 2010 (South Africa)	3	1	1	1	33%
West Indies 2011 (West Indies)	3	1	0	2	33%
England 2011 (England)	4	0	4	0	0%
West Indies 2011 (India)	3	2	0	1	67%
Australia 2011/12 (Australia)*	3	0	3	0	0%
New Zealand 2010 (India)	2	2	0	0	100%
England 2012 (India)	4	1	2	1	25%
Australia 2013 (India)	4	4	0	0	100%
West Indies 2013 (India)	2	2	0	0	100%
South Africa 2013 (South Africa)	2	0	1	1	0%
New Zealand 2014 (New Zealand)	2	0	1	1	0%
England 2014 (England)	5	1	3	1	20%
Australia 2014/15 (Australia)*	2	0	1	1	0%
Total	**60**	**27**	**18**	**15**	**45%**

* *Not captain for full series*

32

VIRAT KOHLI

This chapter is not finished and one would hope, that while it will continue to be updated, it will also take a very, very long time to finish, for the subject is one of a new breed, a new era, Exciting, controversial, but incredibly talented and quite the man to lead India's Test team towards 2020 and beyond.

Born in Delhi into a Punjabi family, he was raised in Uttam Nagar. According to family reports, when he was three-years old, Virat Kohli would pick up a cricket bat, start swinging it and ask his father to bowl at him. He had a great affection for his father who was his biggest support, driving him to practice every day.

Sadly his father passed away in December 2006 and would miss Virat's rising career. His first class debut was in November, a month before his father died.

It should be no surprise that he has come through the ranks at a rapid pace after captaining India's under 19 team to victory in the 2008 Under 19 World Cup. Shortly after that tour, he made his ODI debut for India against Sri Lanka and soon established himself as a regular in the middle-order.

By 2011 he had made his Test match debut against the West Indies at Sabina Park, Kingston. He made 4 and 15. For the remaining two Tests his run tally was mediocre and he was not selected in the first two Tests of the return series against West Indies at home. However he found form when selected for the third Test, scoring half centuries in each innings.

Some would describe the young player as brash and arrogant, and it seemed that he was always up for a confrontation, but the more time he spent with the seniors of the team, the more balanced and tempered his on-field persona became. But it hadn't disappeared completely and the tour of Australia in 2011/12 had some tempers flaring on both teams and on both sides of the fence. He was fined at Sydney for an obscene gesture to the crowd, but he wasn't the only one stirring up trouble. He was the only one however, from the Indian team at least who scored a century, giving the Adelaide crowd a taste what to look forward to in the future.

He finished the series with the highest aggregate (300) and the highest average (37.50), ahead of such greats as Tendulkar, Dravid and Sehwag.

His new found confidence after the Adelaide Oval century saw more runs at home during 2012, first against New Zealand where he picked up another century, and another ton against the visiting English and yet one more against the hapless Aussies of 2012/13. A century and an unlucky 96 away to South Africa in 2013/14. Another ton against New Zealand in the losing series in 2013/14. He struggled in England in 2014, but he wasn't alone there.

The next series was pivotal. By now a permanent fixture in the middle order and new responsibility as vice captain under MS Dhoni.

Australia 2014/15 and a Taste of Captaincy

In Australia for the summer of 2014/15, it was a time of reflection, given the Philip Hughes tragedy, but also a time of renewal. Both Australia and India had to call on their vice captains to lead during the series. Kohli was called upon for the first Test in Adelaide in place of the injured MS Dhoni, making him India's 32nd Test cricket captain.

The match was labelled the Philip Hughes Test but could easily have been labelled the Virat Kohli Test. It had everything. Scintillating batting, excellent catching, great spin bowling and plenty of niggles and a number of fines. It was good hard cricket with a few on both sides stepping over the line, but it ended with a great run chase and a wonderful finish.

Australia's Michael Clarke won the toss and batted, with each of the three centurions, David Warner, Steven Smith and Clarke looking to the heavens upon reaching three figures as a nod to their fallen comrade. Clarke declared seven wickets down for the imposing total of 517.

Kohli took off from where he left last time he was in Adelaide and was in fine form, leading the way with a century in his first innings as Test captain. India fell slightly short of Australia with 444. Warner doubled up with another century and Clarke declared at 290/5 and set India an intriguing target of 364 to win.

What followed was an exciting run chase, Murali Vijay unluckily LBW for 99, but it was the Virat Kohli show and while he was there the game was still on. He was one of Nathan Lyon's seven victims, out when the score was 304. The captain had scored 141, his second century in his captaincy debut. India fell short by 48 runs, but it wasn't through lack of positive intent, or runs from the skipper. His match aggregate of 256 runs was the most by a debut Test captain.

MS Dhoni was back for the second Test, this time in Brisbane, but Australia were missing Michael Clarke, so Steven Smith made his debut as captain, one match after Kohli. What makes that interesting, is that they were on the verge of being the two best batsmen in the world and both a new breed of player, call it the T20 generation, if you will. The prospect of these young men and their teams fighting it out in the ensuing years is a tantalising thought. Smith, like Kohli, scored a century in his first outing as Test captain. He led his team to victory by 4 wickets.

For the third Test, Kohli and Smith both made big hundreds, but the traditional Boxing Day Test in Melbourne ended in a draw and once again, MS Dhoni was in doubt. Virat Kohli would take charge for the fourth Test in Perth. Smith and Kohli head to head for the first time.

Smith won the toss, batted, and scored yet another century and declared Australia's innings 572/7. Virat Kohli replied in fashion, scoring yet another century himself as India replied with 475. He had now batted three times as captain and three times he had scored a century. Both he and Smith were in a glorious purple patch.

Smith set India 349 to chase, and just as he had dictated in Adelaide, Kohli set his team in positive intent to win the game. Unfortunately time was the winner and the Test drawn. Kohli finished the series with 692 runs at 86.50, with four centuries and one half century. His opposite number, Smith, finished with 769 runs at 128.16 with four centuries. These two went blow for blow and entertained along the way.

MS Dhoni pulled up stumps as a Test player after a brilliant 90 Test career and Virat Kohli was now the permanent Indian Test captain. He'd given a good account of himself in the two Tests in Australia and the future looked bright for India's Test team.

A one off Test against Bangladesh away was drawn due to inclement weather, so the next real opportunity for the new skipper was against Sri Lanka, away, in 2015 and it didn't start very well.

Angelo Matthews won the toss for the first Test at Galle International Stadium, and elected to bat. The innings was a disaster for Sri Lanka struggling against the spin of Ravi Ashwin, all out for 183. Kohli and Shikhar Darwan each scored centuries as India made 375 and that should have been enough to put Sri Lanka out of the match, but it wasn't to be.

A magnificent fightback by Sri Lanka, led by an explosive 162 not out to wicket keeper Chandimal, helped the home team scramble their way back into the match and they set India a modest chase of 175 runs. India collapsed against the left arm spin of Rangana Herath who took seven wickets and they were all out for 112, losing the Test by 63 runs.

Kohli won the toss in the second Test at P Sara Oval, Colombo and batted. Lokesh Rahul hit a century, and with half centuries to the captain, Rohit Sharma and wicket keeper Wriddhaman Saha, India scored a good first innings of 393. A century to Matthews saw Sri Lanka get to 306, still 87 behind. This time Kohli and India kept the foot on the pedal, unlike the first Test, a century to Ajinkya Rahane underpinning their second dig and allowing Kohli to declare at 325/8, leaving Sri Lanka 412 to win. Kohli tossed the ball to Ashwin to open the bowling and Sri Lanka never looked like getting the runs, five wickets to his number one spinner. Aided by the spin of Amit Mishra who took three scalps, India bowled Sri Lanka out for just 134, winning the Test by 278 runs. It was Kohli's first Test victory as captain.

Matthews won the toss for the third and final Test, played at the Sinhalese Sports Club Ground, Colombo, and it was game on, series level. The Sri Lankan skipper sent Kohli and his men in to bat and soon they were 14/2. Steady wickets keep falling, but Cheteshwar Pujara the opener carried his bat and his team, remaining 145 not out in the team score of 312. A good score considering they were sent in.

Ishant Sharma's 5-54 did the damage to Sri Lanka and they fell well short, bowled out for 201. Once again Kohli kept up with the initiative. Despite being 7/3 at one stage in the second innings, the lower middle order did what was needed and got the team to 274 all out, setting the home team the target of 385 to win. A century to Matthews, but Sri Lanka were never allowed to get any momentum and were all out for 268, India the victors by 117 runs and India the series winners 2-1 after being one nil down. Kohli had no only won his first series, but to make it sweeter it was an away victory.

For his first home series, Kohli and his team were to host South Africa in late 2015, India still in transition and finding their way, but it was becoming evident, as with all good captains, that Kohli was shaping this team in his image. This was his team now.

South Africa were also undergoing a transition under the captaincy of Hashim Amla but had a good middle order and a bowling attack that featured the evergreen Dale Steyn.

At the first Test in Mohali, Kohli won the toss and batted, but it started dreadfully and India never really recovered. Vijay, at the top of the order and top scoring with 75, India succumbing to the spin of Dean Elgar and Imran Tahir, all out for 201.

What do you do? Toss the ball to Ravi Ashwin and tell him he's opening. It was a plan that could have easily come from Mansoor Ali Khan's text book. It worked. Ashwin weaved his magic, just as the South African spinners had done, and the away team fell for 184. Not much of a lead, but better than conceding one. This was not going to be a high scoring match so the 19 runs were invaluable.

Pujara led the way for India in the second innings as they hit an even 200, leaving South Africa to score the highest innings of the match to win, needing 220. They folded for 109 against India's spinners, this time Ravi Jadeja taking the honours with five wickets, but Ashwin, who opened the bowling with him, picked up three more, India winning by 108 runs.

The second Test, at Bangalore, was lost to the weather with over 3 days of no play and the match was drawn.

Another very low scoring affair at Nagpur for the third Test. Once again Kohli won the toss and batted, and while the wickets fell steadily, South Africa skipper Hashim Amla was too slow to bring on his spinners. India were all out for just 215, but it was to prove a very good score. Ishant Sharma bowled two overs in South Africa's first innings. Kohli opened with Ashwin, stuck with Ishant for 2 overs then had Jadeja bowling, two spinners in operation. South Africa were rolled for 79. Where Amla had kept his quicks on for longer, Kohli read the situation more keenly.

The wicket was not improving and India again struggled in their second innings, but their 173 was about as good as could be expected on this Nagpur wicket. It left South Africa the comparatively gargantuan task of scoring 315 runs to win. They gave it a good try, but it was always going to be a bridge too far and they were beaten by 124 runs.

India won the fourth Test by 337 runs, and the series 3-0. It was won by Kohli's judicious reading of the situation and his handling of the spinners. He had better spinners and used them more wisely than Amla did with his own. Now Kohli had won a home series to go with his away series.

In 2016 Kohli led his team on a four Test series to the West Indies, against a team battling to find its feet under the captaincy of Jason Holder. India was sporting new coach, former Test captain Anil Kumble, an admirer of Kohli's aggressive approach.

It did not take long for that aggressive streak to show itself after Kohli earlier arranged a meeting with the great Sir Vivian Richards. Kohli won the toss at the stadium named after the cricket legend, in Antigua, and elected to bat.

We saw in an earlier chapter how MS Dhoni stamped his authority on a Test series against Australia in 2013 when he came in to bat and destroyed the bowling attack with 224. Virat Kohli scored a century that day too. Did this bold approach rub off on Kohli? Maybe it did for he too stamped his authority on this series in 2016 with a double century. So authoritative was the knock, it set the course of events for the entire series, and but for rain, India might have won 4-0.

Kohli's even 200, backed by a century to R Ashwin and half centuries to Shikhar Dhawan and Amit Mishra, helped the Indian skipper to declare at 566-8. Following on after scoring just 243, the West Indies were crushed by R Ashwin's 7/83, capping off a fine performance for the Indian allrounder, with India victors by an innings and 92 runs.

Rain then began to make its presence felt on the series. Large parts of the second Test at Sabina Park, Kingston, were interrupted by rain and the Test was drawn – frustratingly for India, for they held the upper hand for most of the Test match. A not out century to Roston Chase foiled the Indian's bid for victory.

More rain again for the third Test, this time at Beausejour Stadium, Gros Islet, St Lucia, but Kohli and his men managed to bring off an emphatic victory by 237 runs, despite there being no play at all on day three. Interestingly Kohli made three changes of personnel for this Test despite having outplayed the West Indies in the first two. It would seem that the changes had a positive impact with such a substantial victory margin, but changing a successful side, particularly the batting line-up, is fraught with danger.

That said, this is the way the man leads his team and it is hard to argue that his style of leadership and his brand of cricket is not successful. The impact of T20 has not just affected run rates. It has also impacted the thinking about batting line-ups and their fluidity in the modern age of Test cricket.

The fourth and final Test was another draw, giving India a series win of 2-0. The fact that four days were robbed of play also robbed India of achieving another high watermark: number one Test team in the world. Following a victory in the fourth Test over England in the same month, Pakistan achieved that status and for the first time. With a little less wet weather, India would have been number one, but that is a moot point, and if Kohli had anything to do with it, it was only a matter of time before India retook the number one status in Test cricket.

An emphatic three nil victory against Kane Williamson's young New Zealand team in September and October of 2016 merely confirmed two absolutes: the Kiwis, like their Australian cousins, are yet to find a strategy to combat India's spin bowlers on Indian pitches;

secondly, Kohli's aggressive intent as captain is a style that continues to develop. After a lean start to the series, Kohli's team filled in the shortfall and by the third Test Kohli was back in form, with his second double century of 2016.

The signs for the future of India's Test team under this dynamic leader were looking good and yet there was one more series to play in 2016: Alistair Cook and his England team arrived for a five Test series. Both teams were in the top four Test teams in the world and both had flirted with the top spot. It was shaping as an intriguing series but the Kohli juggernaut rolled an England team that started well, with the better side of a drawn first Test, before the wheels fell off in the second Test, one by one to the point where all four wheels were gone along with all four remaining Tests. Kohli again led with his bat, culminating in a personal high score of 235 in the fourth Test at Mumbai. Three double centuries as captain and all in 2016.

Surprisingly, his 964 runs at 80.33 was not enough for him to finish the year as number one in the ICC Test Player Rankings. That went to Australia's skipper Steven Smith. The prospect of these two locking horns again in 2017 became an even more a delicious prospect.

Australia in India 2016/17

One of the marquee series in world cricket in this century is India versus Australia. Both teams, wherever they sit in the Test rankings at the time always seem to lift a little harder, try that little bit more. Tensions often rise to the surface but always two very tough and committed Test teams leave nothing in the bag and present Test matches of the highest quality. And so it was in March 2017 when Steven Smith brought his Australian team to India for a four Test series.

Going into the series, Kohli and his men had run over all opposition in the home summer of 2016/17. Kohli himself had been a one man wrecking ball with the bat, as we've seen.

Smith's Australians on the other hand, had not enjoyed the most harmonious home summer, losing to South Africa and in the midst of that series, a complete shake-up of the Australian Test team. They bounced back against Misbah's Pakistan outfit, winning 3-0, albeit against a team that was also experiencing some difficulties. Key players were rested in the losing ODI Chappell Hadlee series against New Zealand. Strangely, a programming hiccup saw many of Australia's T20 team in India, leaving a second string team to lose to Sri Lanka. It was not the best lead up into the series against India, but then, the general consensus was that the new look Aussie Test team would be thumped 4-0 by India so none of that really mattered.

Australia played only one tour match, versus India A which resulted in a draw. They had earlier been practicing in Dubai in an effort to become accustomed to Indian conditions without actually being in India.

The first Test match was played in Pune at the Subrata Roy Sahara Stadium, Gahunje and the debut of the ground as a Test venue.

Australia might have felt a little confident, having won their previous four Test matches in the summer, but that shrinks next to the fact India had been unbeaten in their last 19 Tests. While Kohli's India was a Mercedes Benz firing on all cylinders, Smith's Australia was a refurbished Austin Morris.

The pitch at Pune was universally criticized. Oddly coloured, it was expected to take spin from the first ball and Australia's record against spin in Asia had always been poor. Never mind that they would face the indomitable spin twins, Ashwin and Jadeja.

Both captains had spoken to reporters in the days preceding the Test match, making comments about players, plans and pitches, but in reality they were two tigers, circling each other, ready to strike the first blow. They'd met before in the Test arena and both were ready for battle. Their only previous encounter as captains, at the SCG in January 2015, ended in a draw, but that particular series where Australia won the Border Gavaskar Trophy was highlighted by these two captains standing in as captains for their country, and their wonderful batting.

The one piece of luck Smith needed on this raging turner, the toss, went in his favour and he chose to bat. Relative newcomer to the Test circuit, Matthew Renshaw, joined his more experienced vice-captain, David Warner. They were met by the pace of veteran Ishant Sharma and the spin of R. Ashin. Kohli wasted no time in getting spin right into the attack, but the two openers showed good determination in what was ultimately to prove the best part of the day in which to score runs: the morning.

Warner, bowled off a no-ball when he was 20, was the first to go when Umesh Yadav bowled him for 38. Australia were looking steady at 82/1 but Renshaw followed Warner from the field, retired hurt, due to an upset stomach. This meant that Australia was in the unfortunate position of having two new batsmen and in the post lunch session it was tough going.

Shaun Marsh also fell to Yadav, while Peter Handscomb came and went, out to Jadeja. Kohli laid a trap for Steve Smith, tempting him to hit the spinners in the air to mid wicket, and it was the captain himself who took the catch at mid on to dismiss his opposite number. Smith was the first of Ashwin's three wickets. Australia was now 149/4 but it was to get worse.

Mitchell Marsh and Matthew Wade continued the procession to the crease and back again, while Yadav was on a hat trick having disposed of Stephen O'Keefe and Nathan Lyon in successive deliveries. Australia had only just passed the 200 mark with nine wickets down. Enter Josh Hazelwood at number eleven, who, with Mitchell Starc, scored a fighting last wicket partnership of 55 runs. Josh only managed one of those, for it was the big hitting Starc who intelligently carved up the spinners while also farming the strike. On the surface, 260 was a modest Test score for a first innings, but could Australia's spinners conjure up a surprise?

It seemed they could, aided by this wicked wicket. For the first time in a home Test, Kohli, the unstoppable run machine during the summer, made a Test duck. India collapsed in a heap against previously unheralded spinner, Steven O'Keefe, who picked up 6-35 in a team total of just 105. It was as though the world had just stopped for a moment. Australia's second string spinner ripped right through the champion home team's batting lineup.

It got worse. Sure, India accounted for Warner and Shaun Marsh quickly in Australia's second innings, but Handscomb and Renshaw hung around with Steve Smith who seemed intent on giving India some catching practice. They let him off three times with dropped catches as he forged his way to a memorable century. Supported by some more belligerent striking from Starc, Australia posted the formidable total of 285. This left India needing a "mission impossible"

441 runs for victory, with no real chance of escaping with a draw given the time remaining.

The match ended inside three days, India all out for 107, losing by a whopping 333 runs with O'Keefe picking up another six wickets to give him 12 for the match. After the brilliance of the home summer and the expectation that Australia would fail against Ashwin and Jadeja, not to mention India's world class batting lineup, it sent shockwaves across the Test cricket world. Nobody expected this result. It set the series alight and in a nation making preparations for the upcoming IPL season all eyes were suddenly glued to Test cricket.

The wicket was widely condemned, but given that a raging turner should have suited the home side, it was cause for more concern, particularly given that the next Test match was expected to sport a similar surface.

The second Test was at Bengaluru and while there was talk of making changes to the team, indeed momentarily there was chatter about leaving out vice-captain Ajinkya Rahane, given his recent lack of form, but the India selectors stood by their man. They just needed to play better, bat better, than they did in Pune.

The two captains sparred with each other through the media, Smith suggesting that Australia was *"one or two sessions away from retaining the Border Gavaskar Trophy,"* while Kohli insisted he wasn't going to fall for any *"Aussie mind games in the media"*.

Luck turned for Kohli at the toss and he had no hesitation in batting first, just as Smith had done in Pune. Both captains knew that the toss was critical.

What was that about being one or two sessions from retaining the Border Gavaskar Trophy? The batting woes for India continued into this second match and they crumbled against the off spin of Nathan Lyon who took 8-50 in the Indian total of just 189. Lyon's figures were not just a personal best. They were the best figures by a touring bowler in India.

The skipper, on whose batting the team had come to rely fell cheaply again. His blade, so dominant during the summer, was now docile. Had it not been for the rock like stature of opener Rahul, ninth out in a marathon stay of 290 minutes, the India score would have been far less.

Where India struggled, Australia again seemed to find comfort, and despite India's spinners Ashwin and Jadeja collecting eight wickets between them, the visitors posted a good response with 276, leaving India with a deficit of 87 runs to wipe out before setting Australia a target. The Aussies were in the box seat and had one hand already on the trophy.

India's second innings was a complete reversal of the first innings, in that it was the pace of the metronomic Hazelwood and the difficult Starc that troubled the home team. Rahane found some form with a fighting half century, and Pujara showed his class, unlucky to miss a century, out for 92. The home team had nearly matched the Aussie's first innings, with 274, and it left an intriguing run chase for the visitors.

All that stood between Australia and the trophy was 188 runs. And Ravi Ashwin. Once the door was open with the fall of Renshaw, the momentum was with India as wickets fell steadily. Australia were bundled out for 112 and India won the Test by 75 runs. The off spinner took six wickets as he bowled India to victory. After the disastrous first day, India had fought tooth and nail to get back into both the Test and the series. It was "the sweetest victory" for Virat Kohli.

The series, level at one apiece, was alive and kicking. And snarling. There were scowls from both sides of the fence, both on and off the field, and an inference that Australian captain Steve Smith had done the wrong thing by looking to the dressing room for help with a DRS decision. Both the BCCI and Cricket Australia traded barbs, but it was the ICC CEO, David Richardson, who had the final word and chose not to lay any charges.

"We have just witnessed a magnificent game of Test cricket where players from both teams gave their all and emotions were running high during and after the match. We would encourage both teams to focus their energies on the third Test in Ranchi next week. Ahead of that, the match referee will bring both captains together to remind them of their responsibilities to the game." – ICC statement

It seemed the whole cricketing world was gripped by this Test series, right to the very top of the ICC. What did the third Test have in store?

Australia were then hit with injury problems. They lost both Mitches, allrounder Mitchell Marsh and star bowler Mitchell Starc. The selectors wasted no time in calling up Marcus Stoinis and the fast bowler, Pat Cummins, both needing to pack their bags and catch a flight from Australia to India, having not been selected in the original squad. Cummins hadn't played a Test match since 2011, out of action all these years due to injury. He was being nursed back to form ready for the 2017/18 Ashes Test series, but such was the nature of this current contest Australia was prepared to throw everything at it.

Just to keep everyone on their toes, yet another cricket ground was making its debut, Ranchi, the home of Indian great, MS Dhoni. What would the wicket hold, given the first two Test pitches had favoured spin?

Steven Smith won the crucial toss and batted. Where ball won the contest over bat in the previous two Tests, the situation was reversed considerably at Ranchi. The wicket was flat.

Australia piled on 451 runs thanks to a captain's knock of 178 not out from Smith and a century to T20 star Glenn Maxwell. Concerning for India, captain Virat Kohli landed heavily on his shoulder while fielding and left the field during play.

The team rallied around their wounded skipper and overtook the Australian total, with relative ease. A double century to Pujara underpinned the effort and his marathon stay of 672 minutes was supported by wicket keeper Saha. India ended with 603, a lead of 152. It was as though normal service had resumed. While Kohli failed early with the bat, the bigger concern was his injured shoulder.

The relatively docile nature of the Ranchi pitch meant that Australia could ease their way to a draw, with no time to complete their innings. In such an electric Test series, it was a shame that a draw would raise its head. All that meant though, with one Test to play, everything was on the line.

Everything that is, except the shoulder of Virat Kohli. Disappointingly, the skipper was ruled out of the final Test match and would be assuming the unusual role of spectator. What happened in the final Test? You'll see that in the next chapter, as vice-captain Ajinkya Rahane forced a new chapter in this book.

Of his own impact in the three Tests in which he played in the series Kohli had, by his lofty standards, a poor run of form with the bat. The Australians had done what no other team had done for quite some time, nullifying the impact of Kohli's blade. As leader, he won one, lost one and drew one and that had a negative bearing on his excellent overall win/loss record, but those aspects aside, Kohli most definitely left his mark on the series as captain and showed why he is still, from a statistical perspective, India's best performing skipper.

That performance is sometimes questioned, particularly given the sustained run of home Test series over 2016/17. It was answered in emphatic fashion when India toured Sri Lanka in August of 2017. Kohli and his run machine Indian team mauled the Sri Lankan bowlers from Galle to Colombo to Pallekele. Both Shikhar Dhawan and Cheteshwar Pujara scored two centuries. Kohli, Rahane and Hardik Pandya each helped themselves to a century. Two of the Test matches were won by an innings and the third by 304 runs as the Indian batsmen plundered the hapless local attack. It was fortunate for Sri Lanka that Kohli and his charges were only in the country for three Test matches.

Less fortunate for the Sri Lankan team was the prospect of crossing the waters for a return series in India, however they did give India a minor heart palpitation in the first Test by bowling the home team out for 172, including the captain for a duck. However nothing seems to stand in the way of a century in the first Test of a series for Virat Kohli and he responded in the second innings with 104 not out. A bold declaration by the captain, backed by some excellent work by his quick bowlers almost saw the home team pull off a miraculous victory but the match was drawn.

In the second Test, this time at Nagpur, Sri Lanka's Dinesh Chandimal won the toss and elected to bat. The Ashwin/Jadeja show capitalized on the early work of paceman Ishant Sharma to have Sri Lanka bundled out for 205. The visitors hit back to remove Lokesh Rahul for 7. That was the high point of the Test for Sri Lanka, as first Murali Vijay, then Cheteshwar Pujara peeled off centuries. As if that wasn't enough Virat Kohli joined the run fest with his fifth double century as captain of India. Rohit Sharma also scored a century before Kohli declared at 6/610. Sri Lanka folded for 166 giving the home team an emphatic victory by an innings and 239 runs.

The third Test, at Delhi, was a draw, giving India victory in the series 1-0, but of greater significance, Virat Kohli scored yet another double century as captain, six overall, giving him the record for the most double centuries by a captain in Test cricket, overtaking Brian Lara (5), Sir Donald Bradman, Graeme Smith and Michael Clarke (4). The burden of captaincy was having no impact on his batting.

The twin series against Sri Lanka and the never ending yet fruitful home series of 2017 were one thing, but Kohli and his team faced a tougher assignment ahead in 2018. Away series against South Africa, England and Australia. It doesn't get tougher than that for any team in Test cricket.

India in South Africa 2017/18

South Africa and India enjoy a rich history of competitive cricket and this series just after the New Year in 2018 was no exception. As the "story" goes, Indian curators prepare spinning wickets for the South Africans, while green tops are prepared when the situation is reversed.

At Cape Town for the first Test in January 2018 South Africa captain Faf du Plessis won the toss and batted. He may have regretted that decision, for inside five overs both openers and Hashim Amla were dismissed leaving the home side reeling against the pace of Bhuvneshwar Kumar, 3 wickets for 12 runs.

South Africa, through AB deVilliers, Faf du Plessis and the tail then mounted a spirited comeback, getting the home team to what was to prove a good first innings total on this lively wicket, 286. Too lively for India for sure, as du Plessis sent his wrecking ball crew of high quality pace bowlers through the Indian batting line up. One by one, Dale Steyn, Vernon Philander, Morne Morkel and Kagiso Rabada, surely the premier pace attack in the world, humbled India's much vaunted batsmen and save for a brave counter attack by Hardik Pandya would have fared far worse than the 209 they scored. Pandya's 93 run blastathon was the complete opposite of every other innings in the match, save for AB deVillier's.

The wicket was proving just as difficult when the South Africans collapsed in the second innings to be dismissed for just 130 proof that

India's pace attack of Kumar, Jasprit Bumrah and Mohammed Shami were every bit as dangerous in these conditions. It left India the tantalizing target of just 208 runs, by no means impossible, however after a steady beginning by the openers an equally steady procession of batsmen struggling against quality pace on this wicket. Philander took 6-42 as the visitors were rolled for 135, giving South Africa victory in the first Test by 72 runs. However the Test didn't all go the way of the home side and Kohli and his men could draw much from their performance in readiness for the next Test at Centurion Park.

Played in the region of the Highveld, the high altitude grasslands of South Africa, the conditions at Centurion Park long a fast bowler's playground, but can at times the pitch can play dead. On this occasion, the wicket was dry and the spinners would come into play. Yet both sides erred towards the conservative and plenty of pace was loaded on both teams. South Africa's spearhead, Dale Steyn, was out injured and would remain on the sidelines for the rest of the series. Perhaps his absence would help lift Virat Kohli and his Indian team.

Faf du Plessis won the toss and after looking at the wicket, chose to bat. Pace would take a backseat and spin, while evident on day one, would be most difficult to play in the second innings. His decision proved to be the correct one as the Indian bowlers struggled to get any impact. By the third session South Africa was well in control, with half centuries to Aiden Markram and Amla, just three wickets down for 246. It took first Test hero Hardik Pandya to change things up when he ran out Hashim Amla for 82. It was a pivotal moment and instead of the home team amassing a mammoth total, fell away to be all out for 335, R. Ashwin the chief destroyer with 4-113 from 38.5 overs.

An early runout in India's reply had them 28/2 when the captain arrived at the crease. He'd need to put everything from the Cape Town Test behind him and knuckle down for the duration. He would have to lead from the front with his own bat and that's exactly what Virat Kohli did. With his own brand of aggression both with bat and voice, the captain put on a Kohli Special, scoring 153 runs, almost half of the team total of 307. His 379 minute stay was a lone vigil, save for 38 vital runs from Ashwin. Had Kohli been given more support India might have enjoyed a first innings lead.

After Ashwin bowled the first over, it appeared that spin would dominate, but it was Mohammed Shami who was the chief destroyer as India dismissed the hosts for 258. For the second Test in a row, it left India with a gettable run chase, this time 287. Without the experience of Dale Steyn, India were in with a good chance, but it was an unmitigated disaster at the hands of South Africa's least experienced player, Lungisani Ngidi, taking a brilliant 6-39 on debut. India collapsed to be all out for just 151. Kohli was one of Ngidi's victims, LBW for 5. It seemed if the captain wasn't scoring the runs, they weren't getting scored and India lost the second Test by 135 runs and the series with it. It could have been so much more different and indeed it was for the third and final Test, at Wanderers Stadium, Johannesburg.

Kohli finally won a toss and elected to bat first, but the batting difficulties from the previous Test lingered. The two openers were back in the sheds for not many when Kohli joined Pujara, the pair both scoring half centuries. That was it. Kohli out, all out it appears and the team struggled to 187, hardly a dominant first innings total, yet Kumar and Bumrah brought India right back into the contest with three and five wickets respectively, bowling out the hosts for 194. Just as South Africa were laying blows to the body of India with their pace arsenal, India's quick bowlers were dishing out plenty of treatment of their own.

Hard runs again in the second innings. It wasn't pretty, but Kohli and Rahane top scored to take the team to 247, a reasonable score in these conditions against the rampant pace attack of the home team. Chasing 240 for victory, South Africa also struggled and once again Kohli's pace attack, standing an inch or two taller than they did at the beginning of the tour, knocked over the home team for just 177, giving India a consolation win in the dead rubber.

A number of bright things emanated from the tour. Kohli's aggressive style in both batting and leadership were evident at all times. Where previous Indian teams may have been accused of appearing timid, it certainly wasn't the case with Kohli and his band of cricketers. He led from the front and wouldn't take a backward step. Accused in some quarters of being too aggressive, the Indian captain just took it on the chin. That's how he plays. He thrives on that aggression, the confrontation.

Another bonus for India and Kohli was both the standard and the management of his pace bowling attack. Long the lead in the saddlebags of India, Kohli now had a quality pace attack that mixed it with the best in the world. It augured well as India looked towards away series in England and Australia. They'd need that pace attack to fire in both of those countries.

India in England 2018

Kohli has scored runs in every country and in abundance. Every country that is, except England. His one tour there produced a forgettable 13.40 runs per Test innings. In an effort to acclimatize with English conditions, Kohli sought a stint with Surrey before the series in July of 2018. The BCCI was compliant. It meant he would miss the inaugural Test against Afghanistan but it did underline the man's determination to leave no stone unturned in an effort to succeed in the one place he has struggled. It was a good strategy and it was well underway until the super human proved to be, well, human. Kohli's neck gave way during the IPL series and he was sidelined for several weeks. Not only had he now missed the one off Test against Afghanistan, he'd missed the valuable experience of playing county cricket. Would this have a negative impact on the England tour ahead?

The "Fab Four", the premier batsmen of the era was a reference to India's Virat Kohli, Australia's Steven Smith, New Zealand's Kane Williamson and England's Joe Root. Two of the Fabs had locked horns as players and captains, in the epic battles between Kohli and Smith. Now Kohli was to take his bat and his team to take on England and Joe Root. And intriguing contest awaited.

At Edgbaston for the first Test, the England skipper won the toss and elected to bat. Ishant Sharma and Umesh Yadav opened the bowling, but it was the early introduction of spin through R. Ashwin that removed the dangerous Alistair Cook. Plenty of starts for England, but only two half centuries, Joe Root (80) and Johnny Bairstow (70) in what looked like a par score of 287.

Virat Kohli then put on a masterclass, outdoing his Fab "brother" by scoring 149. Unfortunately he had very little support from his team mates and India fell short to be all out for 274. Kohli had come to play but he was on his own with the bat.

India's bowlers stepped up where the batsmen had been found

wanting and through Sharma (5-51) and Ashwin (3-59) and skittled the home team for just 180. It left India needing 193 for victory.

Once more it was Kohli leading the way. He was the seventh batsman out when the score was 141, for 51 hard earned runs. So close, but so far. Plenty of starts but no batsman apart from Kohli was able to stem the tide and Ben Stokes (4-40) led the way with the ball as India were all out for 162 as England won by 31 runs. It was a cruel blow to Kohli, given he'd scored an even 200 runs for the match.

It got worse. In the second Test, at Lords, both Jimmy Anderson with the ball, and Chris Woakes with both bat and ball, destroyed India. Sent in after Root won the toss, India were skittled for just 107, Kohli just 23.

A not out century to Woakes helped England to score 396 and for Root to declare only seven wickets down. It was far too many for India to Match, bowled out for just 130 in the second innings to lose by an innings and plenty.

What had started as tour of opportunity was becoming a tour of hell. The Indian batting was nothing unless the captain made half the runs himself. Something had to change, and change fast. At Trent Bridge, it did.

Root won his third toss in a tow and once more sent India in to bat. A more steady start, but regular wickets falling meant that vice captain Ajinkya Rahane joined his captain at 82/3. Both needed to stand up and both did. Kohli fell short of yet another ton, with 97 and Rahane scored 81. There was precious little else from the lower order but 329 was a decent first innings score after being sent in.

England saw a succession of starts but no more than that as Hardik Pandya (5-28) led the way with good support from the bowling group and the hosts were bowled out for just 161.

Foot firmly on the gas pedal, Kohli made up for his shortfall in the first innings by registering another century. Pandya also chimed in with a half century enabling the skipper to declare at 352/7. Batting clearly easier in the second innings, England began the slow climb to overhaul the target of 520 but steady wickets, despite a century to Jos Buttler and half century to Stokes, England could only score 317 and lost the Test by 203 runs. The series now at 2-1, could India storm home on the momentum?

Root won his fourth consecutive toss at the Rose Bowl, Southampton and elected to bat. Early wickets saw the home side 86/6 at one stage but rallied through Sam Curran (78) and Moeen Ali (40) to post the modest score of 246.

Pujara's 132 not out helped India to a small lead with 273. Assisted by Kohli (46) there was very little appetite for runs from the lower order, particularly against Moeen Ali's spin (5-63).

England again struggled at the top, only to rally around wicket keeper Jos Buttler (69) to post a competitive 271. Once again a delicious prospect of chasing a gettable 244. It wasn't to be, despite half centuries to captain and vice captain, India folded for 181.

It was now a losing series by 3-1 and it became 4-1 at the Oval where Root won his fifth toss. Kohli could not even win a toss in the UK. What started out as a tour of great hope became a disappointment. England were not the better team by 4-1 but it says so in the scorebook and that's all that counts.

An easier time for the Indian team at home with a 2-0 victory over a spirited West Indies outfit led by Jason Holder. The big test was to come: playing in a land where India had never previously won a Test series: Australia.

India in Australia 2018/19

What would have been another round of two heavyweights in the Fab Four - Smith vs Kohli – was dashed when Smith found himself banned from International cricket for his part in the "Sandpapergate" ball tampering scandal in Cape Town six months earlier. Smith, along with team mates David Warner and Cameron Bancroft would take no part in this series. It would be a vastly different Australian side led by new captain, wicket keeper Tim Paine.

The series got underway at the Adelaide Oval where Kohli won the toss and batted. The pace trio of Mitchell Starc, Pat Cummins and Josh Hazelwood were each in the game immediately with a wicket as India slumped to 19/3 when Usman Khawaja caught Kohli from the bowling of Cummins. It soon became 41/4 and 86/5 as India struggled on a first day Adelaide pitch. Thankfully there was an immovable rock at the other end in the form of Cheteshwar Pujara who no bowler could remove. He was eventually run out for 123, the ninth wicket to fall at 250. No further runs were added in what was an under par score for a first innings of an Adelaide Test.

The Aussie quicks weren't the only ones finding juice in the wicket. ODI player Aaron Finch had been promoted to Test opener to replace Warner. Marcus Harris on debut joined him at the other end. It was a short stay for Finch, bowled third ball by Ishant Sharma. Harris made a patient 26 before becoming Ashwin's first victim.

Ashwin continued to baffle the top order, removing Shaun Marsh and Usman Khawaja. Wickets fell regularly and only the young local, Travis Head, showed any lasting application for Test cricket, top scoring with 72 in a total of 235.

Pujara hadn't finished his work. Another fine knock of 71 guided India to an excellent total of 307. Virat Kohli with 34 was one of Nathan Lyon's six wickets. The Aussies were keeping the Indian skipper relatively quiet but it didn't matter with Pujara seemingly on a mission.

Set 323 to win, the locals gave it one heck of a shake, all out for 291. India went up 1-0 in the series. Three to go.

To Perth for the second Test, but not the famous WACA ground. This Test would see the debut of the new Optus Stadium. Would the ball behave the same off the wicket as the WACA? Clearly not. Even the WACA hadn't been the same pitch for some years, how could an entirely new wicket mimic the WACA's past?

Paine needed victory in this Test to stay in the series and got off to a good start by winning the toss and electing to bat. Finch, Harris and Head each scored half centuries as Australia were relatively untroubled in scoring 326.

Starc and Hazelwood removed the openers in quick time and Starc then removed danger man Pujara for 24, however one does not keep Virat Kohli quiet for very long and the skipper 123, with Rahane in support with a half century. India fell short, but a long way off, with 283. They were still in this game.

Mohammed Shami certainly enjoyed the new wicket. He took

Australian wickets as the hosts had no answer. Shami took out the top order, and the bottom. No-one was safe as Australia limped to 243, Khawaja top scoring with 72.

Set 286 for victory, India were all at sea. No-one scored over 30 and the visitors saw themselves bundled out for just 140, losing the Test by 146 runs. Series at 1-1.

Virat Kohli won the toss on Boxing Day at the MCG and elected to bat. With bat in hand one can carve a future and so it was with India's batsmen. In his debut innings Mayank Agarwal scored a steady 76, while Pujara (106), Kohli (82) and Rohit Sharma (63*) all dined out on the Aussie bowling attack.

Tired from bowling or just plain tired, the Australians were all out for 151, top score being 22 from Harris and Paine. Bumrah was the main wrecker with 6-33.

Cummins improved on those bowling figures by takin 6-27 as India also collapsed to be out for 106. Agarwal scored 42 of those on his own. It gave Australia a sniff for victory but it was not to be, bowled out for 261. Cummins top scored with 63. India won by 137 runs to take an unassailable lead in the series, 2-1. A draw in the final Test would have India winning the series.

At the SCG in the New Year Test, that's exactly what happened. Kohli won the toss and elected to bat. The runs flowed as did the champagne on Sydney Harbour on New Year's Eve. Agarwal continued the impressive start to his career with 77. Pujara scored 193. Wicket keeper Rishabh Pant scored 159 not out while Jadeja chimed in with 81. All the skipper had to do was declare and he did at 622/7.

Australia followed on after being all out for 300, and time allowed for no more than four overs in Australia's second innings. Match drawn, series won. Virak Kohli became the first Indian captain to win a Test series in Australia and his crowning achievement to date. From Lala Amarnath in 1948, through Pataudi in 1967 to Gavaskar, Dev, Tendulkar, Ganguly, Kumble, MS Dhoni – no Indian captain had climbed this mountain successfully until now. Kohli stands on the shoulders of those men before him.

Virat Kohli is generation now. It seemed inconceivable many years ago that the great Polly Umrigar's Test cricket numbers would be overhauled. Then along came one Sunil Gavaskar and he mowed down those numbers, then added interest. And it seemed inconceivable that Sunny's numbers would ever be overhauled and then along came one Sachin Tendulkar and he mowed down those numbers and added interest. It seemed inconceivable that Sachin's numbers would ever be overhauled, but Virat Kohli is doing his darndest to do just that. If one looks at where he's been to date and where he's going, only a brave person would suggest that he won't overtake the Little Master.

However, in the captaincy stakes, Kohli has the number of all his predecessors. Statistically at least, he is India's most successful Test cricket captain. The trend continues on an upward trajectory. Where will this modern day great end up?

Captaincy Record	Tests	W	L	D	%
Australia 2014/15 (Australia)*	2	0	1	1	0%
Bangladesh 2015 (Bangladesh)	1	0	0	1	0%
Sri Lanka 2015 (Sri Lanka)	3	2	1	0	67%
South Africa 2015 (India)	4	3	0	1	75%
West Indies 2016 (West Indies)	4	2	0	2	50%
New Zealand 2016 (India)	3	3	0	0	100%
England 2016/17 (India)	5	4	0	1	80%
Bangladesh 2016/17 (India)	1	1	0	0	100%
Australia 2016/17 (India)*	3	1	1	1	33%
Sri Lanka 2017 (Sri Lanka)	3	3	0	0	100%
Sri Lanka 2017 (India)	3	1	0	2	33%
South Africa 2018 (South Africa)	3	1	2	0	33%
England 2018 (England)	5	1	3	0	33%
West Indies 2018 (India)	2	2	0	0	100%
Australia 2018/19 (Australia)	4	2	1	1	50%
Total	46	26	10	10	57%

Not captain for full series

33

AJINKYA RAHANE

Like the Virat Kohli chapter, this too is a work in progress, for while Ajinkya Rahane has only filled the role of stand-in captain, he may well be at the helm one day in the future. If his handling of the India team in the Test matches in which he has been in charge are anything to go by, then one hopes that possibility becomes an eventuality.

Born in Ashwi Khurd, Maharashtra, Rahane is yet another product of Mumbai cricket, playing junior levels right up to first class. He also played with the Mumbai Indians in the IPL, before moving to Rajastan Royals and more recently the Rising Pune Supergiants.

Recognised as a solid middle order batsman from an early age, Rahane made his way through the junior ranks and was selected for the Indian U19 tour of New Zealand in 2007. He was in illustrious company in the team, with Virat Kohli, Ravinda Jadeja and Ishant Sharma. Opposite him playing for New Zealand, future household Test names Kane Williamson, Tim Southee and Trent Boult. In the drawn series of three Test matches, playing as an opener, he scored two 50's, a 47 and finished in grand style with 179 in the final Test.

Like many others of his generation, the pathway to international cricket was via the shorter formats and his international debut for India was in a T20 match at Manchester against England where he top scored with 61.

His Test debut was in the fourth Test of the home series against the

Australian team of 2012/13 where the visitors had lost 3-0 already, had their credentials questioned for lack of "homework" and minus their skipper, Michael Clarke for that final Test. Shane Watson stepped in as captain, but could not reverse the already disastrous tour result, ending in a 4-0 drubbing. Rahane made 7 and 1 and didn't play again until South Africa hosted India in 2013/14. Against the pace of Steyn and Philander, the young right hander was now in the middle order and scored two half centuries including a 96.

He scored his first Test century against New Zealand in Wellington, showing that his love for Kiwi conditions had not abated. By now he was a regular in the Test team and was gaining experience through tours to England, Australia, Sri Lanka, West Indies and Bangladesh. With that came some interesting records.

In England, he became only the 4th Indian batsman to score a century on debut at Lords. Against Sri Lanka, he broke the record for most catches in a match, with eight. Importantly, he'd scored valuable centuries away from home, in Melbourne, Colombo and the aforementioned Lords.

By the time he was unexpectedly presented with the captaincy in the 4th Test against the Australians in 2016/17, Rahane was a most experienced and accomplished Test player. India could not have had a better option to fill the shoes of Virat Kohli.

We have already explored the first three Tests of that series and while Rahane was leading the team in the field for much of the third Test, it wasn't until the final Test of the series that he officially became India's 33rd Test captain.

The series had been electric. There had been great performances from both teams, tempers had flared, both cricket boards became involved and even the ICC stepped in. The pitches were rated as "poor" in Pune and "below average" in Bengaluru. Yet the cricket itself had all the drama and intrigue one would want in a Test series. And, crucially, it all came down to the last Test. A win or a draw for Australia meant they retained the Border Gavaskar Trophy. There was no choice for India. They had to win.

What impact would Kohli's absence make? Who would replace him in the team? What sort of captain would Rahane make? Had he ever captained before? It sent everyone scrambling and all of these questions before the Test match simply added to the atmosphere, both in India and Australia.

On the morning of the first day, it was evident that Kohli wasn't playing and the speculation about his replacement was at fever pitch. Ishant Sharma was replaced by Bhuvneshwar Kumar and Kohli by Kuldeep Yadav, a slow left-arm chinaman who would slot in at number 10 in the batting order. It was an unusual swap, to say the least. Perhaps no more unusual than witnessing Virat Kohli carrying the drinks, injured shoulder or not. There's no keeping Virat out of the game.

The wicket at Dharamsala was potentially more conducive to quick bowlers, something much more to Australia's liking, and when Smith won the toss, he batted, celebrating that with his third century of the tour. However the support for him, aside from Warner and Wade, was woeful. They had been cruising in the afternoon session, but the rot set in once Rahane turned to Kuldeep Yadav. The bowling change was immediately effective, first turning the screws on Australia with tight bowling and good field placement. Those two things often bring about a wicket and in this case, several. Once Kuldeep had Warner, he broke the back of the middle order with the wickets of Handscomb and Maxwell in quick succession, and despite a handy 21 from Cummins, Australia failed to capitalize on both the good start, and the captain's century, bundled out for 300. They needed to score many more than that to put pressure on India.

India, while not advancing much further than Australia's innings, rallied around the skipper with most players getting a start, with, of all people, Ravida Jadeja top scoring with 63, batting at number 8. Once his wicket fell, the tail added little, but there was a valuable lead of 32 runs.

Blink, and you miss it. The Indian quicks knocked over the Aussie top three before the deficit was taken care of. Despite some mild resistance from Maxwell, the rest of the visitors' batting was clueless against the Indian spinners, bowled out for a mere 137. Rahane marshalled his troops well, ringing in the bowling changes and cleverly adjusting his field.

As India passed the target on the 4th day, with Rahul hitting the winning runs to bring up his half century. Ajinkya Rahane was 38 not out at the other end and would have enjoyed being at the crease for the winning runs, as victory for the Test and the series was India's. India had won the Border Gavaskar Trophy and the man who was nearly dropped after the first Test was the victorious captain. He joined Ravi Shastri as a stand-in skipper with 100% record. Was it time to retire?!

Afghanistan in India 2018

No. It wasn't time to retire. Injury to India's captain Virat Kohli meant that Rahane would step up once again to captain his country, this time against newcomers to Test cricket, Afghanistan.

On paper, it seems a relatively comfortable assignment. A Test against a team with no first class competition playing its debut Test on the home turf of the best teams in the world. It all points to an easy victory for India. On paper - but cricket is not played on paper.

While being Test debutants, Afghanistan was no newcomer to international cricket. They had been competing in the shorter formats with distinction since 2007. Their elevation to Test status along with Ireland in June 2017 was a fait accompli.

India on the other hand were without captain and star batsman Virat Kohli. Take the number one batsman in the world out of any team and they drop in quality. Add to that, pace duo Bhuvneshwar Kumar and Jasprit Bumrah were rested, along with Rohit Sharma and Parthiv Patel. All of a sudden India look a little vulnerable.

The Indian skipper showed no concerns however, simply stating before the match that it was important to transition the mindset from IPL to Test cricket. His team was experienced and ready to go. They weren't going to take Afghanistan lightly, but at the same time were not going to give the visitors any favours. Specifically, the word he used was "ruthless".

When India entered cricket uner CK Nayudu in 1932 aginst Douglas Jardine's hardened England line-up, they were true newcomers to international cricket. There were no ODI's in those days. No T20's. They entered the Test arena with zero match experience outside of India. Afghanistan on the other hand had seen the landscape of international cricket for a decade. Domestic T20 competitions allowed players to experience cricket from Australia to

CAPTAINS FILE: INDIA

England. This team had some solid runs on the board.

Ajinkya Rahane won the toss over Afghanistan's skipper Asghar Stanikzai at M Chinnaswamy Stadium, Bangalore and had no hesitation in batting.

Yamin Ahmadzai and Wafadar Momand took the new ball for Afghanistan and began to find out just how tough things are at this level, with the Indian openers Murali Vijay (105) and Shikhar Dhawan (107) both helping themselves to centuries. Dhawan was particularly severe as he collared the Afghani attack, plundering three sixes in the process.

Once those two had departed it was s steady flow of runs, with half centuries to K. Rahul and an entertaining 71 from allrounder, Hardik Pandya. Yamin Ahmadzai gave a good account of himself picking up 3/51 from 19 overs, by far the best of the Afgani bowlers.

Rahane kept up the pressure by allowing India to bat the full innings, all out for 474. It would be a huge mountain for any team to climb and so it proved. Spin twins Ashwin (4/27) and Jadeja (2/18) were too hot to handle. Mohammad Nabi top scored with 24 from a team total of 109. That mountain just got higher as Rahane sent the opposition back for another go.

Despite stubborn resistance from Hashmatullah Shahidi (35*) the second innings was even worse, all out for 103. Among the wickets Jadeja, Sharma and Sharma. India won by a massive innings and 262 runs. In short, the newcomers were hammered by a ruthless India. Rahane was right.

India's vice-captain had now stepped up on two occasions to fill in and his punctuated captaincy career now stands at 100% win record. Time to retire?!

Captaincy Record	Tests	W	L	D	%
Australia 2016/17 (India)*	1	1	0	0	100%
Afghanistan 2018 (India)	1	1	0	0	100%
Total	**2**	**2**	**0**	**0**	**100%**

SUNDRIES

33

THE BEST

"The captain of the All India team can be selected only on merit. Of a dummy who leads a good team and a real leader who captains an average one, the latter will always have better chances of success." – CK Nayudu

So just who was the best? Which of the 33 captains of India were the best and who were less so? Does one merely look at the cold hard stats, or do other aspects, like the resources available and the opposition come into account?

The answer, is that it has to be a bit of everything. By their very nature, the hard facts, the numbers, must have an impact. But if we simply look at the numbers in isolation, take Kapil Dev for example. He captained India 23 times before he had a Test victory. Twenty three times! His overall win percentage is just 12% which puts him right towards the bottom end of the scale. When he finally broke his duck, it was an away win in England, and the series victory was only the second time India ever won a series there and the biggest defeat India had handed to England in England. He won a World Cup in 1983. Of his first 14 Tests as captain, 11 were against Clive Lloyd's powerful unit. Eleven! Ask Australia's Alan Border what it was like playing that team so often. Speaking of Border, he was opposite Kapil Dev for one of the greatest Test matches ever, the tied Test in Madras. So to judge Kapil Dev on numbers alone does him no justice as far as his ability as a captain.

Look at CK Nayudu. Won nothing. Nothing at all. Best he could do was draw one Test match. Does that make him the worst of all, this

Father of Indian Cricket, honoured by the annual trophy that bears his name? Of course not, but the numbers would say so, for his win percentage is zero. However Nayudu was the first and, only one Test captain in the history of cricket, Australia's DW Gregory, has won the first match played by his country. How long did West Indies take to find their feet, or South Africa? By virtue of being the youngest Test nation you are in effect a "minnow" so none of India's first few captains could have been expected to be on the positive side of the ledger. Nayudu didn't take over a settled side and shape it in his own manner. He wasn't even supposed to be captain – it was a last minute choice and even then a contentious one. He was also nearly 37 years old. His record as captain in First Class cricket is excellent. He attacked as a batsman, he attacked as a bowler and he attacked as a captain. That might explain the bulging trophy cabinet.

What about Mansoor Ali Khan? Tiger Pataudi was recognised as the man who pulled the team together to represent India first, and not regional bias. If one were to place a high value on creating an atmosphere of team unity then surely this outranks his win/loss ratio. This was a captain who had no fast bowlers and created the most audacious bowling attack of all time. Yet the selectors must have missed that because he was dumped as captain just when the team was on the verge of success.

The man who replaced him, Ajit Wadekar was the first captain to win in England, in the West Indies, yet his win loss record didn't save him from being dropped either, to be replaced by Pataudi.

After having studied these 33 men for many months, read their books, if able, watched umpteen hours of video footage, read accounts of them by their fellow players and their opponents, and wrote about them, studying every single tour, every single Test match they played, who could be considered the best?

I have whittled it down to three of the captains not any specific order. I have chosen to leave Virat Kohli out of the running while his career is still going. Quite obviously his record speaks for itself and he will one day stand alongside these three as one of India's greatest.

Mansoor Ali Khan "Tiger" Pataudi

The Tiger must be included here, for he is the man who got his players thinking about the success of India above all else. Across regional differences, cultural differences, religious differences, language differences, something every single Indian captain must contend with, this is the man who first managed to corral those disparate forces and get them working for the collective goal of winning Test matches for India.

His creative captaincy in the face of a drought of available fast bowling options meant that he turned a liability into a potent weapon. That he won India's first overseas tour is significant even today. What team in this current era is regularly winning away from home? Not one, so reaching this milestone was a significant achievement. He laid the groundwork for others to follow and in fact his immediate successor, Ajit Wadekar, benefitted from Tiger's efforts. Tiger Pataudi took the Indian Test team to places it had never been before and his captaincy legacy is that just about every captain since has built on Tiger's work.

MS Dhoni

Just on statistics alone he makes the top three, and a 45% win ratio maintained over sixty Test matches is the best, discounting part-time skippers and Virat Kohli who is still playing. Dhoni has done it successfully across three formats, and while we are only interested in Test cricket here, it must be said that the job is made that much more difficult captaining across the three. It means he can't simply focus on Test cricket and forget the rest. Each requires vastly different strategies.

It must be said that while he is in the best position to marshal his troops from behind the stumps, the job of wicket keeper is a fulltime job in itself. To sustain himself and maintain his form in sixty Tests as captain is a remarkable feat. To guide the team to so much success during his tenure shows he's a leader who leads from the front, always thinking, always calculating, unorthodox at times and a man his team would follow to the end of the earth. A captain of his team and a captain of his time.

Sourav Ganguly

As with Dhoni, Ganguly's statistics alone mean he's worth a look, with a win percentage of 43%. He inherited a very good side, but it was a team that while it looked good on paper was underachieving. Names like Tendulkar, Laxman, Dravid, Srinath, just to name a few. He was a captain with great self-belief and led the team through what was a tumultuous time in Indian cricket with the match fixing scandal bubbling away in the background during his early captaincy. He was aggressive and astute and unafraid to take an unorthodox approach.

His unusual mannerisms sometimes annoyed the opposition captains and players, but if they are concentrating on that, they are not concentrating on the game at hand. Ganguly I suspect played this card as often as possible. Whatever he was doing, it worked and he remains one of India's greatest captains.

These are my three best. It was difficult to exclude the Father of Indian Cricket, just as it was also to leave out colossal names such as Gavaskar and Tendulkar, and of course the emerging talent of Virat Kohli. As with any selections in cricket I am sure these will be debated vigorously and that's as it always should be.

Finally, as seems traditional with "criclit" there has to be collective Test team across the expanse of time, which brings us to the Centenery Tour of 2032…

34

THE CENTENARY TOUR 2032

We've just stepped into the future. It's 2032, the centenary of England and India Test rivalry. One hundred years after the Maharaja of Porbandar set foot on English soil, so too is a side bound for England once again. This will be a full tour against the county teams and a healthy five Test programme, the first of which will be played at Lords commencing Thursday June 10th. The King will meet the players at tea on the third day. It is expected to be a mighty battle for the Pataudi Trophy.

Much has changed since 1932. There were no helmets, no coaches, no TV rights, no DRS, no third umpire. The advent of world cups, one day cricket, T20, and the more recent version, introduced in 2025, Ten10, designed for a younger audience, to rid the game of the predictable middle 10 overs in T20.

Our touring party of 17 will be selected from a very special pool of players: from Nayudu to Kohli, the 33 Test captains of India. Fifteen of India's greatest players will not be picked. Given the heavy schedule of tour games the tourists will be nine batsmen, seven bowlers and a wicket keeper.

Like many Test nations, India's captains have mainly been batsmen, so the bowling ranks, particularly the pace department, will need to be given good consideration and the available batting spots will need to be filled by players who can bowl, and preferably medium pace.

The spots in the Test matches will be determined by the form of the players in the lead-up games so as to give every player equal opportunity. Current form on this tour is the only criteria. The Board has already selected a captain for the tour. In keeping with the name of the trophy, the Board is pleased to announce that Mansoor Ali Khan, Tiger Pataudi, will be the captain.

The selection panel of Tony, Arun and myself spent many hours going through statistics and debating the merits of the various players. Our task was a little difficult facing the dilemma of India's Test selectors since 1932: a lack of fast bowling options!

Opening Batsmen:

We're choosing three openers to share the load. There are six regular openers (seven if you count Vinoo Mankad) who have captained India:

- Datta Gaekwad
- Pankaj Roy
- Nari Contractor
- Sunil Gavaskar
- Krishnamachari Srikkanth
- Virender Sehwag

The selectors have chosen Sunil Gavaskar, Virender Sehwag and Nari Contractor. Roy and Gaekwad were not considered purely on the basis that they had not performed well in English conditions at all. Contractor on the other hand, had a better average in English conditions than the previous two players combined. Gavaskar had mediocre form in his early tours to England but improved considerably in subsequent tours. Srikanth only had one tour and at 17.50, his batting average in the UK means he misses out and Sehwag gets the nod as his form in England was pretty good.

It is expected of all three openers that they will be utilised quite often during the tour for their medium pace bowling as they are all capable of doing. It may be that the deciding factor in the selection of the two openers in the Test matches may come down to their bowling form, if all other things are equal.

Middle Order: (positions three to six)

We are choosing six of the following 18 middle order batsmen to have captained India:

- Cottari Kanakaiya (CK) Nayudu
- Maharajkumar of Vizianagram
- Iftikhar Ali Khan Pataudi
- Vijay Hazare
- Polly Umrigar
- Hemu Adhikari
- Mansoor Ali Khan Pataudi
- Chandu Borde
- Ajit Wadekar
- Gundappa Viswanath
- Ravi Shastri
- Dilip Vengsarkar
- Mohammad Azharuddin
- Sachin Tendulkar
- Sourav Ganguly
- Rahul Dravid
- Virat Kohli
- Ajinkya Rahane

There is such a glut of talent in this section that selection will come down again to ability in English conditions and medium pace bowling. One of the places has already been decided by the selection of captain. That leaves five spots.

You'd want to find a spot for CK Nayudu, given that he twice scored over 1000 runs on tour during his two trips to England, but his lesser form in the Tests is something we can't overlook. However we would like a man of the Colonel's standing on tour, so he will be offered the position of team manager. His disciplined approach will ensure good behaviour, early nights and no drinking!

Maharajkumar of Vizianagram, "Vizzy" is another early casualty, unless we can convince every English bowler to bowl long hops and full tosses. However, as he was a great servant to the game, we have given him the same position he got in 1932 and that is deputy vice-captain – non playing.

The father of our captain, the 8th Nawab of Pataudi, is well known in English conditions but his Test average for India in England is only 11.00 so sadly we must leave the Nawab at home.

Vijay Hazare had one mediocre tour in 1946, but a very good one in 1951/52 when he was captain. He also bowls medium pace. Let's leave him as a strong possibility.

The great Polly Umrigar had some excellent overseas form, however not in England. Unfortunately we must leave Polly at home. For the same reason we must leave out Hemu Adhikari and Chandu Borde. Ajit Wadekar had two pretty good series in England, but one disaster and also cannot be considered.

Gundappa Viswanath, "Vishy" had four tours to England, two good, two not so good and would be well across the conditions, so let's put him with Hazare in the possibles.

Ravi Shastri had three tours to England, two dreadful and one very good. We're not going to take Ravi as a player but we will enjoy his presence as coach, and the ocassional stint in the commentary box.

Dilip Vengsarkar had four tours to England and acquitted himself well on all four. We shall put him with Hazare and Vishy in the possibles.

Mohammad Azharuddin had one very good tour to England, a mediocre one and a disaster. While we note his ability to bowl medium pace, given the other talent on offer, we regretfully must leave Azhar at home.

Sachin Tendulkar. His worst tours to England are better than many other's best tours. Of course he's in.

Sourav Ganguly liked England conditions better than anyone, including Tendulkar. Ganguly is in. Dravid thrived in English conditions also. He's in too. Both of those players are rock solid in the Old Dart.

Current superstar Virat Kohli had a brilliant tour in 2018 but unfortunately his one and only previous tour to England, in 2014, returned the very modest average of 13.40 so Virat misses the cut for now.

Ajinkya Rahane has only modest form in England, so we must leave the latest member of the captains club home.

That leaves two remaining spots to be filled by Hazare, Vishy and Vengsarkar. Given that Vengsarkar performed in four out of four tours, one of them averaging 90, we must give the "Colonel" a run.

The selectors were in complete agreement up til this final middle order spot. Tony had chosen Ravi Shastri, while Arun and I had chosen Virat Kohli, with an eye to the future. None of us had initially chosen Vijay Hazare, and on returning to the stats, it was agreed that he would be our final choice.

Our six middle order batsmen, painstakingly chosen from a high quality offering of 17 players:

- Mansoor Ali Khan Pataudi
- Dilip Vengsarkar
- Sachin Tendulkar
- Sourav Ganguly
- Rahul Dravid
- Vijay Hazare

We now move to the wicket keeper's spot. Any ideas there? You'd be forgiven for thinking there's only one option, MS Dhoni and we have chosen MS Dhoni, of course, but note that there are two other captains who have kept wickets at international level: Rahul Dravid and Lala Amarnath. Rahul Dravid is already selected so we have a reserve keeper if Dhoni needs a day off. (Unlikely)

Bowlers

To the bowlers. This is much easier, for while there is high quality on offer, the number of options is limited.

- Lala Amarnath
- Gulabrai Ramchand
- Ghulam Ahmed
- Srinivas Venkataraghavan
- Bishan Singh Bedi
- Kapil Dev
- Vinoo Mankad
- Anil Kumble

The selection of bowlers was a matter of fitting eight players into seven spots. By virtue of the fact that they were the only pace bowlers, Kapil Dev, Lala Amarnath and Gulabrai Ramchand all made the cut, leaving four spots for the remaining five.

Bishen Bedi, with good results across several tours of duty is selected and for the same reason, both Mankad and Kumble make the cut, leaving a choice between Venkat and Ghulam Ahmed. Both are the same style of bowler, off break, and both have similar results from their England tours, perhaps going a little in Ghulam's favour. However, Venkat went on four tours so his experience is stronger so we're going with Venkat.

The final seventeen to tour are:

MAK Pataudi (c), S Gavaskar, N Contractor, V Sehwag, S Ganguly, R Dravid, S Tendulkar, D Vengsarkar, V Hazare, MS Dhoni, B Bedi, A Kumble, V Mankad, K Dev, G Ramchand, L Amarnath, S Venkataraghavan. Manager Col CK Nayudu

BIBLIOGRAPHY

Books

Arlott, John, *John Arlott's 100 Greatest Batsmen,* Queen Anne Press, London 1986

Amarnath, Rajender, *Lala Amarnath, the Making of a Legend,* SportsBooks Ltd, London, 2007

Benaud, Richie, *Willow Patterns,* Hodder & Stoughton, London 1969

Bose, Mihir (contributor), *Test Match Grounds of the World,* Willow Books, London 1990

Bose, Mihir, *A History of Indian Cricket*, Andre Deutsch Limited, London 1990

Cardus, Neville, *A Fourth Innings with Cardus,* (Kindle Edition)

Souvenir Press, London, 2012

Chappell, Greg, *Fierce Focus,* Hardie Grant Books, Melbourne 2011

Coward, Mike, *Champions: the World's Greatest Cricketers Speak,* Allen & Unwin, Sydney 2013

Douglas, Christopher, *Douglas Jardine: Spartan Cricketer,* Methuen, London 2003

"Escari", *CK Nayudu: a Cricketer of Charm,* Illustrated News, Calcutta, 1945

Harvey, Neil, *My World of Cricket,* Hodder & Stoughton, London 1963

Lloyd, Clive, *Living For Cricket,* W.H. Allen &Co, London 1983

Majumdar, Boria, *Lost Histories of Indian Cricket: Battles Off the Pitch*, Routledge, London, 2005

Menon, Suresh (Editor), *Pataudi, Nawab of Cricket,* Harper Sport, India 2013

Mukherjee, Sujit, *An India Cricket Century,* (Kindle edition) Orient Black Swan, Hyderabad, 2012

Ramaswami, N.S., *Indian Cricket – A Complete History,* (Kindle edition) Shakti Malik Abhinav Publications, New Delhi 1976

Ramaswami, N.S., *Porbandar to Wadekar,* Abhinav Publications, New Delhi 1975

Sarkar, Saptarshi, *Sourav Ganguly: Cricket, Captaincy and Controversy,* Harper Collins, India 2015

Wadekar, Ajit, *My Cricketing Years,* Vikas Publishing House, Delhi 1973

Waugh, Steve, *Out of My Comfort Zone,* Penguin, 2005

Tendulkar, Sachin (with Boria Majumdar), *Playing it My Way, My Autobiography,* Hodder & Stoughton, London 2014

The Nawab of Pataudi, *Tiger's Tale,* Stanley Paul & Co, London, 1969

Whitington, RS, *The Lindsay Hassett Story,* Wren Publishing, Melbourne 1969

Wisden Cricketer, *Flying Stumps and Metal Bats,* Aurum Press, London 2008

Online

ESPN Cricinfo (http://www.espncricinfo.com)

Cricket Archive (http://cricketarchive.com)

Wisden Almanac Online Archive1864-2015, ESPN Cricinfo: http://www.espncricinfo.com/wisdenalmanack/content/story/almanack

Articles

C.K Nayudu- The First Indian Captain, Sourav Das, Sporteology: http://sporteology.com/c-k-nayudu-first-indian-captain

Captains Galore, Gerald Howat, ESPN Cricinfo: http://www.espncricinfo.com/cricketer/content/story/143983.html

A far from straightforward delivery, Martin Williamson, ESPN Cricinfo: http://www.espncricinfo.com/magazine/content/story/299244.html

A right royal Indian mess, Martin Williamson, ESPN Cricinfo:

http://www.espncricinfo.com/magazine/content/story/303898.html

Teething problems, Partab Ramchand, ESPN Cricinfo:
http://www.espncricinfo.com/ci/content/story/117152.html

Captains Galore, Martin Williamson, ESPN Cricinfo:
http://www.espncricinfo.com/magazine/content/story/541112.html

Sailing by banana boat to face the Three Ws, GS Ramchand, ESPN Cricinfo *(first appeared on wisden.com)*:
http://www.espncricinfo.com/wivind/content/story/244926.html

Former cricketers react to Ramchand's death, Nagraj Gollapudi, ESPN Cricinfo:

http://www.espncricinfo.com/india/content/story/133488.html

The bouncer that ended a career, Martin Williamson, ESPN Cricinfo:
http://www.espncricinfo.com/magazine/content/story/807661.html

We did not drop a single catch in 1971, Ajit Wadekar Interview, Subash Jayaraman, ESPN Cricinfo:

http://www.espncricinfo.com/magazine/content/story/813005.html

The Vaseline affair, Martin Williamson, ESPN Cricinfo:
http://www.espncricinfo.com/magazine/content/story/594464.html

High Court strikes down Azharuddin's life ban, ESPN Cricinfo:
http://www.espncricinfo.com/india/content/story/590339.html

Became captain by default – Kumble, Staff, ESPN Cricinfo:
http://www.espncricinfo.com/india/content/story/789475.html

Candy upstages cricket, Andrew Miller, ESPN Cricinfo:
http://www.espncricinfo.com/magazine/content/story/304635.html

'Dhoni led by example, not rhetoric' – Dravid, Staff, ESPN Cricinfo:

http://www.espncricinfo.com/australia-v-india-2014-15/content/story/815145.html

ABOUT THE AUTHOR

Rob Harvey is an Australian author residing in Naracoorte, South Australia. His previous works include the comedy fiction *"Bringing the Cows Home"* and the travel adventure, *"Gweilo in the Diaolou"*.

His passions include history, culture, writing and Test cricket. And Indian food. Nearly got the whole lot into this book.

More recently he has published the second in this series, *"Captains File: From Peden to Haynes, Australia's Women Test Cricket Captains"*.

For more information about Rob's upcoming titles, please visit www.kovac.com.au.

Printed in Great Britain
by Amazon